BARBED WIRE
& BABUSHKAS

BARBED WIRE & BABUSHKAS

A River Odyssey Across Siberia

Paul Grogan

First published in 2005 by

Virgin Books
Thames Wharf Studios
Rainville Road
London W6 9HA

Copyright © Paul Grogan, 2005

The right of Paul Grogan to be identified as the Author of the Work
has been asserted by him in accordance with the Copyright, Designs
and Patents Act 1988.

This book is sold subject to the condition that it shall not, by way of
trade or otherwise, be lent, resold, hired out or otherwise circulated
without the publisher's prior written consent in any form of binding
or cover other than that in which it is published and without a
similar condition including this condition being imposed on the
subsequent purchaser.

ISBN 0 7535 0938 5

Typeset by Phoenix Photosetting, Chatham, Kent

Printed and bound by Clays

CONTENTS

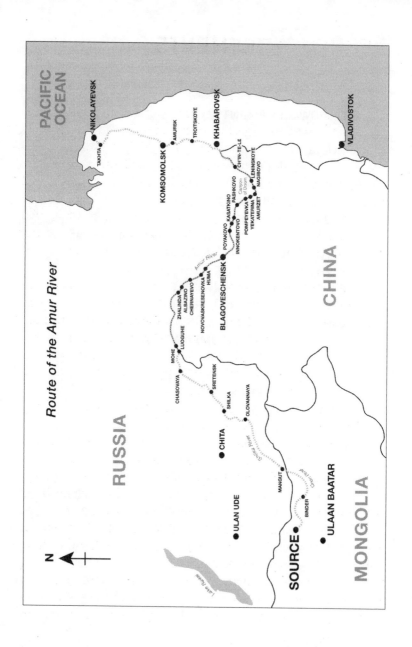

Route of the Amur River

ACKNOWLEDGEMENTS

Of all the duties an author has to perform, writing the acknowledgements is arguably the most important, and certainly the most enjoyable, so I make no apology if the following vote of thanks seems a little on the long side. First and foremost, I would like to thank Richard Knight, honorary Colonel of Kentucky and radio producer extraordinaire, for giving me the confidence to put pen to paper in the first place, and Emma Longhurst, who was instrumental in ensuring that my ramblings reached a wider audience; without their belief and enthusiasm, this book would never have been written.

I am also grateful to Sir Henry Beverly and everyone at the Winston Churchill Memorial Trust for all their help and support. The grant I was awarded by the Trust was established in memory of Mike Jones, a pioneering paddler who made countless first descents of some of the world's most daunting rivers, and who died saving the life of a friend on Pakistan's Braldu River in 1978. Today, his legacy continues to inspire paddlers from all over the world, and his sense of fun and adventure lives on in every journey that is undertaken in his name.

In terms of equipment, Rich and I are indebted to Alistair Wilson at Lendal Products: his ingenious Paddlok paddles were, quite simply, a work of art. I would also like to thank Bob Vardy at Avoncraft and Wolfgang Haupt at Prijon for donating the boats which carried us so safely and comfortably towards our goal. Thanks also to Andy Knight at Palm, Stephanie Smith at Sprayway, Aline Peat at First Ascent, Lillian Sullivan at Terra Nova, Sue Taylor at MASTA, and Pete Forey at Sartech.

When it came to advice on our chosen destination, Peter Knowles couldn't have been more helpful, and Dave Manby, in his capacity as chairman of the British Canoe Union's expedition committee, was no less supportive. It would also be remiss of me not to mention Chippy Powell, whose assurance that 'talking to shepherds can frequently get you bits of sheep' turned out to be mercifully wide of the mark. As for the journey itself, we couldn't even have attempted it without the help of Dmitry Shparo and his tireless secretary Helena Mokrous. In this regard, we would also like to thank His Excellency Grigory B Karasin, Russian Ambassador to the Court of St James, who was almost certainly more influential than we realised when it came to ensuring our safe passage along the river's all-important border section.

I would also like to say a big thank you to my editor Kerri Sharp for her invaluable comments and suggestions, to my uncle Peter Jackson, for his wit and wisdom on all matters pertaining to spelling and grammar, and to my agent Veronique Baxter, for her constant advice and encouragement, and for giving me the kind of support that most first-time authors can only dream of.

Emma and Sarah won't expect a mention, which is precisely why they deserve one: neither of them thought anything of their boyfriends disappearing off to Siberia for four months, and for that (and for much else besides) they deserve the Nobel Prize for patience. Richard Boddington, meanwhile, is truly a king among men: it was an honour and pleasure to be his door man, and I'm especially grateful to him for agreeing to drop his libel suit in return for a share of the royalties.

Finally, and perhaps most importantly, I would like to thank everyone we met along the way for their boundless warmth and generosity, and their seemingly endless capacity for kindness. It is to them that we owe the entire experience.

To Mum and Dad . . .
for giving me the confidence
to follow my dreams

The contract between me and you persuing witnesseth in the name of God – Amen and so forth.

(One)   That me and you will settle this matter together; i.e. to be Kings of Kafiristan.

(Two)   That you and me will not, while this matter is being settled, look at any liquor, nor any Woman, black, white or brown, so as to get mixed up with one or the other harmful.

(Three) That we will conduct ourselves with Dignity and Discretion, and if one of us gets into trouble the other will stay by him.
         Signed by you and me this day.
         Peachey Taliaferro Carnehan.
         Daniel Dravot.
         Both Gentlemen at Large.

'There was no need for the last article,' said Carnehan, blushing modestly; 'but it looks regular.'

                    Rudyard Kipling, *The Man Who Would be King*

PROLOGUE

Hearing footsteps outside the tent, I begin to question my decision to wander around naked just a few minutes before. We've been told these hills are teeming with bears, but the thought of contributing my own sweetmeats to the proverbial picnic is enough to make me hold my breath for a fraction less than nine minutes.

My only previous experience with bears, I have ample time to recall, was while sleeping out under the stars in Canada's Banff National Park. On that occasion, the first hint that I might be in bear country came when I woke to find a tongue noisily licking the crown of my head. Then, as now, I did the only sensible thing: in one fluid motion I reached up to the hood of my sleeping bag and pulled it down over my head. For almost an hour I hardly dared to breathe, scared as stiff as someone who's just had his head licked by a bear. With nothing but a thin layer of rip-stop nylon between me and the top of the food chain, I eventually tensed myself to sleep, wondering vaguely if the manufacturer's guarantee extended to bear claws.

The next morning, I looked around the clearing for irrefutable evidence of my nocturnal visitor: footprints, the odd moose carcass, that sort of thing. Only when I looked down at my camping mat did I find the proof that I'd been looking for; but instead of bear prints, I found half a dozen porcupine needles sticking out of the foam. Some time later I learned that porcupines love salt, and that the little bastard had simply been after the ample supply of sweat from my brow. At the time, however, all I could think about how close I'd come to being nuzzled to death by a small mammal with a saline habit.

Back then, I was only a few miles from the nearest road and a few hours from the nearest bite-unit. Now, I'm five days' walk from the nearest track, and at least another two days' drive from the nearest road; there are, I realise with alarm, astronauts in space who could get to a hospital quicker.

Still, at least I'm not alone: lying asleep beside me is Rich, blissfully unaware of the carnage fast unfolding in my imagination. Between us (by which I mean clenched in my right hand) is a can of bear spray, which looks – and feels – reassuringly like a grenade, complete with plastic pin. If the bear is still hungry after eating Rich, I reason, at least I should be able to avert further slaughter with some particularly piquant pepper (bears, apparently, aren't partial to spices, although I've never been convinced that they'd be stopped mid-snack by a pinch of seasoning, however strong).

Thus reassured, I start thinking about our imminent journey, in the vain hope that it might take my mind off the big surprise lurking outside.

We're camped on the banks of the Onon River, a tributary of the Amur, which begins its life high in the mountains of northern Mongolia: 30km upstream is the river's source; 4,400km downstream is its mouth, on Russia's Pacific seaboard. Our only goal is to travel the entire river from source to sea; our only problem is that we don't have the faintest idea what we're doing.

In fact, that's not quite true. Geographically speaking, we know that the Amur is the eighth-longest river in the world. For its first 600km it flows east through Mongolia, before crossing north into Siberia. From here it continues east, becoming first the Argun and then the Shilka, each change of name corresponding to its confluence with other, smaller tributaries. Eventually, 1,400km from its source, it becomes the Amur, the name by which it's known throughout Siberia. Maintaining its progress east, the river then follows the 1,800km-long border between Russia and China (where it's known by the more colourful – and frankly more dangerous-sounding – name of Black Dragon River). Finally, 1,000km from the Pacific, it heads northeast, back into Russia, and ultimately to its mouth at Nikolayevsk-na-Amure – or Nicholas-on-Sea to you and me.

Politically speaking, the Amur is no less daunting. The Mongolian section of the river passes so close to the Russian border that it's closed to non-military personnel. The point where the river actually crosses into Russia is also considered off limits, as foreigners are only allowed across the border by train, and only then at one of two designated checkpoints. Beyond that things are even more precarious, particularly along the Russia–China border: bitterly disputed for centuries and the scene of armed conflict right up until the late 1980s, the entire area remains strictly out of bounds. According to one of our Russian contacts who has travelled in the area, even locals aren't allowed within 25km of the heavily patrolled border fence.

Help, though, is at hand: far from hoping that we can charm our way past the odd watchtower or 500 with a bottle of vodka and a packet of Lucky Strikes, we've enlisted the help of a mysterious fixer called Dmitry. For months (and for a not inconsiderable fee) our man in Moscow has been wearing holes in the corridors of the Kremlin on our behalf. Now, on the eve of our departure downriver, we still haven't got permission to cross into Russia, we haven't got permission to paddle *in* Russia, and we most emphatically have *not* got permission to travel along the Russia–China border. Another few hours and I'd say we were cutting things a bit fine.

Still, such minor details are rarely a match for mindless optimism: our hope remains that the gradual thawing of relations between two of the world's largest superpowers might yet persuade them to roll out the red carpet for two of the world's smallest canoeists (figuratively speaking, of course; Rich is actually quite large).

Politics aside, there's also the small matter of Siberia's weather to consider: we know, for example, that the river is frozen for seven months of the year, and from the sound of rippling water outside our tent it's obvious that we're now well into spring, but we've no idea when it will freeze over again, or if we'll be able to reach the Pacific Ocean before it does.

Finally, there are the all-important questions of actually living on the river. Will we be able to find food? Will we meet many other people along the way? Will the weather be freezing? And, perhaps most importantly of all, will we be able to grow beards like David Bellamy?

Once again, our intelligence is scarce for the first section of the river, and almost nonexistent for the rest. Just before we left the UK, we received an enigmatic email from Chippy Powell – an implausibly named friend of a friend who's spent some time canoeing in Mongolia – warning us that food might be hard to come by in the hills. The locals, he explained, often don't have enough for themselves, although he assured us that 'talking to shepherds can frequently get you bits of sheep'. Thanks to our forty-year-old maps, we also know that there are isolated settlements further downstream, but we have no idea how big these settlements are, or even if they still exist.

In terms of weather, we're no better informed; our best guess from the information that we could gather before leaving the UK is that it will be cold and wet at the beginning, warm and wet in the middle, and cold and wet again at the end. As for David Bellamy, we'll just have to let nature take its course and hope for the best.

Oddly enough, it's this very thought that brings my mind alarmingly back to the subject in hand: namely, bears. Only when my senses return to their immediate surroundings do I realise that the sound of footsteps outside the tent has stopped. Anyone who's ever slept in a tent will know how darkness seems to amplify sounds beyond all reason – particularly those of wild, man-eating beasts – but as I doze off to sleep, I can't help but feel a little relieved.

At least, that is, until I hear the sound of wolves howling in the distance.

1 INTO THE LION'S DEN

I felt so nervous I thought I was going to throw up.

'Your trip sounds exciting,' said the imposing woman across the vast expanse of mahogany that lay between us.

'Yes, yes, it is!' I began enthusiastically, but before I had a chance to continue, a door opened to my left and a voice said, 'Whenever you're ready, Mr Grogan.' The secretary I'd been speaking to did a quick lap of her desk, wished me luck and beckoned me in.

They say a winning smile can do wonders for your chances at interview; an inane grin, such as the one I then gave, is probably marginally less effective. In front, or rather all around me, sat three of the most distinguished people I had ever met: to my left was Mrs Susan Pegler LTA LSSM (Dip), a professional tennis coach (I had no idea what the letters stood for, but they sounded intimidating); in front of me was Mr Ian Beer CBE JP, a former rugby international and Chairman of the Sports Council for England (I knew exactly what his letters stood for, and they *were* intimidating); and finally, to my right, in the darkest corner of the room, sat Sir Henry Beverly, Director-General of the Winston Churchill Memorial Trust, which every year helps to fund around a hundred worthwhile travel projects all over the world. I'd been given brief biographies of the first two before I went in (presumably to shatter any last vestige of confidence that might remain), but there was nothing next to Sir Henry's name. All I knew was that, as the man from the Trust, he was the linchpin of the lynch mob.

'You'll have to forgive my appearance,' began Sir Henry, indicating the brace fastened around his neck. 'I got into a tussle with a taxi yesterday,' he explained, laughing at his own joke. I laughed too, out of politeness, but it came out as more of a cackle; it was, I thought, a promising start. Eventually though, I began to relax, and once we started talking about my travel plans, I felt I was on solid ground. Then came the final question: 'So, tell us everything you know about Sir Winston Churchill?'

I couldn't believe it. I almost let out a groan of despair. Here I was, being interviewed by the Winston Churchill Memorial Trust, and I hadn't done a minute's research on the great man himself. I knew he'd led Britain through the Second World War, that he smoked cigars, and that he was a bit of a wag when it came to parliamentary speeches, but I felt certain my inquisitors were after something a little less obvious. After an agonising pause, and equally agonising thought, I came up with the stunning and decisive response: 'Not a lot actually.'

I might as well have pulled down my trousers, offered them the stars and given them the moon. I tried to recover, muttering something about his travels in Uganda (I'd been there the year before) and his penchant for painting (who'd have thought a degree in Art History would ever come in useful?) but it was too late. As I stood up to leave, my worst fears were confirmed:

'Thanks for coming in to see us, Paul,' Sir Henry began, 'and don't worry if we decide not to award you a fellowship – I'm sure you'll have a great trip anyway.'

Of course, it all started long before that fateful fifteen minutes. It was at a university mountaineering club slide show in 1992 that I first met Richard Boddington, a man whose popularity with women is matched only by his penchant for the same. Our eyes met across a glass of cheap white wine, and I knew then that it would be the start of a beautiful relationship.

Actually, that's a lie. All I knew was that (a) everyone else in the room seemed to know everyone else, and (b) that I couldn't feign interest in the wine label much longer without arousing uncertain glances and certain derision. 'So, you're thinking of getting into mountaineering?' I ventured, tentatively addressing my fellow connoisseur. 'Yeah,' he replied, with measured nonchalance, apparently unwilling to commit himself any more to the subject in hand or, for that matter, to our fledgling conversation.

'I might give canoeing a go tomorrow,' I enthused, trying to elicit more than a one-word response. 'Cool,' came the inspired reply. Nodding politely, I was just about to resume my study of Bulgarian bouquets when I realised there was more to come: 'I was thinking of either canoeing or rowing, but I'm not sure I can be arsed with rowing,' he finally shrugged. Overwhelmed by this sudden rush of syllables, I blurted out that perhaps we should meet up and go down to the beginners' canoe session together? 'Yeah,' he replied, 'cool.'

In Rich, I realised, I had found a kindred spirit: I, too, had decided to try canoeing, not out of any deep-rooted desire, but because I couldn't face the early-morning starts that seemed to be *de rigueur* for the more traditional university sport of rowing (well, that and the fact that I was six inches too short and six stone too scrawny to ever be an accomplished oarsman). Ironically, Rich *did* have the right build to be a rower, but because of his aforementioned affection for the fairer sex, he didn't believe in mornings, and consequently distrusted anyone who got out of bed before midday.

Given this allergy to early starts, it was hardly surprising that – for us at least – canoeing was more recreational than competitive. As an excuse not to do any work, it was second to none: just getting to the river could take the best part of a morning, and by the time we'd bobbed down a few rapids and picked up a fish supper on the way home, it was invariably too late to do much more than plan our next trip. And so it was that for the next three years we splashed and snacked our way around Scotland, determined to see as little of the inside of the university library as possible.

At some point we thought – albeit half-heartedly – about canoeing one of the world's great rivers from source to sea, again not because of any obsession with paddling per se, but because we liked the idea of making a long journey somewhere that was a world away from the commotion of our day-to-day lives. After university we went our separate ways, but we kept in touch and met up whenever we could. I went to America for a year and then landed a job with a travel magazine based in Essex. Rich, meanwhile, found employment as an environmental scientist, handing in his notice a few months later to become a river guide on the Zambezi. When he returned home he was offered some work on a slurry pit in Slough, and soon became something of a leading light in sewage assessment.

Needless to say, neither of us was over-keen on our respective working environments, but for two years we endured our nine-to-five lives without giving much thought to our source-to-sea ambition, which had been filed well and truly in the 'one day' category. And then, quite unexpectedly, 'one day' became today and our pipe dream became a reality.

The nudge we needed was provided by a book called *Running the Amazon* by Joe Kane, about the first ever source-to-sea descent of the world's second-longest river. The story itself was as compelling as it was remarkable, but it was the last page – and more specifically the last few lines – that made the greatest impression: 'All I *can* say is this: for a while at least, the Amazon sucked me out of my cocoon, and my life has been better for it. To anyone seriously considering a flying leap into the void, I say: go.'

The next day I dropped Rich an email suggesting it might be time to meet up. His reply was uncharacteristically enthusiastic, and a couple of weeks later we converged on the map room of the Royal Geographical Society in London, as much for inspiration as for advice. With the help of an atlas the size of a small mattress, we compiled a list of the world's ten longest rivers. After making a few notes, we emerged into the gathering dusk of Hyde Park. Even then, I was acutely aware that I was at a turning point in my life: come what may, our big adventure had begun.

Over the coming weeks we started to think about what we were looking for in a river, and what we really wanted to get out of our journey. For us, a source-to-sea descent was something of a Holy Grail, equivalent, say, to a mountaineer climbing a mountain from sea level. Rich and I had obviously done shorter trips together in the past, but we both felt that the only way to really experience a river, to truly get to know it, was to start at the top and finish at the bottom. Similarly, it needed to be long – hence our list; all of our previous jaunts had been frustratingly short, but this time we were determined to savour life on the river to the full.

In many respects, the Nile would have been ideal: it was the longest river in the world and as far as we knew it had never been travelled all the way from source to sea in a single journey. Perhaps more importantly, it was also somewhere hot, another condition near the top of our wish list. Even higher on the list, however, was staying alive, and continued civil war and political uncertainty in Sudan meant the Nile was out of the question.

So, too, were the Congo and the Niger, the former because of an ongoing civil war in the republic of the same name, the latter because its source lay in Sierra Leone, which at the time was undergoing violent political upheaval. The Zambezi was another option, but we'd already travelled the length of Lake Kariba on a previous trip and had no wish to repeat it. North America and Europe, meanwhile, were ruled out for being too populated and too well known. With that in mind, our attention turned to South America and Asia.

The Amazon had already been paddled, as had most – if not all – of the major rivers in South America, but the Amazon's tributaries looked more promising. One, the Madeira, stood out as a favourite, so we duly added it to our shortlist.

Across on the other side of the world were the mighty rivers of Asia, all of them in the top six of our longest-rivers list: the Yangtze in China, the Lena and Yenisei in Russia, and the Mekong, which flowed through Tibet, China and Thailand. The Yangtze was ruled out for being too industrialised, a characteristic that seemed to go against the wilderness picture we'd built up in our imaginations. The Lena and Yenisei, both flowing into the Arctic Ocean from deep in the heart of Siberia, looked too desolate and cold – we might have wanted wilderness, but we weren't stupid. The Mekong, meanwhile, had only recently been travelled *upstream* by a team intent on following the river from sea to source by bike, although quite why anyone would want to cycle *up* a river when it's perfectly viable to let gravity do all the hard work is beyond me, but that's by the by.

Another river, slightly shorter than the Mekong at 2,900km, also caught our eye, as it was one we'd never heard of before: the Brahmaputra. Like the Mekong, its source was in Tibet, and from the map it looked as though it flowed through some pretty mountainous terrain. Whether or not it was navigable in a canoe we had no idea, but we popped it into the melting pot alongside the Madeira. The only other river that seemed suitable was the Amur, which, like the Brahmaputra, we'd never heard of. It started its life as two tributaries, both of which began within a few kilometres of each other, high in the mountains of northern Mongolia. The northernmost tributary flowed into Russia, while the slightly longer, southernmost tributary flowed into China. From the point at which these two tributaries met, the river followed the Russia–China border for some 2,000km, before veering northeast, back into Russia and – ultimately – to the Pacific Ocean.

It seemed remarkable to us that two tributaries which started life on separate sides of the same mountain should meet for the first time over 1,500km later, and this added to the river's appeal. We knew from experience that we would have little hope of crossing straight into China, so we decided to confine our thoughts to the shorter of the two tributaries, in the vague hope that the Russian authorities would be marginally less resistant to any unorthodox requests. This failed to address the more pressing issue, namely that the Amur followed the Russia–China border for over half of its length, but we decided it was worthy of further investigation. The fact that it also crossed Siberia, and therefore qualified for automatic inclusion in the 'desolate and cold' category, somehow seemed to escape our attention.

Now all we needed was some advice from someone who knew what they were talking about. After a few tentative enquiries we were told there was only one man who had the depth and breadth of knowledge we were looking for, and his name was Green Slime. I have since discovered that his real name is Peter Knowles, but at the time everyone we spoke to simply referred to him as Slime. When I phoned him, I didn't know whether to address him as 'Mr Slime', 'Green', or simply 'sir'. 'Hello there!' I exclaimed, immensely pleased at my solution to the problem. 'You don't know me,' I continued, 'but you might just be able to save my life.'

A few weeks later Rich and I went to meet Slime at a pub in southwest London, where we were greeted by a bespectacled grin on legs. Slime seemed even more enthusiastic than us about our little adventure, and when we told him that we were allowing six months for the journey, he became positively giddy with excitement. 'Ooh,' he gushed, with *Carry On* enthusiasm, 'you could canoe any river in the world in that time. Where are you thinking of going?'

Opening Slime's atlas in amongst half-finished pint glasses, we outlined our plan and pointed out the three rivers that were on our short list. First up was the Brahmaputra, which was instantly greeted with a slow intake of breath: 'The gorges in this section here,' Slime said, indicating the sweep of river dropping down off the Tibetan Plateau, 'are unimaginably deep, with mile after mile of continuous white water.' Rich's eyes lit up, but Slime continued to shake his head. 'It's been tried. In fact, people have died trying, but no one's done it yet.' Somehow, the phrase 'died trying' didn't quite capture the spirit of what we were hoping to achieve.

Of the two remaining options, Slime wasn't impressed by the Madeira, hinting that any of its tributaries would be as long, flat and boring as the Amazon itself. In fact, we knew this from our own research: after dropping over 5,000m in its first 800km, the Amazon then drops less than 300m in its remaining 5,500km, an average of just five centimetres per kilometre. Ocean-going liners can navigate 3,700km upriver, and even the tide sweeps 800km inland. 'Not only that,' he said, 'but there's nothing there: the only thing you'll see for thousands of miles will be trees.'

With South America ruled out, all that was left was the Amur. 'Hmm,' mused Slime, pausing for thought, 'that might work. Of course, they may not let you into Russia from Mongolia, they probably won't let you near the Russia–China border, and even then you might not be able to reach the end before the river freezes over, but apart from that it looks promising.' How very reassuring. It wasn't until much later (too late, as it turned out) that we learned the Amur also flows through the largest forest on the planet. This forest – or *Taiga*, as it is known in Siberia –

covers an area the size of all 48 mainland US states, and is twice the size of all the world's tropical forests put together. So much, you might think, for riverside views.

By the time we'd decamped to Slime's house, he was already making plans. 'You could call it "Mongolia to the Pacific: Journey from the Centre of the Earth",' he enthused, pulling out bundles of press clippings that he thought might be of use. 'I wouldn't worry too much about the border,' he added. 'If it comes to it you can always sneak down without telling anyone.' But of course! Rather than paddle, we could just tiptoe 2,000km along one of the world's most sensitive borders …

In fact, the only appealing thing about the Amur was that we didn't know the first thing about it. We had no mental picture of what it would be like, and as such it was just the flying leap we'd been looking for. Now all we needed to do was buy a boat or two, apply for a couple of visas and then jump on a plane. Oh, and dig out the odd thousand pounds that might have fallen down the back of the sofa; our priority was obviously to obtain permission to travel on the river, but equally important was finding sponsors to help fund our journey. In the end, we decided the best way forward would be for us to tackle one of these tasks each, so while Rich set about wooing various embassies with scented letters, I began to think about robbing a bank.

My main concern was cash: we already had a lot of our own camping equipment, and even if we couldn't persuade a manufacturer to lend us some suitable boats, I felt sure that we'd be able to cover these costs ourselves. What I was less sure about was how much it would cost to get the permissions we needed, how much things would cost on the river, and how much we'd need by way of 'administrative fees' along the way.

After a few false starts, my quest for sponsorship eventually led me to the doors of the Churchill Trust, and my triumphant interview. Ironically, I'd made a point of speaking to past interviewees to make sure I wouldn't get caught out. 'Make sure you've got a contingency plan. They like to think that what you're doing is safe, even if it isn't,' urged one. 'Give them all a smile when you enter the room, and look them in the eye when you're speaking,' suggested another. No one, but *no one*, said anything to the effect of 'if you don't swot up on Winston, you might as well walk in there backwards with your trousers down'. As I left the building along the Trust's cavernous corridors, I felt like I'd fed myself to the lions cheek-first.

Rich wasn't having much luck either. Before setting about getting hold of visas, he tried to learn more about the river, with mixed results: he discovered, for example, that on 18 May 1998 a riverside town called Shilka experienced some unseasonably cold weather; that 12,422 hectares of land in the river's Khabarovsk region is set aside for agriculture; and that, on average, the Amur discharges 346km^3 of water into the Pacific Ocean per annum. All fascinating stuff, I'm sure you'll agree, but it struck me that we needed something a little more substantial, such as where we might be able to buy bread, or – I don't know – where we'd be most likely to get shot at?

There was *some* promising news, however: following centuries of conflict between Russia and China, ownership of the river's 3000-odd islands had finally been ratified in a treaty signed less than twelve months previously. It wasn't much to go on, but it was better than a pie chart of the region's rodent population.

At this stage we still had no idea if we'd even get as far as the source, but that wasn't the point: as far as potential sponsors were concerned, we could practically smell the Pacific. In fact, mindless optimism proved to be something of a winning hand when it came to equipment manufacturers, and it wasn't long before we had all of the extra gear – including boats and paddles – that were required for our journey. Now all we needed was some cool, hard cash.

The letter from the Churchill Trust arrived about a month after the interview. As I picked it up, all I could think about was a story I'd once read in a book called *Danziger's Travels*: like me, the author had applied for a Churchill Fellowship, and about a month later he'd received a sizeable package in the post. Reasoning that a letter of rejection was unlikely to merit an entire package, he'd guessed (quite rightly) that he'd been granted an award before he even opened it. With this in mind, I fingered my svelte little envelope with a sinking heart. Resigned to rejection, I prised it open and read the first line. I got about as far as 'I'm very pleased to inform you …' before running up and down the stairs. Twice. I yelled, 'Come on!' at an annoyingly loud volume. I introduced myself in Russian (I'd recently enrolled in a night class at the local college), and was very pleased to make my acquaintance. I was, I thought, one of the nicest people I'd ever met.

Rich was typically excited when I phoned to tell him. 'Cool' was about the best he could manage, although he may have thrown a 'nice one' in there for good measure. But it didn't matter: we were on our way to Siberia, and no one could stop us. No one, that is, apart from the entire Russian Army, the Chinese Embassy in Moscow and the Mongolian Consulate in London. Even the Foreign & Commonwealth Office weren't keen: 'This is clearly a sensitive region, and any inconsistencies in your documentation would incur the immediate attention of local police. Were you to get into trouble, you would be a long way from any assistance.' Given that we didn't actually have any documentation, the risk of inconsistencies seemed like something of a moot point.

By now it was early February and we were hoping to fly to Ulaan Baatar in late April: as far as we could tell, if we left any sooner all the rivers in Mongolia would be frozen; if we left any later there was a chance that the river would freeze over again before we reached the Pacific. Estimating we could travel 30–40km a day, we guessed it would take three to four months, assuming nothing went wrong along the way. If we were delayed at the Mongolia–Russia border or the Russia–China border, there was no telling how long it would take.

This gave us less than two months to sort out all of our permissions and visas and organise the rest of our journey. Repeated letters to the relevant embassies went unanswered, and emails to other organisations might as well have done: 'Unfortunately there is big problem,' declared the reply from the Mongolian Outdoor Sports Federation. 'It isn't possible to travel by the rivers through Russian boundary. Permission can only be given to citizens of neighbouring countries.'

The advice from one Moscow-based adventure-tour operator was even less encouraging: 'Evacuation from Amur can be arranged only by special charter of helicopter. During the summer in Amur region there is "super moskitos" period when even local citizens avoid going to Taiga. In the end of summer big storms can took place, so the canoeing can be onerous.' The letter from the Chinese Canoe Association probably said much the same thing, but it was in Chinese, so it was hard to tell. Thus far, Slime's prediction was proving all too accurate, and now – with only a few weeks to go – we were battling an overwhelming tide of bureaucracy.

Clearly we needed help, so, following the advice of a number of people, we got in touch with Dmitry Shparo, the director of another adventure-tour company in Moscow. All we knew about him was that he'd once helped Sir Ranulph Fiennes in his attempt to drive from London to New York via the Bering Strait. That particular expedition, we discovered, never took place because the sponsor withdrew the funding, but it had established Dmitry as something of a mover and a shaker in Russia's expedition community.

With time fast running out we had little choice but to entrust our outstanding visa problems to him. While Dmitry paced the passageways of power on our behalf, we got on with sorting out the trip's minor details, such as booking our flights to Mongolia.

We didn't even try out our new canoes until a few weeks before we left. Our testing ground was a stretch of the River Thames between Henley and Marlow. The distance was about 20km – only half of what we were planning to cover every day on the Amur – and it just about finished us off. We had to stop at the halfway point for an ice cream, and even then I was willing it to end (the paddle that is, not the ice cream). It all seemed far too cold and wet for my liking. I convinced myself that on a river as long as the Amur we'd get fitter as we went along, but psychologically I was beginning to wonder if we hadn't bitten off more than we could chew.

The week before we were due to leave, a friend of Rich's threw us a good-luck party. Our host thought it would be fun for everyone to dress up as a character that we might meet along the river: in addition to a border guard, a UN peacekeeper and a KGB agent with an alarmingly convincing accent, two people came as angels, and no fewer than three of our closest friends decided that the grim reaper was a fairly safe bet. Oh, how we laughed.

The last week passed in a frenzy of activity. Although Dmitry was working on our permissions to travel on the river, we still had to queue for standard tourist visas at all of the relevant embassies and consulates in London; we had to get vaccinations for every ailment known to medical science; and we had to take a PhD in electronics to learn how to charge our camera batteries with a solar panel. The fact that the camera itself didn't arrive until three days before we were supposed to leave didn't help matters. Our spray-decks – the only thing that would prevent our canoes from being swamped in the event of a capsize – arrived with just a day to spare. And then, just when we thought things couldn't get any more hectic, we got an urgent email from Dmitry: the next day, he said, he'd arranged for us to meet the Russian Ambassador in London. Never mind that in the next 24 hours we had to pick up our money, buy all our food, pack all our gear, waterproof all our maps, solder wires to our solar panel, say goodbye to our grannies and get a haircut; when the Russian Ambassador wants you to pop over for afternoon tea, you go.

'The Ambassador will be with you in a minute.' We were standing self-consciously in an imposing anteroom not much bigger than a football stadium. Only a few minutes before we'd been wandering equally self-consciously along London's Kensington Palace Gardens, trying to find the Russian Embassy. I half-expected to see at least one shifty-looking character standing outside in the rain with a copy of *Pravda* peeking out from behind folded arms, a consequence, perhaps, of having read too many spy novels as a child. Disappointingly, we found nothing more sinister than a two-way intercom.

When we were buzzed inside it was like walking into a different country. The people at the reception desk were gossiping animatedly in Russian. I tried to introduce myself, but I couldn't find the words quickly enough. I finally managed something that sounded like 'glasnost sputnik vodka bratwurst', which was greeted with a barricade of blank looks. For the first time, it finally began to dawn on me just what we were letting ourselves in for.

While we waited we were joined by the Ambassador's personal assistant, an earnest young Muscovite with a cynical smirk on his face. He must have known something about our trip, but he didn't know where we were going. When we told him, he smiled a smile that said: sounds great, but you do know you're going to die? 'And what about the *super moskies*?' he added conspiratorially, letting slip his first laugh of the day – he probably allowed himself four.

Before we had time to answer, we were called in to see the Ambassador. His name, we'd had little time to learn, was Grigory B Karasin. I was grateful when he greeted us in English, but I was less grateful when he asked if either of us spoke Russian. After my linguistic triumph of earlier, however, I was prepared for just such an eventuality. Drawing on months of night-class knowledge, I took a deep breath and launched into my reply. 'A little,' I said finally, beaming with satisfaction. 'Oh well,' he continued in English, 'at least you've still got plenty of time to learn. When are you leaving?' Tomorrow, I told him, and at this he laughed out loud, shaking his head and patting me paternally on the shoulder.

Over tea he quizzed us about our journey. Dmitry had mentioned that the Ambassador was a big fan of adventure sports and he seemed genuinely interested in our plans. 'So tell me,' he asked sincerely, 'how long is the Amur?' 4,400km, we replied. 'And how long do you expect the journey to take?' About four months, depending on the weather and other 'considerations', I said, trying to be diplomatic. 'And have you made such a journey before?' Well, I shrugged, we once spent seven days on a river in Turkey. With that, the Ambassador let loose another bellyful of laughter. We laughed too, but more out of hysteria than amusement. I was starting to feel sick.

When we finally rose to leave, he became serious for a moment: 'Here is my card,' he said, holding out his hand. 'If you ever need anything, just let me know.' It was a heartfelt gesture and for a fleeting moment I wanted to tell him everything: about the difficulties we faced crossing into Russia on the river, about the problems posed by the Russia–China border, and about the possibility that the river might freeze over before we even reached the end. But I didn't. I just shook his hand, said thank you, and left. And with that, we were on our own.

I continued to feel sick for the rest of the day and most of that night. We were due to leave at 6 a.m., but with twelve hours to go we *still* had to pack our canoes, waterproof our maps and solder connections to our solar panel. At 3 a.m. I found myself siphoning tea granules into sterile urine bottles (presumably unused) donated by the local surgery; we still didn't know what food we'd be able to buy in Mongolia, but without tea there was a chance we'd never even get to Mongolia.

Before I went to bed, I stood over the maps that were spread out to dry, and looked at them closely for the first time. There were nine of them, each more than a metre square, and pieced together they looked decidedly daunting: our route seemed to traverse nothing but a vast expanse of forest, hundreds of kilometres from anywhere. It was exactly the wilderness we'd set out to find, and yet now, on the morning of our departure, it seemed impossibly remote.

At around 4 a.m. I finally nodded off. A minute later, I heard Rich cursing next door. 'It's six-thirty!' he cried, running past my door. 'We're going to miss our flight!' For a moment, I just lay there. In a little over twelve hours we'd be in Ulaan Baatar. We didn't have permission to canoe in Mongolia, we didn't have permits to cross into Russia, and the Russia–China border was still strictly out of bounds. And now we were late.

It was, I thought, a promising start.

2 GREASING THE WHEELS

'A private dance,' said the captain, outlining the in-flight entertainment options on the Moscow leg of our journey, 'consists of a client taking the girl of his choice to a room for five minutes, where she dances to loud music and takes off her clothes in close proximity to the gentleman …'

It took me a few moments to realise that I was hallucinating from lack of sleep: in the absence of anything as sophisticated as a video, radio or life jacket to keep me amused, I'd turned to the agenda-setting *Moscow Times* in the hope of some insight into Russian culture: a spread on Moscow's burgeoning strip clubs wasn't quite what I had in mind; nor was the equally entertaining 'Linguist's Corner', which gave me the chance to swot up on my vocabulary with everyday phrases like 'withered on a stalk' and 'acute abdomen'.

Alas, there wasn't a strip club in sight on arrival at Moscow's Sheremyetevo Airport, but I did have to ask a young airport attendant where we needed to go to catch our connecting flight to Mongolia. After a promising start I got confused with the word 'go' (there are approximately 973 variations in Russian) and promptly announced that Rich and I were travelling to Mongolia *on foot*, and could we please be directed to the nearest lunatic asylum? Not surprisingly, the first girl simply fled in panic, and it took a few minutes of loud, drawn-out syllables before our second victim had any idea what we were talking about. But it was worth it: once on board our onward flight we were served a meat stew covered in lightly icicled onions, both of which contributed rather neatly to an all-out assault on my acute abdomen and the withering that duly ensued.

To kill some time on the six-hour flight – and having given up on the 'Linguist's Corner' crossword some hours previously – I read up on our destination: Mongolia, I soon learned, has a population of just 2.3 million people, all living in an area six times the size of the UK (put another way, that's equivalent to having most of Western Europe inhabited by a population that habitually squeezes into London's Underground every weekday morning). The sense of space is staggering, and nowhere is this more starkly illustrated than from a plane at 30,000 feet: as we crossed the mountains that straddled the border between Russia and Mongolia, I could see the steppe stretching to the horizon like an impossibly smooth fairway, interrupted only by the occasional ribbon of river. It was this view that gave me my first mental picture of what the start of our journey might be like, and I felt a familiar surge of excitement at the thought of being somewhere new for the first time.

This was closely followed by an equally familiar feeling of abject fear: I was, as they say in polite circles, soiling my britches. It wasn't so much the thought of being immersed in a completely new culture without knowing how to speak a word of the language, but of doing it with two sixty-kilo canoes as carry-on. We had tried sorting out some sort of airport shuttle to the nearest guesthouse when we were back in the UK, but in the end we decided it would be easier to organise locally. And by easier,

I mean cheaper. And so it was that we arrived in Outer Mongolia (somehow the word 'Outer' makes it sound so much more daunting) without a clue as to how we might get out of the airport, let alone how we might get to the source of an impossibly remote river.

The first thing I noticed as we walked off the plane was how hot it was, particularly after Aeroflot's Siberian acclimatisation program. Equally striking was how quiet the airport was: after having our passports and papers stamped, stamped and (if you wouldn't mind) re-stamped, we emerged into the arrivals hall to be greeted by ... absolutely no one. The only people there were our fellow passengers, a handful of hostel owners, and a big, bearded American wearing cowboy boots and a lumberjack shirt. Somehow, we decided that Grizzly Adams looked like our best bet, and that if we stared forlornly at our canoes for long enough, his curiosity would get the better of him: by and by he'd come over to say howdy, offer us a lift, insist on looking after our boats for a few days and introduce us to a local guide, who'd be more than happy to take us to the source of our chosen river for a very reasonable sum indeed. Which, as it transpired, is exactly what happened.

Our saviour's name was Jim Glembowski, a Christian missionary who lived and worked in Ulaan Baatar. He was involved in all sorts of community projects, he told us, and he hadn't even started spreading the word of God, having spent the last four years just learning the language and getting to know the people. 'How can you expect people to put their faith in God if they can't even put their faith in you?' he explained.

I was waiting for him to ask us if God was our saviour, but the question never came. Instead, he just went out of his way to help us: within a few hours of our arrival, all of our equipment was safely stored in a lockup on the outskirts of the city and we were poring over maps in the front room of his modest apartment. Once we'd outlined our plans, he arranged a meeting with a local guide that very evening, before dropping us at the nearest hotel.

After a few hours in a light coma, we met Gal, Jim's guide, in the hotel bar, which was just about dark enough for a million-dollar arms deal. He was older than I expected, and very softly spoken, but his English was good, and he assured us that getting close to the source by jeep would be no problem, and that once we were there, we'd be able to hire horses to take us the rest of the way.

His only concern, he said, were the canoes. When we told him they were twelve feet long, he looked like he was going to cry, but something had clearly been lost in translation: in his mind's eye he had a picture of two wooden rowing boats complete with oars, and he seemed somewhat relieved to learn that our own boats only *weighed* that much. Thus reassured, he agreed a price and suggested we meet again early the next day, to buy a roof rack for his jeep.

In the cold light of the following morning, the roof rack in question looked like it had been soldered together by a partially sighted pensioner wearing boxing gloves, but the salesman was nothing if not loyal to the brand. To demonstrate its strength he leaped precariously from strut to strut, and even invited me to do the same, but by that stage I was prepared to accept that his handiwork was at least as strong as my ankles. Gal seemed unconvinced, but when we pointed out how useful it would be for future trips, he was soon spending our money with gay abandon.

The next stop on our cultural tour of Mongolia's capital was the food market, where we hoped to buy supplies that would last us all the way to the Russian border; we had no way of knowing what we'd be able to find en route, so we had to assume the worst. When we'd packed just 24 hours before, we'd had no idea what we'd be able to find in the way of staples, but the weight of our already-laden canoes meant we'd had to leave all the pasta, noodles and rice behind. What we had included were all of the things that didn't weigh very much, but which we'd thought might be more difficult to come by in the Siberian Styx: powdered soup, garlic salt and stock cubes, dried vegetables and chillies, Bird's custard powder and, of course, tea granules.

As it turned out, we needn't have bothered: with the words of Chippy Powell still ringing in our ears ('talking to shepherds can frequently get you bits of sheep'), we walked into the Mercury Market in downtown Ulaan Baatar with tongues practically basting the vast array of goods on display. All around us were rows of tables piled high with food, from pigs' trotters to Swiss chocolate. We found everything we could possibly have needed and more, including two large salamis and a kilo of dried meat-shavings, the latter simply stuffed into a plastic bag. We had no idea what it would taste like – or indeed if it was really meat – but the fact that it was the most expensive item there seemed to suggest that it was something of a local delicacy.

So we had food and we had transport; now all we needed was some local diplomacy. And by that, I mean asking Gal to find out if we'd even be allowed near the river in the first place.

While Gal busied himself emailing one of his contacts in the Ministry of Foreign Affairs, we embarked on a mission to phone Dmitry in Moscow, to find out if we'd been given permission to so much as sneeze in the direction of Russia. I say mission, because that's precisely what it was; for those who've never had the pleasure, standard operating procedure goes something like this:

(1) Become fluent in Mongolian before proceeding to the nearest post office.
(2) Fill out a form (whereabouts unclear) detailing the name and number of who you want to call.
(3) Pay at a cash desk for the length of call you are about to make (ignoring the fact that you won't know how long the call is until you've made it).

(4) Wait in a big hall full of gossiping Mongolians until your name is called (in Mongolian).

(5) Wait another five minutes until a kind stranger points to you and indicates (via sign language) that they've been calling your name for the last five minutes.

(6) Proceed to your booth to complete your call.

(7) Realise you've got the wrong number and return to step (2).

When we finally got through to Moscow, Dmitry was out. 'Would we mind calling back in an hour?' his secretary asked innocently. We called back an hour and thirty seconds later. Dmitry had come and gone, but he wanted to know why we were phoning? 'Oh, nothing really, just to chat about the weather, the news … oh, and the small matter of what we're supposed to be doing for the next five months.' In the event, it had to wait: Gal had heard from his man at the ministry, who had arranged for us to meet with a colonel at the headquarters of the Mongolian Border Guard Federation later that afternoon. It wasn't an invitation we felt we could refuse.

Two hours later we were standing nervously in front of a big desk belonging to a big cheese. 'So,' the colonel barked suspiciously, 'tell me again why you want to cross into Russia by river?' With the help of Gal and an impressive floor-to-ceiling map, I outlined our route.

Our aim, I began, was to travel the Amur from its source in Mongolia to its mouth on Russia's Pacific coast. Following the blue squiggles on the map with my finger, I traced the river's two main tributaries: 'The longer of the two, the Gerlen, heads southeast into China,' I explained, 'but we've been refused permission to enter Chinese territory. Our only option,' I concluded confidently, 'is to follow the Onon, which heads directly into Russia. The problem,' (and here's where I sighed my most forlorn sigh), 'is that foreigners are only allowed to cross into Russia on the Trans-Mongolian Railway, five hundred kilometres to the west.'

The colonel seemed impressed, not so much by my powers of persuasion, but by the length of our trip. Slowly warming to the idea, he told us a Russian general was in town to discuss border relations; he couldn't promise anything, but for a small 'administrative fee' – preferably including a few portraits of Mr Washington – he'd be delighted to discuss our case.

On our return the following morning, the colonel was all smiles; everything was arranged. When we arrived at the Russian border, he assured us, there would be no problems. We felt immensely relieved. The alternative didn't bear thinking about – so much so, in fact, that we'd actually thought about it rather a lot: the only other option would have been to meet Gal where the river crossed the border (assuming there was a road nearby), drive back to Ulaan Baatar with our boats, and then catch the train into Russia. Once inside Russia we'd have to catch another train to Chita (still trailing our sixty-kilo canoes), and then hitch a lift the last few hundred kilometres to the river. The irony was that this would have meant rejoining the river at exactly the same place we'd got off, only with *slightly* longer arms. The detour, we'd worked out, would have been about 2,000km, but it wasn't that so much as the interruption that mattered: to us, it just seemed important to follow the natural flow of the river.

As we were getting up to leave, the colonel asked when we'd be likely to cross the border. At this stage we still hadn't heard anything from Dmitry about whether we'd be allowed to continue *beyond* the border, and I guessed it would take at least the rest of that day to reach him. The river was a day's drive from Ulaan Baatar, and from what Gal had told us it would take another two days to get to the source on foot. As I began adding up the days in my head, however, our kindly colonel started to get impatient. 'How does the first of June sound?' he demanded, addressing Gal in Mongolian. Today was 16 May; providing everything went to plan, that would still give us twelve days to travel the 600km from the source to the border. We had no idea what the current would be like, or even if the river would be navigable, but I had to make a decision.

'The first of June sounds fine,' I said finally, anxious not to push the colonel's patience any further. This expiry date was duly added to our visas before we were shown to the door. '*Bayarlalah, mash Bayarlalah*,' I enthused, thanking our deliverer with all the enthusiasm of a prisoner being given a stay of execution. It seemed to go down well, but I probably wouldn't have been nearly so grateful if I'd known the problems this new deadline was about to cause.

For the time being, though, visa deadlines were the least of our worries: before we could go anywhere, we had to run the gauntlet of the great Mongolian phone stampede all over again.

When we at last managed to speak to Dmitry later that day, he had some good news … sort of. He'd managed to secure permission for us to travel on the Russian parts of the river in June and September. In July and August, he explained, the Amur was going to be the focus of a massive military exercise and would be strictly out of bounds. We still didn't have permission from China to go anywhere near the border, but what's a few thousand kilometres between friends?

That evening we picked up our gear from Jim's lockup and loaded the boats onto our shiny new roof rack, before bidding Jim a fond farewell. We spent the rest of the night knee-deep in maps, camping gear and meat shavings, trying to pack everything so that it would be easy to carry. Paddling equipment, camera gear, first-aid kit, stove, clothes, books and the odd kilo of non-sequential dollar bills – we had to find a home for it all. It was gone 2 a.m. by the time I clipped my last dry-bag shut and shuffled into bed. As I dropped off to sleep, however, I couldn't help but feel that everything was going a bit too smoothly.

3 WALKING ON WATER

Gal picked us up at first light, but before we could hit the open road we had one more rendezvous to keep. On the outskirts to the east of the city, Gal's driver, Cholon, turned up a rough dirt track. A few rights, lefts and lurches later, we pulled up outside his home, a round felt tent – or *ger* – nestling in a sprawling shantytown of similar dwellings. *Gers*, or *yurts* as they are known in Russia, are the abode of choice for many Mongolians, even in the cities; they provide a warm shelter during the severe winter months (temperatures as low as -40°C are not uncommon) and a cool haven during the country's scorching summers. A dung-burning stove, or *zuukh*, provides the focal point, with beds arranged around the outer walls and a small table placed near the centre for serving food, tea and *airag* (a milky concoction that's vaguely alcoholic). The position of family members and guests is dictated by a strict hierarchy in which elders enjoy pride of place.

Traditional rituals are also closely observed: when approaching a *ger*, for example, it's polite to call out *'nokhoi khor'* (literally 'tether your dog'), but it's impolite to whistle inside or touch other occupants' hats. Visitors who step on or kick someone else's feet should immediately shake their hand. But for Mongolians, arguably the most important ritual of all is blessing a long journey, which in our case involved Cholon's wife sprinkling yak's milk in the path of our waiting jeep.

Thus prepared, we at last rolled out of the city under darkening skies, rain lashing at the windscreen. Not surprisingly, the fact that this was exactly the kind of weather we'd been expecting was no consolation at all. An hour later, though, the clouds started to clear, and as we crested the first pass into the mountains I could see the vast, sun-mottled valley of Ulaan Baatar framed in the back window of the jeep. The road we were on, Gal told us, had been built in the 1950s, during a time of rare co-operation between the Chinese and the Soviets, but when the goodwill had run out, so had the road; 70 km east of Ulaan Baatar, we bounced off the tarmac and headed into the hills.

Gal's driver, I can happily attest, was a certified lunatic. Apart from short stretches of dusty track, the route we were following was marked by little more than tyre tracks in the steppe, but Cholon was clearly on a mission to hit as many bumps as possible, as fast as possible. It didn't seem to matter if I tried to look out for these bumps or not – the back of the jeep had a mind of its own, bucking and lurching independently of the front, while the exposed metal ceiling had an irritating habit of dropping onto my head after every fourth bump. The only way to take my mind off the ceiling (would that it had been the other way round) was to chat to Gal between blows.

His name, he told us, meant 'Fire Hero' in Mongolian, something which seemed to cause him a great deal of embarrassment. He was born and bred in Ulaan Baatar, but retained a great respect – as most Mongolians do – for the countryside. As we drove, we passed an abandoned Russian army base, and Gal lamented the damage that the Soviets had done to his country's environment; from 1921 until the collapse of communism in 1991, Mongolia was – to all intents and purposes – an occupied country, providing a convenient buffer-zone between China and the Motherland. When the Russians finally withdrew, Gal explained, they left nothing but pollution and waste in their wake. They were, he said, a swallowing nation, intent only on eating other countries whole.

Before we'd left the UK, I'd read up on the Soviet occupation, but I'd taken for granted the fact that most Mongolians speak Russian and that Mongolian is now written in Cyrillic. Even the name of the country's capital wasn't sacred: the correct, Mongolian, spelling was in fact Ulaan Baatar (the stress in *Baa*tar is on the first syllable, and not, as is commonly thought, on the second). It was only when I spoke to Gal that I realised what it must have meant to everyday Mongolians to rediscover their own country – their culture, their religion and even their language – after seventy years of oppression. The language, in particular, had enjoyed something of a revival in recent years, and as part of my continued education, Gal insisted on teaching me a few words. Of all the phrases I tried to learn, however, only two seemed to stick: *oodz oodsk* (I'm hungry) and *ta eech sechan hoohoon* (you're a very pretty woman). It was, I felt sure, enough to get me out of all but the stickiest of situations.

As we drove from valley to valley, we occasionally passed herds of horses or camels, sometimes so densely packed and so far away that they looked like stubble on the landscape. There are hardly any fences in Mongolia, so herdsmen spend about half of their lives just looking for stray animals in the vast, open grassland that characterises much of the country. We saw very few wild animals, but Gal assured us they were abundant further north, where we were headed, and further south, in the Gobi Desert: Bactrian camels, elk and moose; bears, wolves and snow leopards; and even wild white stallions. Mongolia's native stallions, he said bitterly, had been wiped out by the Soviets, but recent attempts to reintroduce them from Europe had so far proved quite successful.

But it was for his Russian-made jeep that Gal reserved his greatest wrath. After twelve hours of driving, by which time we should have been comfortably close to our destination, we were still four hours short, and the jeep's engine was starting to make decidedly unhappy sounds. Before long, these sounds became really rather sad, and when we stopped for petrol at a tiny, one-pump outpost in the middle of nowhere, the engine gave a last, lingering whimper, and died. 'Russian jeeps,' said Gal, shaking his head, 'very bad. That's why Russia only sells them to Mongolians,' he added angrily, before giving in to a sly grin: 'Oh, and maybe Saddam Hussein.'

Russian reliability aside, I'd always assumed that a grease gun was something Freddie Mercury sang about to maintain his reputation for romance ('… put your hand on my grease gun, don't wanna listen to no run-of-the-mill talk son …'), but it turns out there is such a thing and, what's more, we needed one. There can't have been more than a dozen dwellings in the village, but one by one we solicited them for help. By the time we got to the third or fourth tent we had assembled an impressive entourage of experts in the procurement of grease guns: fortunately, one was eventually found, and the axle was duly lubed in all the right places; unfortunately, the whole process (including dismantling and reassembling the grease gun), took over an hour, during which time the temperature fell almost as fast as the sleet that came with it. By the time we were finished, we were bitterly cold, and looking forward to snuggling down for the night under obscene quantities of felt, with or without the village chief's eldest daughter for company.

Alas, it wasn't to be. A few hours later, as dusk rallied itself for a final stand against the onset of nightfall, Cholon managed to park our jeep axle-deep in the middle of a muddy bog. The next morning, after a cold night under canvas, the full irony of our predicament became clear: not only was our bog little bigger than a small Russian jeep, it was the only bog for miles in any direction. The good news was that the weather had cleared, and any remaining cloud was soon chased across the steppe by the rising sun. The bad news was that there was no sign of Gal or Cholon.

An hour passed, and then another. I was just beginning to wonder if we'd been left to the vultures in favour of a vodka breakfast, when they both emerged from the landscape on horseback. It turned out they'd been up since first light canvassing nearby settlements for another vehicle to help drag ours out of the mire, but to no avail. Instead they'd brought with them two nomads, both traditionally dressed in thick woollen gowns and soft leather boots with distinctive, upturned toes (no one knows quite why boots are designed like this in Mongolia, but one theory has it that they prevent the disturbance of loose earth, which is considered sacred). Minutes later, and as if from nowhere, more nomads appeared, and before long they were all hard at work, digging out the wheels of our jeep and fetching stones from a nearby stream to place under the tyres.

After an hour or so of ineffectual scraping, however, we didn't seem to be any better off, so a couple of the younger lads sped off on their motorbike to fetch help, returning instead with two bottles of vodka. The first of these was promptly dispatched, presumably as a way of shedding some light on the situation in hand, but the problem remained: even when the wheels did catch, the axle was buried so deeply that it acted like an anchor in the mud. The only way to free it was either to lower the bog or to raise the jeep.

The answer, as often seems to be the way in Mongolia, soon happened along on the back of a horse: balanced precariously across its saddle were two tree trunks, which were used to lever the vehicle out of the mud just long enough to place more stones beneath the wheels. Inch by inch it was lifted clear, until we could see daylight beneath the axle. Only then did Cholon dare to start the engine again. No sooner had he eased his foot off the clutch, however, than the jeep was spat headlong from its hole, eliciting a huge cheer from the assembled crowd. Eighteen hours after that first, sinking feeling, we were at last back on track.

But before we could get away, we had the second bottle of vodka to attend to. With Gal acting as our interpreter, we thanked our friendly neighbourhood-watch committee, and presented them all with copies of the postcards we'd had printed back in the UK, of us paddling on the River Thames in Henley (we'd thought this would mean more to people than pictures of Big Ben or Buckingham Palace, and would make for a better souvenir). In return they offered us a share of the refreshments, urging us to toast the land, the sea and the sky by dipping our ring fingers into the vodka and flicking them into the air three times. Once the bottle was empty they drifted away as quickly as they'd appeared, grinning through leathery faces and wishing us luck on the rest of our journey.

It was early evening by the time we reached Batshireet, the first and last town before the river. This was cowboy country, complete with wooden fences, log cabins and a police chief wearing a pullover straight out of the *Starsky & Hutch* catalogue. We paid for the permits we needed to travel beyond Batshireet and stocked up on provisions from a tiny roadside hut that sold little more than sugared peanuts, chocolate and – curiously enough – breadsticks. Before we continued, Gal ordered us some food from the village 'hotel', which in reality was little more than a cold canteen with a few empty rooms attached. We ate generous helpings of noodles and mutton (the dish of choice outside of Ulaan Baatar), and drank as much yak's-milk tea as there was milk to be squeezed out of a yak; it was the first time we'd eaten since exhausting our meagre supply of salami and bread some twelve hours earlier, and although we weren't to know it at the time, it was to be our last square meal for over a week.

At dusk, a few kilometres beyond Batshireet, we saw the Onon for the first time. To many Mongolians the Onon Valley is considered sacred, for it was here that Genghis Khan, warrior leader of the Mongol hordes, was born. In the west his name is synonymous with rampaging armies and brutal subjugation, but he was also a consummate ruler: until the end of the twelfth century, the Mongols were little more than a disparate collection of warring clans, but under his unswerving leadership they established the largest empire the world has ever seen (at its height, it stretched all the way from the Middle East to the Pacific). Such was the importance of his place in Mongolian history, in fact, that his name and image were banned during the Soviet occupation, presumably to quell any nascent feelings of nationalism. Following the collapse of communism, however, he re-emerged as a national hero, a much-needed symbol of strength and unity in a time of political uncertainty, and his likeness began to appear on everything from banknotes to beer bottles.

To us, of course, the Onon was significant for a very different reason: it was these very waters, we hoped, that would carry us all the way to the Pacific Ocean. This was the first time we'd had any indication of what the river would be like this high up, or indeed if it would even be navigable by canoe. We were only 120km from the source, but the river was already quite wide – maybe 50m across – and at least a metre or two deep in the middle. One thing was clear: if we wanted to start paddling from as high up as we could float our boats, we needed to head further upstream.

Before continuing, though, we had to check in at the Mongolian border post across the river. Russia was only a few kilometres to the north, and no one – not even Mongolians – were allowed to continue past the post without permission. We were invited into a small, candle-lit cabin and questioned by a young border guard. His maps were incredibly detailed, and as he traced the river upstream, he warned us of dangerous rapids, fallen trees, forest fires and, inevitably, bears. As he spoke, I sat back to take in the scene, and caught Rich's eye in the flickering light. His look summed it up: here we were, in a remote Mongolian border post, poring over maps by candlelight. This was the stuff, he seemed to be saying, that dreams were made of. When we finally left the hut, he could hardly contain his excitement: 'I've been trying to catch your eye for the last half-hour,' he admitted. 'I didn't want to interrupt, but I'm absolutely bursting for a pee.'

Beyond the border post was a military track set into cliffs high above the river. We continued our journey by moonlight, keeping one eye on the phosphorescent glow of the white water down below, and one eye on the loose boulders that threatened to send us there at every twitch and turn of the steering wheel. Eventually the boulders became too big and too numerous to continue, so we stopped for the night and camped in a clearing, tantalisingly close to the river.

The going, however, was little better the following morning: the track was only just wide enough for the jeep, so we continually had to scout ahead on foot to look for turning places – not to mention landslides and rockfalls – as reversing back along the track would have been difficult, if not impossible. Whenever we came across a boulder that was small enough to move, Rich and I would roll it to one side while the jeep edged along behind us. Progress was slow, but occasionally the track dropped back down to the river, providing us with a chance to make up the miles. Not only that, but the weather was warm and bright, giving us great views of the Onon Valley as it rose almost imperceptibly to meet the distant Mongolian Highlands.

Finally, about 40km upstream of our overnight stop, we reached the end of the road – upstream, the ground was simply too rough and boggy to continue by jeep. This put us about 80km from the source. The first thing we realised was that the river wasn't looking any smaller, or steeper. The second thing we realised – bearing in mind Gal's promise that we'd be able to hire horses to carry our canoes the rest of the way – was that there wasn't so much as a donkey in sight; in our determination to make up for the delay in the bog, we'd completely forgotten about beasts of burden. When we pointed out the apparent dearth of said beasts, Gal was nothing if not pragmatic. 'Ah,' he nodded knowingly, 'that's because there aren't any horses this far upriver.'

Whether or not it was because he felt guilty about the horses, Gal was clearly concerned about us going on without him. 'This is the best place to canoe,' he declared adamantly. We tried to explain that we couldn't travel as far as the ocean *knowing* that we'd missed out the first 80km, but he still wasn't happy. As soon as all of our equipment was unloaded, we started packing it into our boats. As the piles got smaller, the boats got heavier, and each time Gal tried to lift one end he shook his head and apologised for not being able to take us further. 'It's not possible,' he kept insisting, 'they are too heavy. It would be better to start here, I think.' Once our boats were fully packed, he and Cholon delayed their departure for as long as possible, shaking our hands repeatedly. When at last they ran out of excuses, they cranked the jeep into life, waved a worried-looking goodbye, and left behind a silence that we'd been looking forward to for months.

Our first thought was to use our canoe trolleys to continue up the riverbank: they were based on a simple system that involved placing two wheels (on a collapsible steel frame) underneath the canoe, just behind the cockpit. The frame could then be lashed to the boat using a couple of bungee cords. As most of the heavy gear was stored in watertight hatches in the stern (the majority of the bow being needed for other essential items, like legs), the trolley bore the bulk of the weight. The problem was, despite rigorous testing on Rich's patio back in Hertfordshire, we weren't sure how long they'd hold up in the Mongolian marsh. Thirty seconds later, we had our answer.

This presented us with something of a quandary: at 60kg apiece, our boats were too heavy to carry, so instead we rigged up a couple of makeshift shoulder harnesses using some climbing slings, and dragged them across the ground like sleds. This worked well up to a point, but it clearly wasn't going to see us through the next 80km; the tussocky grass was just too dense, and that was before we'd even thought about climbing up and down bluffs or hacking our way through thick forest. The only solution, we realised, was to float the boats up the river, letting the water take the weight while we waded through the shallows. In theory, it was a great plan. In practice, however, the water was painfully cold; it was late spring, and the river was draining the last of the snowmelt from the hills. Not only that, but the rocks on the riverbed were *covered* in slimy algae: slippery at best and utterly frictionless at all other times, they soon had us floundering around like drunks on a skating rink.

All in all, it was a nice walk, if you liked swimming. Initially the shallows were just that, but as soon as we reached the outside of the first big bend, the riverbed dropped away, forcing us to wade out into the main channel to get to the shallower water on the other side. The first few times we tried this, the water came up to our knees (we were wearing shorts to minimise drag), but with each bend it got higher and higher, eventually reaching our chests. Each time the initial shock was enough to make us gasp, but just when we'd start to get used to it, we'd reach shallower water, where the wind would start to exact its toll on half-frozen muscles. Still, it wasn't all bad news: the water didn't feel nearly as cold once our legs had gone numb.

There were times when we tried clambering onto the bank to avoid the deeper water, but this meant taking the harness off both shoulders and holding the towline out over the water so that it was parallel to the shore (if we kept the harness on, it just dragged the canoe into, rather than along, the bank). While this sounds quite sensible on paper, in reality it was as awkward as it was tiring, putting added strain on our arms and backs. Far better, we found, was just to plod on regardless and hope that the water never got deeper than our chins.

That afternoon we covered just two kilometres in as many hours. At that rate, it was going to take us weeks to reach the source, but thanks to the colonel's visa deadline imposed back in Ulaan Baatar, we now had only twelve days to reach the Russian border. It didn't take a great leap of reasoning to realise that the longer we waded upstream, the further we'd have to paddle back downstream, and the less time we'd have to paddle it. The colonel, I couldn't help thinking, was a complete git.

We made our first camp on a beach beside the river, glad to be out of the water and on our own. A miscalculation back in Ulaan Baatar meant we could only afford to eat half as much pasta as we'd planned, but after such a long day anything was better than nothing. In celebration of our first few hours on the river, we also gave the dried meat-shavings a whirl and found them to be distinctly meaty, in a dry and tasteless kind of way. Still, they must have had some animal content – at the end of the meal, there was a reassuringly greasy residue on the inside of our cooking pots.

The following day, we established something of a routine on the river: after a strictly rationed breakfast of porridge and muesli (both Russian and both tasteless) we started the day's wading at nine in the morning. We divided the walk into two three-hour sessions and a final two-hour session, with a twenty-minute break between each. We also took a five-minute rest every hour. In terms of food we allowed ourselves half a bag of sugared nuts and a chocolate bar each; during the longer breaks we went crazy and devoured a dozen breadsticks between us. Despite such unabashed gluttony, however, I felt low on energy all day, and I couldn't work out why Rich was always so far ahead. Then, towards the end of the afternoon, I started to feel quite chilly, despite the fact that it was mercifully warm (at least out of the water), and that night I shivered myself to sleep.

By the next morning my chill had become a full-blown cold, but far from making things worse, it actually made me feel a little better – at least now I had an excuse for always being so far behind. All day I craved sugar and daydreamed about French toast and maple syrup. At each break I made sure that I drank my water *before* eating any chocolate so that it wouldn't wash away the taste.

The only other thing I had to contend with was the chafing in my nether regions. In truth, it was the top of my thighs, but there's something tender-sounding about 'nether regions' that the word 'thigh' just doesn't quite capture. I digress: the fact was that after twenty hours of being scoured by ice-cold river shorts, my crotch was as raw as a steak that's still mooing. Rich was having similar problems with his feet, but at least he could wrap his sores in long strips of duct tape; all I could do was walk like John Wayne and hope that the blood wouldn't attract any bears.

The sun continued to shine and there was very little wind to speak of, but the forested hills that flanked the river weren't anything like the mountains we were expecting, and the river itself wasn't getting any steeper, both of which made the walking monotonous. The water didn't seem to be getting any shallower, either, and after two days of gasping through chest-deep glacial water we were beginning to wish we'd brought a couple of canoes with us to cross the deeper pools ...

I'd like to be able to say that overlooking the enormous, brightly coloured craft we were hauling upstream was an indication of just how tired we were, but in reality it was an indication of just how stupid we were. Still, for the rest of that afternoon, we stayed blissfully dry, jumping in and out of our boats whenever the need arose. It didn't always make sense (sometimes it was just as easy to wade across the smaller pools) but it was infinitely preferable to deep-freezing the family baubles.

At the end of our second full day on the river we took a GPS reading, and were pleased to learn that we were averaging a blistering twelve kilometres a day. There were, I felt sure, grannies in Grimsby who could walk faster. But in a sense the distance didn't matter: as long as the river was still deep enough to float our canoes, we had no choice but to keep going. We also knew, however, that things were starting to get tight: we'd now spent almost three days wading upstream. That gave us just ten days to cover the 600km to the Russian border. In the end we decided to compromise: if we hadn't reached a suitably shallow starting point after one more day of walking, we'd set off anyway – the last thing we wanted to do was miss our deadline for the sake of a few kilometres.

And so it continued. On the final day we slipped and stumbled our way upstream for almost twelve hours. Slowly, almost imperceptibly, the river began to narrow. At one point we passed within shouting distance of the Russian border, but all I could think about was the chafing between my legs. It was the same with the wildlife: we'd been told these hills were thick with bears, but I was too busy pouring Mycil foot powder down my shorts to worry about something as trivial as being eaten alive. By the end of the day, I was swearing in frustration at the algae-covered rocks that had sent me sprawling more times than I had the energy to remember. I was tired, cold and decidedly irritable. Still, I consoled myself, at least we could start paddling tomorrow.

'I think we should keep going upstream for another day,' Rich announced as I pulled my boat up the bank at dusk. Bastard. He was right of course: although the river was now little more than a stream, and the shingle banks were only a few inches shallow, the main channels were still deep enough to warrant going higher. Our only consolation was the fact that we'd now seen most of the river between here and Batshireet, and we felt sure that we'd be able to cover the ground faster once we were travelling downstream.

Finally, after four and a half days of walking, wading and stumbling, we reached the confluence of two tiny streams. They were too narrow and too shallow to canoe individually, but together they would hopefully provide enough water to float our boats all the way to the Pacific. It was a significant moment, but there was no time to celebrate. Getting to this point had taken us four days longer than originally planned, leaving us only eight days to reach the Russian border before our visas expired. And that was assuming we'd be allowed across; if we were denied entry into Russia, we'd be stuck in Mongolia illegally. We also had no idea how long it would take to cover 600km, but if I were a betting man, I'd have said eight days. Give or take a week.

We had plenty of time to reflect on our surroundings before the sun went down. We were, our GPS reliably informed us, just thirty kilometres from the source of the Amur. If we'd had more time, we could have continued further upstream, but there didn't seem to be much point; purists would argue that a true source-to-sea descent demands starting at the summit of the mountain from whence the river springs, but we weren't interested in mountaineering, or in dragging our boats across country, unless there was a way to float our boats back down. As far as we were concerned, this was a paddling trip, and paddling was what we'd set out to do. Which was just as well, really: from where we were sitting, the Pacific Ocean was a little over 4,400km away, which by my reckoning was around three million paddle strokes.

Frankly, though, after all that walking upstream, I couldn't wait to sit down for hours at a time and let gravity do its thing. If I'm honest, I could hardly believe we'd made it this far. It only seemed like a few weeks before that we'd made the decision to travel one of the world's great rivers, and here we were, near the source of one of the greatest. We were five days' walk and two days' drive from the nearest village, and ahead lay the adventure of a lifetime. Mind you, it could so easily have become the misadventure of a lifetime: later that night I heard footsteps outside the tent, and began to question my decision to wander around naked just a few minutes before ...

4 BAPTISM OF FIRE

Our first day of paddling dawned as crisp as the frost on our boats. The night before we'd decided to celebrate the start of our journey proper by going for an early morning dip, but what had sounded like a good idea from the warmth of our sleeping bags didn't seem nearly as inviting in the cold light of day.

It took us almost three hours to have breakfast, strike camp and make our boats river-ready – we later had it down to little more than an hour, but nothing was routine yet, and everything took time. Of all the little tasks we had to perform that morning, however, the most significant was assembling our paddles. Their ingenious design meant we'd been able to bring them from the UK in four separate pieces; now all we had to do was slot these pieces together and tighten them with an Allen key. We fervently hoped that the next time we'd need to take them apart would be in four or five months, and not – as seemed increasingly likely – eight or nine days.

We finally pushed off at half past ten. Five minutes later, we were still pushing off. I'd pictured starting the journey as I meant to go on, with half a dozen deep and satisfying paddle strokes, but thanks to the river's shallow shingle banks, the best I could manage was an ungainly, inch-by-inch shuffle that involved using my arms like stunted ski poles. The difference here was that instead of a slope of one in four, we faced a heady gradient of one in four thousand.

Still, once we were under way, it felt great to be paddling, even if the riverbed did scour the hulls of our boats at every other bend. Once or twice we got completely stuck and had to repeat the 'shoulder shuffle', but in many ways this was reassuring, as it meant we'd ventured *just* far enough upriver to be able to scrape back down. In deeper water, the canoes felt reassuringly fast, and the current was quicker than it had seemed from the bank; after just two hours, we'd already passed our campsite of two nights before, and were having to pole less and less frequently. Surely, I argued, this called for a celebration: a slice of week-old salami, perhaps, or half a bag of peanuts? In the event, we went crazy and had both. We even tried them at the same time, but soon discovered that the salami overwhelmed the taste of the peanuts, and that the peanuts spoiled the texture of the salami. Could things get any more exciting, I wondered?

Actually, they could: after lunch, we had our first imaginary lunch – no less essential but much less satisfying. Rich went for avocado and bacon on a toasted baguette, while I had chicken and Brie on warm ciabatta. Rich declared his own choice delicious, but I felt mine was lacking a certain *je ne sais quoi*. In the event, a generous dollop of cranberry jelly was all that was required.

Satisfied that we were at last making headway, I also found myself having a proper look around for the first time, taking in views that I'd failed to really appreciate on the slog upstream. For a start, the weather was glorious, the azure of the sky interrupted only by occasional, cotton-bud clouds. The mountains weren't as big as I'd expected, but the broad river valley rose up to forested hills on either side of us. Eagles and other birds of prey soared on the thermals created by these hills, keeping tabs on our position as we continued downstream.

Most striking of all, though, was the forest itself: great swathes had been decimated by fire, leaving behind a charred, skeletal landscape. Isolated splashes of colour looked out of place in this blackened world, which perhaps explained why we hadn't seen any bears yet. Not that we were hoping to run into one, mind, just that the odd cub at the water's edge wouldn't have gone amiss; nor, too, would a moose or elk, or perhaps a wild argali sheep, apparently common in these here parts. Most welcome of all, though, would have been a glimpse of the rare and elusive snow leopard. Alas, the only sizeable creature I caught sight of all day was the rare but not so elusive Boddington.

We called it a day after six hours, having paddled a section of river that had taken us two days to cover on foot. We celebrated with the last of the chocolate we'd bought back in Batshireet almost a week before. As the sun eased itself onto the horizon, the temperature dropped dramatically and we were soon huddled around the stove, half-inside our sleeping bags. My distinct lack of training before leaving the UK meant that my body was now paying the price: my ankles were swollen from pushing on the footrests of my boat and my lower back was stiff and bruised. I found it hard to picture another 120 days of paddling, so instead I focused on easier goals: getting to the bridge we'd crossed on the way here; getting to the Russian border; and, easiest of all, getting to sleep.

The next morning, we agreed that if we were to stand any chance of reaching the border on time, we'd need to paddle nine hours a day, with food breaks every three hours. Again, I tried to focus on short-term goals: the first hour of the morning session flew by, but the second seemed to drag on interminably: the novelty of the first hour had long worn off, while the third was still to come. Hour three was the best, because there was food to look forward to at the end, but the final ten minutes somehow managed to last about half an hour. I soon realised that if I wanted to survive the next 4,000,000 seconds of paddling, I'd have to stop counting them down one by one.

The morning wasn't completely without interest, however: we saw dozens of fish flapping in the shallows, and we continued to be shadowed by eagles, sometimes at alarmingly close range. We even saw two elk carcasses in the river, and guessed the animals had been drowned in the spring floods. We also noticed a change in the surrounding scenery; the burned-out black of the day before giving way to a vivid spring-green. Curiously, trees grew only on the northern slopes of the surrounding mountains, presumably because the southern slopes were simply too dry during the long, hot summer months, and the resulting landscape looked like a ragged patchwork of half-dressed hills.

After another six hours of paddling, we camped near the starting point of our walk upstream. So far, it had felt like we were going over old ground; now, at last, we were making real progress. Unfortunately, the same could not be said for our battered bodies; by this stage Rich's lower back was almost numb, and my fingers had been in and out of the water so often that the ends were starting to split open (in my experience the only way to treat this particular problem is to wrap each finger in reams of duct tape, leave them for a week, and hope for the best).

Some of our equipment was also showing signs of wear and tear: the filthy Mongolian fuel we were using for cooking had clogged up our stove so badly that it no longer worked. Some judicious cleaning soon had it up and running again, but this turned out to be just the start of a stove saga that was to last the rest of our journey. The day's fantasy meal, in case you were wondering, was poached salmon in a sweet dill sauce – the day's real meal was dried meat-shavings in sweaty noodles.

The following morning Rich gave me a home-made card which read: 'In honour of your 27th birthday I've caught a large fish, which I've put in this convenient river for safekeeping.' How very amusing. To mark the occasion (my birthday, that is, not catching the fish) we both had an extra spoonful of dry muesli in our tasteless porridge. I can honestly say it was the best birthday breakfast I've ever had. The weather didn't disappoint either, blessing us with clear, cobalt skies.

By now, we'd left the shallows far behind and the river was really starting to pick up speed. Our first session was a birthday-inspired blast, heralded throughout by a heron leading the way. According to our GPS we covered thirty kilometres in just three hours, which was exactly the injection of pace we felt we needed if we were to reach the border in time. We continued for another hour and a half to reach the bridge that we'd crossed with Gal over a week before.

Soon after this, the landscape underwent a sudden and dramatic transformation, from deep, forested valley to sweeping, baize-green steppe. So, too, did the weather: as we paddled, three or four towering clouds reared up behind us, but despite the ominous claps of thunder coming from within, they rolled harmlessly past, before squatting on the horizon, gun-metal anvils heavy with unspent rain.

Speaking of which, I was absolutely bursting for a pee. And for 'bursting', read 'fainting'. Perhaps I should explain: back in Blighty, our spray-decks – the thick skirts of neoprene worn around the waist and stretched over the canoe's cockpit to keep water out – had arrived the day before we'd left. Pushed for time, we'd only tried one on for size. When I'd finally stretched the other one around my cockpit on the eve of our departure downstream, the dense rubber cord that was meant to hold it in place had promptly ripped away from the neoprene, leaving a gaping hole that would – in the event of a capsize – ship water faster than a sinking supertanker. Since then I'd managed to repair it, but this had done little to solve the initial problem: namely, that the deck was just too small. Together, Rich and I had figured out a system of heaving and grunting that got the thing on, but this required both of us to burst a jugular at precisely the same moment; as such, we tried to avoid taking it off between food breaks at all costs. Because the deck's narrow top was secured almost as snugly around my waist, I was effectively a prisoner in my own boat.

Now, on this particular occasion, I'd started needing the toilet about an hour into our three-hour session. When it finally came time to siphon the proverbial python two hours later, the force was such that it almost knocked me off balance. As you can imagine, the feeling of release was ... well, biblical. In my joy, I thought it might be fun to time how long it lasted: the result, in case you were wondering, was 63 seconds (you may also be interested to know that I now time myself, without fail, every time I've had a few scoops, and have since improved this PB by 4.6 seconds).

That night, at the end of our second nine-hour day, we camped on a beach at the very edge of the steppe, opposite the mouth of a narrow ravine. We'd long since given up hope of finding any white water or waterfalls on which to test our rapidly-waning skills, but somehow not being able to see around the next corner added to our sense of anticipation, and gave us something to look forward to.

For the first time since we'd set off, our chosen campsite was crisscrossed with footprints, and it wasn't long before the culprits emerged from the woods. They sported matted hair, torn clothes and worn plimsolls, and carried what looked like long birch twigs, with film reels attached at one end and dead mice dangling at the other; I couldn't work out if they were fishing for bream or bear. Acting as though we were the third pair of crazy canoeists they'd seen that day, they nodded a cursory greeting before heading straight for the water's edge. Minutes – and I mean minutes – later, we heard a triumphant cry and looked up to see one of them wrestling a two-foot pike onto the bank. It was clearly putting up a fight and was covered in sand by the time he brought it over, still writhing in his arms. '*Padarak!*' he announced, beaming with pride. Unfamiliar with the nuances of fish classification in Mongolian, I couldn't do much more than return his grin, but as I rolled the word around in my head, I realised he wasn't speaking Mongolian, but Russian: he was offering us the fish as a present.

Taken aback by such a generous gesture, I politely refused his first catch, but the second and third were fair game as we sat around a campfire sharing food and stories. Our benefactor's name was Andrei. He lived in a village a few hours' walk to the north, he told us, and only came across the border to fish. Apart from his rod, all he had with him was a Hessian sack slung over his shoulder on the end of a short stick. His companion was a Mongolian who lived nearby; he didn't speak a word of Russian, let alone English, so while I did my best to translate for Rich, Andrei did the same for his friend. As we talked, Andrei opened his bag to reveal a blackened pot, a loaf of bread and a mysterious foil parcel. Filling the pot with river water, he dunked two or three small fish into it before popping the whole lot on the fire's ruby embers. The fish were called *leenok*, he explained, and were best eaten with hunks of bread dipped in salt – hence the mystery parcel.

After we'd all eaten our fill, Andrei's friend indicated that we should follow him into the woods. It was now completely dark, and I had visions of being despatched in much the same way as the two pairs of paddlers who'd passed this way just a few hours before us. What transpired was much less disconcerting, but no less strange. Our abductor led us to a tree near the edge of the river and pointed to a hollow in its trunk. No sooner had Rich shone his torch in that direction, however, than something darted from the shadows. The next thing we knew, a hand was opening in the narrow beam of the torch to reveal a tiny, brightly coloured bird. Once we'd both had a look, a second hand gave it a paternal stroke before placing it carefully back in its nest and beckoning us back to the campsite.

It was gone midnight by the time we decided to turn in but, despite an invitation to shelter in the porch of our tent, our companions insisted on sleeping outside under their coats, only rousing themselves to heap a few more logs onto the crackling fire.

The next morning our tent, our canoes and our companions were covered in a thick layer of hoarfrost. I was amazed that they'd been able to endure such a bitter night out in the open, but neither of them seemed to think anything of it. What they *did* think a lot of was all the equipment that appeared from the depths of our tent when we began to pack our boats later that morning. Of particular interest was a bright orange object with a rubber antenna poking out of the top. '*Chto?*' Andrei wanted to know: 'What is it?'

And so it was that on my second day of Russian for Dummies, I had to explain the inner workings of an Emergency Position Indicating Radio Beacon, or EPIRB for short. This was our only way of reaching the outside world, but as methods of communication go, it wasn't exactly designed for back and forth banter: essentially, pressing a button on the device or immersing it in water sent an instant and irretrievable signal via satellite to HM Coastguard in Dartmouth. Dartmouth would then call our insurers in London, who would contact their opposite numbers in Moscow. Finally, Moscow would alert the Russian military with our precise location and have us airlifted to safety by the nearest passing helicopter gunship. Suffice it to say, the aforementioned button was well taped up, and we tried to avoid water at all costs.

Relying heavily on the words *sputnik* and *telefon,* plus the odd *thucka-thucka* of helicopter blades thrown in for good measure, I tried to make myself understood. For his part, Andrei was agog, although whether with wonder or confusion I couldn't quite tell. When it was at last time to push off, he and his companion shook our hands and wished us luck, and by way of saying so long and thanks for all the fish, I gave each of them one of the postcards we'd had printed back in the UK, with the word *spaseeba* scrawled on the back in Cyrillic.

Our goal that day was Binder, the first village marked on our maps. Having badly miscalculated how long it would take to reach the source, we were now completely out of sugar, and down to our last few spoonfuls of everything else, including porridge, pasta and, most disturbingly of all, meat-shavings. On the river we'd been rationing ourselves to 50g of salami, half a bag of nuts and a bar of chocolate each a day, but now they too were gone. We just had to hope that our maps, made by the US military at the height of the Cold War, weren't past their sell-by date. We had tried to get hold of more up-to-date maps back in the UK, but Russia just isn't the sort of country that publishes detailed maps of its most sensitive military regions, and the only western maps we'd been able to find simply weren't detailed enough for day-to-day navigation.

To pass the time during the first session we compiled a list of the top ten films of all time, and – because that didn't take long enough – the top ten film moments of all time. All of the usual suspects were there, including – coincidentally enough – *The Usual Suspects*. Other films that made the cut were *Zulu* ('Zulus sah, thaasands of 'em'); *Cool Hand Luke* ('Shakin' it up here, boss!'); *The Great Escape* (cue jaunty whistle); and *Butch Cassidy and the Sundance Kid* ('Are you crazy? The fall'll probably kill ya'). Doubtless as a result of all this deliberation, the paddle into Binder seemed to take no time at all, and before we knew it, we were tying up our ponies and wandering into the village in search of the local sheriff. In the event, the best we could manage was the local cobbler.

Batserk (for that was the cobbler's name) introduced himself in halting English and asked if we needed any help. He was wearing a North Face jacket and a carefully groomed goatee, and wouldn't have looked out of place in Piccadilly Circus (it later transpired that he'd been given the jacket by a missionary who'd taught English in the village a few years before). When we asked where we could buy food, he showed us down a corridor in a long wooden hut. Each room had its own speciality, but they all sold much the same thing: namely nuts, noodles and chocolate. It was almost as if they'd known we were coming. We cleaned one poor woman completely out of *Duna* bars, and stocked up on everything else we could find; we had no idea when we'd be able to resupply again, so it seemed prudent to buy enough for a few weeks. Among our purchases were two kilos of semolina and two tins of pilchards, a selection that – as it turned out – was a few kilos heavy on the semolina and a few tins short on the pilchards; the fifty bars of chocolate, though, were just right.

The more Batṣerk chatted the less halting his English became, and he was soon nattering to us like we were old friends. When we'd finished shopping he ordered us some food in the local restaurant, which – conveniently enough – was at the end of the same corridor. It boasted as many dishes as it had tables (by which I mean one). This time, though, the ubiquitous mutton and noodles came with a dash of chilli sauce: it was, we all agreed, a meal fit for a canoeing king.

By this stage, Batserk was clearly warming to his role as Binder's cultural attaché, and insisted on showing us around. Armed with a well-thumbed Mongolian–English dictionary, he took us past the municipal buildings (built by the Chinese), the derelict water-heating plant (built by the Russians), and the school (built by both). Even in this remote outpost, a tiny village miles from anywhere, the legacy of Mongolia's oppressors was all too apparent. *Gers*, too, skirted the edge of the village, as if unable to decide whether they belonged inside or out. The monastery, though, was in no doubt: cast far into the surrounding steppe, this modest Buddhist shrine, with its long-neglected ornaments and pyres, was the only thing of any lasting beauty in the whole village.

Inexhaustibly enthusiastic, Batserk then asked us if we'd like to go for a beer. I half expected a night of debauchery, guzzling fermented horses' milk in some felt-lined drinking den, but instead we found ourselves supping Korean lager in a chintzy 70s bar, complete with glitter balls and UV lights. Batserk was obviously trying to impress us, but I felt oddly out of place, and was relieved when he finally decided to call it a night.

We stayed in a wooden building identical to the one that housed the shops. Although it wasn't exactly a *ger*, it was much more inviting than the club: at one end of our room was a wood-fired stove, providing an endless supply of hot water for tea and washing. Lining the walls were four beds, colourfully painted and laden with dense blankets and fabulous felt throws.

During the night, I dreamed that I was Steve McQueen, riding along the Russia–China border on a motorbike, jumping over barbed-wire fences, and generally being a bit of a dude. I was gutted when I woke up to discover that I was just me.

Before we left Binder the following morning, we paid a visit to Batserk's workshop. The walls were lined with boots, all made from leather that was as soft as felt. Beaming and bashful by turns, Batserk showed us his raw materials, his sewing machine and his giant pair of samurai-sharp scissors, which cut through quarter-inch leather like it was paper. The finished boots were a snip at $18, and they looked like they would last a generation. I was tempted to buy some myself, but I couldn't bear the thought of carrying all that extra weight in my canoe.

Wheeling our boats down to the river, we were accompanied by a vast entourage of well-wishers. One was Batserk's father, a sombre-faced, bearded man riding his horse with obvious pride. Another was an excitable, grey-haired fellow who spoke Russian thirteen-to-the-dozen, little caring if we understood or not. He told us that his brother had once worked in London. I had no way of knowing if this was true, but I couldn't fault his discerning description: 'Not much grass in London,' he said with a frown, 'and always raining, raining.' When he wasn't gassing to us he was giving the assembled throng a guided tour of our boats, explaining which end was which and how the rudder worked.

At the water's edge, I lightened my load by a postcard or two and shook Batserk warmly by the hand, before easing out into the current. It was a few minutes before the last cheers ebbed away behind us, but it wasn't until we'd been paddling for almost an hour that Batserk's father reappeared, galloping along the riverbank on his horse and waving a final farewell.

Our night in Binder meant we now had some serious paddling to do. I remember very little about the following day, and even my diary is pretty vague: 'Another nine-hour stretch. Felt really rough, and couldn't keep up with Rich. By the end he was half a mile ahead. "Great paddle!" he enthused as I hauled my boat up the beach. I'm already beginning to hate him.'

After almost throwing up on my chipper chum soon after we made camp, I realised that I was badly dehydrated. A rehydration sachet was the obvious solution, but the thing about rehydration sachets is that if you've reached the point where you're close to throwing up, one sip is usually enough to tip you – and your lunch – over the edge (think sea water with a hint of raspberry). The good news is, if you get past the initial gagging reflex, rehydration sachets are nothing short of miraculous, and I was soon tucking into my pasta'n'pilchards as though it was almost edible.

The next three days were almost as arduous, even without the effects of dehydration. It wasn't long before I gave in to temptation and listened to my Walkman, an activity which soon became known as 'plugging in'. Originally I'd planned to save this luxury for hard times at the end of the journey, but after just five days my boredom got the better of me. I'd brought a handful of tapes with me, but the best of these was undoubtedly Tchaikovsky's *1812 Overture*, not because I was particularly into classical music, but because it was over fifty minutes long. Suffice it to say that anyone walking along the banks of the Onon that day would've seen someone in a bright-yellow banana boat having some kind of seizure. In fact, I was conducting the St Petersburg Symphony Orchestra – to considerable critical acclaim, I might add.

In addition to this new-found appreciation of the classics, I realised with alarm that I was addicted to sugar. The symptoms were obvious: I craved chocolate all day, but when I finally allowed myself some, I felt guilty that I'd eaten too much. Once I started feeling guilty, there seemed little point in holding back, so I ate more. It wasn't long before I was eating sugar straight out of the bag, dipping a damp finger deep into the granules and swirling them around my salivating chops.

Biscuits, too, were fast becoming a problem. Since stocking up in Binder, we now allowed ourselves a daily ration of eight and a half biscuits each. We'd eat the first one and a half whole, by way of an *hors d'oeuvre*. The next six could then be split into two (they had cream fillings), effectively making twelve biscuits. These could be further divided into eighteen portions, by first eating the side without the cream, then licking the cream off, and finally eating the remaining side. The last biscuit could then be eaten whole, by way of a final binge.

The wilderness around us remained completely unpopulated, alternating between open steppe and short sections of steep-sided gorge. Wildlife became more plentiful, with deer drinking at the water's edge and swans following us downstream. But most impressive of all was the weather: although the mornings were still chilly, the afternoons were now so hot we had to strip down to our shorts. Not only hadn't it rained since we'd set off, but there'd rarely been a cloud in the sky, and with very little in the way of wind, the river was often quicksilver still. It was also quite wide now, often stretching up to 100m across, although this didn't seem to affect its cantering current.

Finally, after nine days of paddling nine hours a day, we got to within seven kilometres of the border with a day to spare. It had been a baptism of fire, to say the least. We camped on a sandy spit and took stock of our situation: at first glance, we both looked tanned and fit, but this belied the inevitable wear and tear of paddling 600km in eight days. Rich was still taking painkillers for his back, and although my fingertips had been under wraps for over a week, my nails were starting to come away from the skin, causing bleeding around the edges. I was also itching all over, but the fact that I'd been wearing the same clothes for a week was, I felt certain, entirely coincidental.

We'd also encountered none of the dangerous rapids that we'd been told to expect by the Mongolian border guard. In retrospect, this was almost certainly a good thing, but at the time I couldn't help but feel slightly aggrieved; we were white-water paddlers after all, and so far the only white water we'd come across was the stuff we spat into the sand during our daily ablutions.

Other than that everything seemed fine, but we were apprehensive about the fate that awaited us at the border. We were armed with a portfolio of official-looking documents, all translated into Russian, but out here in the middle of nowhere, they hardly seemed to be worth the paper they were written on. If all else failed, we always had our brick of dollar notes to fall back on, but this was clearly a last resort. If we *were* turned away we'd have to hitch a lift – with our boats – back to Ulaan Baatar before making the arduous journey overland through Mongolia and Russia to reach exactly the same point on the river. Either way, we were now just seven kilometres away from finding out. At least, we thought we were seven kilometres away – it was difficult to tell from our maps where Mongolia finished and Russia began. We'd just have to head for the duty-free lounge and hope for the best.

The next morning, we couldn't find the duty-free lounge – just kilometre after kilometre of forest. Anxious not to cross into Russia unwittingly, we stopped at a beach to discuss our options: the way I saw it, we could either keep going as far as the bridge just *beyond* the border, or we could ask for directions from the heavily armed soldiers who were barrelling down the bank towards us.

5 CAPTAIN COOL &
THE TANKER TWINS

When I paddle, I like to start my day staring down the muzzle of a semi-automatic weapon. Don't get me wrong, I've had my fair share of run-ins with Welsh farmers, and I do enjoy the odd length of barbed wire deliberately stretched across the river, but when it comes to morning wake-up calls, there's nothing quite like the business end of an AK47 to really get the adrenalin flowing.

I couldn't make out the flag on the soldiers' uniforms, but they were the most European-looking Mongolians I'd ever seen. As they drew closer, one of them barked a question. I caught the odd word of Russian, but still the rouble didn't drop. 'You're Mongolian, right?' I asked him in Russian, aware that most Mongolian soldiers speak both languages. 'Nyet!' he said with a finality that suggested it wasn't open to discussion.

I had visions of giving evidence at the KGB tribunal: 'Awfully sorry. There we were, paddling along, when all of a sudden we slipped and fell into Russia. Bit embarrassing, really.' How had this happened? How had we not seen the border post? How had they ever managed to spot our gleaming red and yellow canoes in broad daylight?

Without saying another word, they motioned us to sit down on the riverbank and wait. After an anxious couple of hours, an officer finally arrived, all starched sleeves and aviator sunglasses. 'Velcome to Russia!' he said, in heavily accented English. I half expected him to add, 'I've been expecting you, Meester Bond.' Before we knew what was happening, we were whisked off to the nearby border post where we were served tea and cakes. The good captain even presented us with a lapel badge as a souvenir, and a good-luck card signed by all his personnel. I couldn't help but notice that most of them were female, and that they were all stunning. Vodka Martini, anyone?

It turned out that the crumpled scrap of paper we'd been given by the colonel back in Ulaan Baatar was – quite literally – just the ticket; against all the odds, we were now officially in Siberia.

The name Siberia comes from the Altai word *sibir*, which literally translated means 'sleeping land'. Essentially, the region comprises all of Northern Asia, and as such its statistics defy comprehension: it makes up one-twelfth of the earth's landmass; it straddles seven time zones; and from east to west it measures over 6,000 miles, or a third of the northern hemisphere. But it is perhaps best known for its weather: for seven months of the year, the entire landscape literally freezes solid, with temperatures regularly dropping to −40°C (Verkhoyansk, where temperatures as low as −70°C have been recorded, is the coldest inhabited place on the planet). In the summer, all but the top few feet of this landscape remain frozen in a rock-hard layer of permafrost that can be hundreds – even thousands – of metres deep. Not for nothing have Russians dubbed Siberia 'the land east of the sun'.

Siberia is also known for its salt mines, its exiles and its gulags. For over 300 years, it was used as a dumping ground for the detritus of Russian society, first by the tsars, and then by the communists. Criminals, dissidents and undesirables were sent to Siberia to die in their millions. Those who survived (and there were precious few who did) often chose to remain, preferring to scratch out a living from the frozen wastes than to return to a life of renewed persecution and certain penury. Today, the whole of Siberia – which comprises an area bigger than mainland America, Alaska and Europe put together – is home to just 33 million people, most of whom live in the towns and cities along the Trans-Siberian railway, or in the isolated villages that litter the banks of the Amur.

The captain drove us back to the river and had a good look around our boats. I wanted to take a photo of what for us was quite a momentous occasion, but because the border zone was so sensitive, I didn't dare ask. As if reading my mind, the captain proceeded to take an enormous, steam-driven video camera from the back of his jeep. He went on to film the entire proceedings, right up until the moment we waved goodbye. Thinking I should say something poignant as we pushed off, I plumbed the depths of my night-class Russian before giving a rousing cry: 'To the sea!' I yelled, holding my paddle aloft in triumph. Only much later did I discover that what I'd actually said was: 'To war!'

If our first impression of Siberia was overwhelming, what came next was something of a shock. A few kilometres past the border we stopped at Mangut, a village of rambling log cabins and the odd statue of Lenin. While Rich watched the boats, I set off to find somewhere to stay. I asked a dozen people if there was a hotel in town, but they all looked at me like I'd just stepped out of a canoe. Just when I was about to give up, I met two young girls who said they might be able to help. Their names were Julia and Natasha, they told me, and they were both thirteen years old. They took me to see a stern, middle-aged matron who eyed me suspiciously. When I explained where I was from, her frown softened, but only a fraction. Yes, there was somewhere we could stay. 'How much is it?' I asked. 'A dollar,' she replied quickly. And then, almost apologetically, 'Is that too expensive?'

I followed her tottering heels along the village's dusty dirt roads to a squat municipal building with a spectacularly unattractive mosaic at one end, and a concrete portico at the other. 'This is the house of culture,' she said, without a hint of irony. Unlocking a fist-sized padlock on the massive wooden door, she heaved her way in. The inside was more impressive than the outside, boasting a vast lobby, a grand staircase and even a ballroom. It was also dark, cold and empty, and didn't look like it had been used for years. Comrade Matron beckoned me through the lobby to a small room with floor-to-ceiling tiles and a porcelain basin. The adjacent room was similarly tiled, but instead of a basin it featured four beds piled with blankets. This, it seemed, was to be our room for the night. She handed me the keys, told me she'd return at nine the next morning, and then clacked her way back across the lobby and out through the front door.

Thrilled at the prospect of sleeping in a converted toilet block, I ran back the way I'd come, aware that I'd now been gone for over an hour. As I neared the river, a big, oily tanker roared up beside me and two young lads leaned out of the window. 'Give us five roubles!' they demanded. I pretended not to understand. 'Give us five roubles,' they repeated, this time with more venom. 'Nyet,' was the best I could come up with. Clearly angry, they started to drive off, but then turned around, revved the tanker's engine, and headed straight for me. I only avoided being hit by clambering up a nearby fence.

When I eventually reached Rich, I discovered he'd already had a run-in with the Tanker Twins; he'd only stopped them from driving over our boats by standing in front of them and refusing to move. He didn't seem too bothered by it all, but I was quite shaken up. The more I thought about it, the worse it got: this was, after all, only our first night in Siberia, and already it felt like one night too many. I was tired and I was angry, and I was really dreading the months that lay ahead.

I was also scared. My biggest fear was that the Tanker Twins would come back during the night to steal our boats. When we eventually got to the Dom Culturi, we made a point of locking them to the banister railings of the lobby staircase. We were too dispirited to go in search of food, so Rich set up the stove in our room and put on some pasta, while I sat around feeling sorry for myself. Just when I was about to call the whole trip off, I heard a knock at the door, and Julia appeared clutching a brightly wrapped package. 'A souvenir,' she said shyly, before dashing off down the corridor. Inside was a Christmas card that played a traditional Russian carol. It was only the first of June, but for me it hadn't arrived a moment too soon.

Before we turned in, we took stock of our progress: by crossing the border on the river, we had avoided a costly, two-week detour. More importantly, the integrity of our journey had been preserved: we'd been able to go where the water went, unimpeded by people or politics. To my mind, this lay at the very heart of what we were trying to achieve: somehow, 'Canoeing the Amur River from Source-to-Sea via Ulaan Baatar and Ulan Ude' didn't have nearly the same ring to it.

So, 600 kilometres down, 3,800 to go. From our conversation with Dmitry back in Ulaan Baatar, we knew we had permission to travel on the Russian part of the river until the end of June. After that, the whole region was supposedly closed for military manoeuvres. We estimated that the Russia–China border was about 1,000km downstream, so we decided that we should aim to get there by the end of the month. That way, we reasoned, we could address the twin problems of continuing our journey in July and August and paddling in Chinese territory at the same time. We also thought, perhaps naively, that if we were prepared to paddle 1,600km just on the off chance that somebody might say yes, they wouldn't actually have the heart to say no.

The next morning Comrade Matron arrived at nine on the dot. She was much less guarded than she'd been the day before, and insisted on taking us to a shop to buy bread and provisions. We talked while we walked. Her name was Aleva, she told us, and she was the director of the Dom Culturi. The job paid about $30 a month, but she made a little extra selling milk and cheese on the side. Aleva's situation was nothing unusual, I knew. Despite a growing middle class in the big western cities like Moscow and St Petersburg, the average wage in Russia was still less then $100 a month, and 20 million Russians lived below the poverty line of $31 a month. Like Aleva, many of them were forced to diversify to make ends meet, and in Siberia that often meant living off the land.

'It's still not enough,' she shrugged. She asked me what I was paid. I thought about lying, but decided against it. Instead, I took care to explain the price of property in England, and the cost of everyday items like bread and beer. She wasn't shocked at the amount I earned (Hollywood sees to it that everyone in the West is wealthy), but she was aghast at how much I spent on rent. Still, I didn't doubt for a second that life for her was much, much harder. She blamed the government in Moscow, which she said was making itself rich at Siberia's expense. 'And then there's the corruption ...' she sighed, leaving the thought hanging in the air as if she didn't need to say more.

In Siberia, *corruptsia* is a way of life. Following the collapse of communism in 1991, three-quarters of state-owned enterprises were privatised. Former party *apparatchiks* made millions overnight, while the rest of the country – no longer supported by the safety net of the Soviet state – struggled to keep their heads above water. Because there were no laws to protect those without power, those with power – including the police, the security services and the politicians – thrived.

But not everyone in authority prospered: those at the bottom of the ladder – the lowly village policeman, the security-service pen-pusher, the young border guard conscript – were paid so little (and so rarely) that they were forced to run little sidelines to make up any shortfall: a little extortion here, a little bribery there, perhaps even some poaching when prices were high. In effect they became black-market businessmen, with a finger in any pie that might bring in a few extra roubles. As we'd learned to our cost, everything in Siberia had its price. Want to paddle the Amur? Sure, but it's not going to be cheap. Want to cross the Mongolian border? No problem, but it'll cost you. Anything, it seemed, was possible, so long as you had the money to pay for it.

The shop, owned by one of Aleva's friends, was surprisingly well stocked. Before leaving the UK, I'd had visions of us having to queue around the block to buy bread. Instead, we were able to find everything we could have wished for, including orange-flavoured drinks powder and sachets of instant soup. On Aleva's recommendation, we also agreed to buy some home-made, rose-petal jam, which turned out to be every bit as revolting as it sounds. Finally, and perhaps most intriguingly, we bought our first mystery tin, which featured no descriptive labelling whatsoever.

After our shopping spree, Aleva gave us a tour of the Dom Culturi and brought us tea to drink outside on the steps. She seemed delighted that I'd be writing about Mangut when I got back to England, and was most insistent that I told everyone how kind and friendly the locals were. I promised I would; she and Julia had restored my faith in human nature – thanks to them, I'd gone from hating the place to not wanting to leave. Alas, we had another deadline to meet. Thankfully, though, it wasn't nearly as urgent this time around: with just a thousand kilometres to cover in thirty days, we'd still have a day or two in hand, even if we only managed six hours a day instead of the usual nine.

We finally left Mangut at midday, but it took us the best part of an hour to make our way back to the main flow of the river through a series of braided channels. After all the excitement of the day before, we couldn't get into the paddling, and only managed a single three-hour session. This left us plenty of time to sample the delights of our generously stocked larder. The highlight, if only for novelty value, was the rose-petal jam, which on further consideration was actually quite edible, if a little soapy. The biggest disappointment was the mystery tin, which contained a bland, anaemic-looking meatloaf dripping in unappetising jelly.

Despite this early experience, we soon got into the habit of buying a mystery tin whenever the opportunity presented itself, and the opening of each tin invariably involved a great deal of pomp and circumstance. Rich even made up a little poem to accompany the opening of the tin itself, which he uttered with all the enthusiasm of an evangelist praying for a sign from on high: 'Oh mystery tin, oh mystery tin, what lies within the mystery tin?' Well, maybe you had to be there. Other offerings from the god of canned goods included seaweed in brine, a startling variety of fish pastes, and a few more meat stews that defied description.

Thanks to a curious quirk of the local time zone (for some reason, this side of the border was a whole two hours ahead of the Mongolian side) it didn't get dark until midnight, which meant we also had plenty of time to sunbathe. In fact, it was so scorching that the beach we'd chosen as our campsite was too hot to walk on, let alone lie on, so we spent most of the afternoon languishing in the shallows near the riverbank. It didn't start to cool down until well after eight, by which time my shoulders were smouldering; so much, you might think, for Siberian weather.

We adopted this relaxing regimen for the next week, paddling three, two-hour sessions a day with a swim and a snack between each. This meant we were only on the water for six hours out of every twenty-four. We were, I realised with mounting guilt, a couple of lazy toads. But we were a well-fed couple of toads: although we were paddling a lot less than before, we were eating a great deal more. The first break – or elevenses – usually comprised eight slices of bread between us, each buttered and smothered in whatever we happened to have to hand: on a good day this meant chocolate spread; on a bad day it meant rose-petal jam, or – as was the case during one particularly bleak, four-day spell – cocoa-flavoured butter (we'd bought this thinking that it might be tasty. It wasn't). This was invariably followed by half a bar of chocolate each: Nestlé white chocolate was a favourite, while Russian-made cooking chocolate definitely wasn't. The lunch stop, meanwhile, involved two sardine sandwiches apiece, followed by another half bar of chocolate. Whenever possible we bought sardines in tomato sauce, as this gave the sandwiches added flavour and helped to provide much-needed moisture to four-day-old bread. We tried experimenting with other fillings, but we soon learnt that tinned fish was the only thing we could buy with any confidence.

Our evening meals were no more adventurous. We'd start with a large bowl of soup, usually mopped up with any bread that was left over from lunch. After that it was noodles or pasta with yet more tinned fish, which we flavoured with garlic, dried chillies and, when we could get hold of them, dried vegetables. This worked well up to a point, but because we were eating the same meal every day, our taste buds soon got used to the garlic. The obvious solution was to add more garlic, but the more garlic we added the more we got used to it, and it wasn't long before we were chucking seven or eight cloves into the mix. In fact, such was the damage done by this daily overdose, that even now I can't taste garlic in food unless it's swimming in the stuff.

The main course was then closely followed by another small bar of chocolate, usually accompanied by a large bowl of hot chocolate or coffee. Oh, and then we'd have another half bar of chocolate before we went to bed, just to keep our energy levels up during the night. Needless to say, with a diet like this, it wasn't long before we became the proud fathers of two, perfectly-formed pot bellies.

Part of the problem (I tried to convince myself) was that the river was now moving quite quickly, which meant we had to make a lot less effort to cover the same sort of distance. If I fancied a quick break, it was quite possible to drift with the current for a minute and still not fall too far behind. On one occasion I even dozed off midstream, thanks to a combination of temperature, tedium and general toadiness. This would have been fine but for the fact that while I was sleeping I dreamed that I was best friends with Zöe Ball. When I woke up, I was understandably alarmed – and frankly a little put out – to find myself on some godforsaken stream in the middle of Siberia.

Another dream I had, oddly enough, involved us paddling on some godforsaken stream in the middle of Siberia: we were just drifting around a bend in the river when the horizon line suddenly seemed to disappear in front of us. I back-paddled furiously to avoid being swept over the drop, but Rich decided to go for it. Luckily, it was only about 20ft high, so I followed him down before pausing for breath in an eddy below. Rich, meanwhile, was swept over a second fall that was at least 100ft high. In my dream, I saw his boat getting smaller and smaller as he fell, until he landed in the shallow plunge-pool at the bottom with a sickening crunch. When I eventually clambered down to find him, he was dazed but unhurt. 'Blimey,' he said casually, 'that was quite interesting.'

The next morning, I thought it pertinent to ask Rich what he would do if either of us died while we were in Siberia (obviously if *he* copped it, his options would be pretty limited, but you know what I mean). In the event, we both agreed that after a suitable period of mourning (say, three or four minutes), we'd carry on alone, as a mark of respect for the other. For his part,

Rich was quite aggrieved at the thought of having to carry both halves of the tent, but he seemed to cheer up considerably when I pointed out that he would also stand to inherit my brand-new video camera.

If Rich met his maker, I'd be the first in line for his radio, an item which I quietly coveted. Before leaving the UK, I'd decided that a Walkman would be preferable to a radio: I liked the idea of being cut off from the rest of world, and besides, if I ever got bored with my tapes, I could always just swap with Rich. It soon became clear, however, that he was far too attached to his daily fix of the World Service, and that he'd never give up *Woman's Hour* without a fight.

Another thing that Rich benefited from was his tongue. Unlike most tongues, his was made of asbestos, which meant he could eat much larger spoonfuls of porridge than me without burning it. Since we ate from the same bowl, it stood to reason that he was getting more than his fair share. I thought about kicking up a fuss, but then decided – on balance – that I was being a complete arse.

On the morning of 6 June it started to rain for the first time since we'd set off over three weeks before, and for the next two days, it positively pissed it down. The temperature plummeted, and for the first time in days we were forced to wear more than just our river shorts. In fact, I put on almost everything I had with me, including thermal leggings and waterproofs, and I was still cold. This was exactly the sort of weather we'd been dreading. It was a timely reminder of how good we'd had it up till now, and how much worse it could've been. Over the last few days I'd been praying for a quick thunderstorm, just to cool things down a bit, but that didn't mean I actually wanted to get wet. I vowed there and then never to go out in the rain again.

Thankfully, 8 June dawned cool and misty, the sun forming a completely circular rainbow as it tried to burn through the haze. By midday it was back with a vengeance, more intense than ever; it was so hot that my back began to blister, and Rich's nose turned an alarming shade of crimson. What I wouldn't give, I thought ruefully, for a quick thunderstorm, just to cool things down a bit. The end of the rain also signalled the arrival of the infamous 'super-moskies,' which up until now hadn't been much of a problem. By happy coincidence, the zip on our tent decided to stop working that very evening. Luckily, we'd brought along a couple of spare mosquito nets, but it took us a few days to perfect a system of rigging them up around the tent door so that they were utterly impervious to invasion. In the meantime we were bled dry by the little bastards.

Still, apart from the odd bite or two hundred, my body was now in pretty good shape: my fingertips had at last softened up, my back was no longer giving me grief, and my spare tyre was coming on nicely. Most crucial of all, though, was the fact that my beard was starting to look gratifyingly bushy.

The day before we reached Olovannaya – the next village marked on our maps – we crossed the 2,000ft contour on our maps. It was surprising, and more than a little depressing, to learn that we would only drop 600 metres in the next 4,000 kilometres. Put another way, this was less than 20cm for every kilometre we paddled. There were, I felt sure, parts of the Pacific Ocean that had more of a gradient.

We needed to stop in Olovannaya to resupply but, after our experience in Mangut, I couldn't help but feel apprehensive. I was also reluctant to give up the solitude that we'd enjoyed for the last few days: without a schedule to keep to and with no real demands on our time, we'd established a routine that was as relaxing as it was idyllic; we paddled, we swam, we ate and we slept. The biggest decision we had to make each day was whether to have porridge or semolina for breakfast. It was exactly how I felt a source-to-sea journey should be, and I dreaded having to give it up, even for a minute.

The night before we were due to reach Olovannaya, I decided to prepare for our imminent shopping spree by digging out my

Russian phrase book. Flicking absent-mindedly through the pages to avoid actually doing any work, I came upon a chapter simply entitled 'Encounters'. Intrigued, I decided to investigate further, and was soon glad that I did: by the end of the night I could say 'I'd love to have some company', 'Shall we go somewhere quieter?' and 'May I kiss you?' Significantly, I felt less inclined to learn the likely responses, namely 'Leave me alone', 'I'm afraid we have to leave now' and, my personal favourite, 'Sorry, I'm not ready for that yet.'

The view from the river as we approached Olovannaya the following morning was dominated by the distant, orange and white smoke stacks of a power station. Nearing the upstream end of the village, we passed directly beneath a swathe of high-tension cables, and a few minutes later a huge diesel locomotive screeched into view, tugging an endless line of trucks filled with coal. We even saw a bus in the distance, and wondered – as you do – if it might be carrying a troupe of Swedish dancing girls. On reflection, however, we realised that neither of us had ever met any dancing girls on our travels, Swedish or otherwise.

We also saw legions of fishermen along the riverbank, and as we approached the vast railway bridge that linked the town to the power station, one of them started shouting at us. To begin with we ignored him, but when he became more aggressive, I yelled back, assuming he was just another angler. Rich politely pointed out that he didn't know many anglers who fished with an AK47.

6 THE GREAT OLOVANNAYA HOTEL HUNT

After weighing up the options, we decided it might be prudent to pull over at the nearest beach. We waited anxiously while a welcoming party stumbled down the steep bank to confront us. AK Angler was joined by an overweight policeman wearing a sweaty string vest and a scowl that could have killed a small mammal at twenty paces. When he got close, I tried to break the ice with a cheery greeting, but he didn't bat an eyelid. '*Dokumenti!*' he spat, his hand resting conspicuously on the butt of his holstered pistol.

He looked over our papers before launching into a tirade of Russian. 'I don't understand,' I shrugged. Another tirade, this one slightly louder than the last. Again I shrugged. Infuriated, he turned around and heaved himself back up the bank. We waited for a moment, not sure what to do, before AK waved his gun in the direction of his panting boss.

He led us along an oily, soot-caked railway track to a wooden building that was guarded by a pack of child-eating wolves. I tried to look nonchalant, but when one of them lunged at me, it was all I could do to stifle a muffled miaow. Just when I thought I could make out the molars at the back of the beast's gnashing jaws, its head was snapped abruptly backwards by a long chain. In the long seconds that followed, I became a fully fledged member of the Christian community.

We were shown to a back room, which contained a large desk, a few rickety wooden chairs, and a telephone which looked like it had seen service in the Bolshevik Revolution. On one of the walls was a giant poster showing how to strip down and reassemble an AK47 (AK47s, it seemed, were all the rage in Siberian circles). Hauling himself behind the desk, Serpico motioned us to sit down. He studied our papers some more, before cranking up his phone. A series of urgent monologues followed, none of which I could understand. I just hoped that whoever he was speaking to could vouch for our permit to travel on the river – and that they didn't feed spies to ravenous Alsatians.

When at last he replaced the phone in its cradle, he was all smiles. We were free to go, he said, and he apologised for any misunderstanding, saying something like, 'You can't be too careful these days.' Well, quite. He told us where there was a hotel in town, wished us luck, and led us out past the dogs, which were still baying for blood. So much, I thought, for *Glasnost*.

And so began the Great Olovannaya Hotel Hunt. The place he'd suggested turned out to be a derelict squat, so we asked some lads on a street corner if they knew of anywhere we could stay. One of them, with short blond hair and bright, searching eyes, seemed more welcoming than the rest, and invited us to stay in his house. We refused, guessing that his parents might be less than thrilled, but it was getting late, so when he insisted, we gave in. He led us through a labyrinth of dusty dirt roads to a small, well-kept cabin that he said was his own.

It seemed ideal, but when we asked where we could put our boats, he motioned us to follow him back the way we'd come. When we reached the place we'd met him, he pointed to the river and suggested that we'd be better off camping downstream. I was a bit taken aback – I couldn't understand why he'd changed his mind. It dawned on me that perhaps he'd been thinking of robbing us, but he was still smiling, as though nothing had happened – he even pointed out a shop where we could buy food.

By this stage, we'd had enough of hauling our boats back and forth across town, so we decided to take Blondie's advice. Before we left, though, we needed to stock up on bread, sugar and other staples. The small shop he'd indicated was owned by a tanned, thickset man with a silver crew cut and three gold teeth. We told him who we were and where we'd come from, and he seemed fascinated by the details of our journey. He asked us if we had somewhere to stay, and when we said no, his smile became a beam. 'I know just the place,' he enthused. It wasn't far, he added, and he'd be happy to take us there – in the meantime, we could store our boats in his back garden.

Something about his manner reassured me that he was on the level, so we duly dumped our loads in the vegetable patch behind his shop and followed him to the hotel. On the way, he told us his name was Nikolai, or Kolya for short. He was originally from Moscow, he said, but he'd been working in Olovannaya for ten years. I told him more about our journey, and with each new revelation he shook his head, gold glinting in a disbelieving smile. As we walked, he gave us a guided tour, pointing out the town hall, the police station and the bakery. Everywhere we went he shook hands with people, greeting them fondly and introducing us both as if we were old friends.

The hotel was more like a row of whitewashed apartments, featuring threadbare furniture and well-used bathrooms, but as far was we were concerned, it was the Ritz. Kolya left us to it, insisting that we came by his shop once we'd had a chance to clean up. When we did reappear an hour later, he had a couple of cold beers waiting for us on the shop counter, compliments of the house. I can't be sure, but I think I might have kissed him. Thankfully, the beer was Siberian, not Korean, and we sucked it down with greedy gulps. Once we'd finished, he took us across the square to a small stone building with a nondescript door. It was a restaurant, he said, owned by a good friend of his from Georgia. It wasn't open until ten, which was still an hour away, but we were welcome to wait. In the meantime, he suggested, we could have a look around the town.

The square itself was dominated by a large tank and a jet fighter pointing dramatically skywards; Soviet sculpture, I was beginning to realise, was nothing if not subtle. As I gazed in wonder at the plane, I also realised there was a small child playing in the cockpit, and – perhaps more alarmingly – that the cockpit was a good thirty feet off the ground; the only way to reach it was to shin up the length of the impossibly steep fuselage. In fact, the whole time we were in Olovannaya, it always seemed to contain at least one underage aviator risking life and limb for Mother Russia.

The trees that lined the streets around the square were thick with a white, cotton-bud blossom that drifted down like snow when the wind blew. But for the roads themselves, which were little more than dusty tracks, we might just as easily have been in America's Deep South, with its wooden decking and sun-kissed screen doors. Even at nine o'clock, the shops near the square were still doing a brisk business (mostly in vodka), and before long we fell in with a party of revellers, all decked out in their Sunday best. Two of them, Yuri and Nastia, were twins celebrating their 25th birthday. When they realised we were English, they insisted we join them for dinner.

While we waited outside the restaurant, they asked us about life in England, and one young lad – slightly the worse for wear – insisted that London was always foggy. We tried to convince him otherwise, but he stood – or rather, swayed – his ground. Only much later did I learn that Sherlock Holmes was still a standard text in many local schools, and that a generation of Siberians had an image of London based entirely on the stories of a nineteenth-century author with an opium habit.

And then, before you could say *shashlick* and stuffed pork parcels, we were inside the restaurant, supping our second bottle of beer and tucking into a tantalising array of pig produce. With just half a dozen tables and no windows, it had what can only be described as a cosy, intimate feel. Within half an hour of it opening, it was packed to the rafters and, perhaps not surprisingly in such a small town, everyone seemed to know each other. The more we drank, the more vocal we got, and before long we were both fluent in Russian. While the girls danced their way out of tight-fitting dresses, we danced like John Travolta in *Saturday Night Fever*. The music – or what little I can remember of it – was a mixture of Russian pop and Abba, with the odd Boney M medley thrown in for good measure. It was, I thought giddily, the best party I'd ever been to.

When the vodka appeared, I knew it was all over. Yuri showed us how it was done, necking a shot not much bigger than a bucket before chasing it down with a beer. I followed his lead and immediately wished I hadn't. Rich, however, couldn't get enough of the stuff, and was soon dancing with every girl in the room. In the interests of cross-cultural relations, I thought now might be the time to try one of my new phrases – 'Shall we go somewhere quieter?' perhaps – but it wasn't to be. The party, along with my brain, finally dissolved at around 4 a.m., at which point we reeled back to our hotel room, feeling like a million dollars and grinning like complete cretins.

The next morning I felt very rough indeed, but I found some consolation in the fact that Rich felt *so* much worse. Blinking our way into the painfully bright, mid-morning sun, we went in search of bacon and eggs, and mugs of steaming black coffee strong enough to stand a spoon in. Instead, we had to make do with lashings of beef goulash and mashed potato at the nearby *stolovaya*. The food, though, did nothing to quench our raging thirst, so we bought a bottle of mineral water each and sat on the steps outside, watching the world go past and trying desperately to stop it spinning.

While we were sitting there, our heads resting gently in our hands, we were approached by the owner of a nearby shop. I felt too tired and jaded to speak to her, but when she sat down next to me, I realised I didn't have much choice. She was quite young – maybe in her mid-thirties – and had a round, attractive face and a mischievous smile. Somewhat worryingly, she seemed to know exactly who we were. She introduced herself as Maria. She was originally from Samara, she told us, on the Volga River. She'd only been in Olovannaya for a year, and was hoping to move back in another year, once she'd made enough money from her shop.

'I have two kids, aged twelve and seven,' she explained, 'and they both miss their home. The school here is OK,' she added, 'but there are lots of breathing problems in Olovannaya. I don't know if it's the coal or the nuclear reactor, but either way, it's not a good place for them to grow up.' Like Kolya, she spoke slowly and clearly, aware that I might find her hard to understand; maybe it had something to do with the fact that she was well travelled and that she, too, was a long way from home, but it offered a rare and welcome respite from the usual rush of syllables.

As we talked, a shiny black car sped past in a plume of dust. Maria tutted. 'Armenians,' was all she said. I asked what she meant. 'They're bad people,' she said simply. 'Mafia?' I suggested, still not sure I'd understood. 'No,' she said, rubbing her thumb and forefinger together, 'just corrupt businessmen, always doing deals.' As I was to learn later, shiny black cars were the vehicle of choice for those with power and money.

After we'd been talking for about half an hour, she asked us what we were doing later. I said that we weren't sure, but that we were thinking about getting back on the river. 'I'm closing up shop now, to take my kids to the beach,' she beamed. 'Why don't you come with us?' After the night we'd had, it was all the excuse we needed.

But before we could enjoy the plutonium-rich delights of Olovannaya Sands, we had some unfinished business with Kolya. We found him enjoying a midday snooze in his shop. Once he'd supplied us with everything we needed for the coming weeks, he showed us around his garden, pointing out the greenhouse where he grew tomatoes, the vegetable patch where he grew potatoes, and the sturdy metal bar where he grew his biceps. 'I work out every day,' he said proudly, pumping his chest up to its full size. 'I'm not as strong as I was when I was your age,' he confessed with a smile, 'but I'm not bad for an old man!' His home-made gym also included an old wooden plank for sit-ups, and a ramp for some hernia-inducing exercise that I couldn't quite fathom. I asked him if I could take a photo of him doing a chin-up. 'Tomorrow,' he said shyly, 'you can take one tomorrow.' He might have been proud, but he was clearly no poseur.

When we eventually wandered down to the river, we couldn't find Maria and her tribe; the beach was actually quite wide – maybe half a kilometre across – and was surprisingly busy with kids, families and middle-aged men working on their sunburn. Not sure where to start, we made a beeline for a quiet area at the water's edge, stripped down to our shorts, and went for a swim. After our sweaty night on the town and the debilitating heat of the morning, it felt fantastic: the water was cold and clear, and the current was so fast we had to work hard just to stay in the same place. Drying out on the beach, we filmed a piece to camera about the rigours of expedition life, little knowing at the time just how rigorous things were about to get.

A few minutes later, a skinny girl in a tiny, bright-pink bikini strode purposefully towards us. She looked maybe eleven or twelve. 'Hi,' she said in Russian with unabashed enthusiasm, 'Mama is calling you over.' As we wandered over towards where Maria was sitting, we introduced ourselves. 'I'm Helena,' she smiled in reply, and then, in stilted English, 'My name is Helen.' She stressed the second syllable, which somehow made it sound more endearing, and with that, we were firm friends.

'How's life?' I asked Maria in Russian as we wandered up. 'Eh,' she shrugged with a smile, '*Normalni*.' She introduced us to her younger daughter, Angelica, who was very blond and very shy, and to her friend Natasha, who also had two young kids, Zhena and Olga. Once the introductions were over with, she whipped away the tablecloth at our feet to reveal plates piled high with food, and produced a bottle of wine from behind her back.

'Russian champagne,' she announced with aplomb, 'it's traditional!' As she spoke, she flicked her throat with two fingers, before rolling her eyes and falling into a fit of giggles. I was soon to learn that, in Siberia at least, throat-flicking was a universally understood sign for getting well and truly whammed.

Natasha, we discovered, ran a market stall in town. Twice a month she crossed into China to buy clothes, but she didn't think much of the Chinese. 'They're all thieves,' she stated pointedly. I asked her what she meant, but either she didn't hear me, or she chose to ignore me. 'Mind you,' she continued, 'at least their customs men are fast. The Russians take hours, checking every last item of clothing.' After our little AK47 scare the day before, that didn't surprise me in the least.

As we swapped stories over sausages and champagne, Helena pointed to the pendant around Rich's neck and asked what it was. After some frantic flicking through our dictionary, we revealed it was a snake, representing the god of the Zambezi River. 'It's supposed to protect paddlers from harm,' I explained. '*Kak talisman?*' Maria suggested. 'Exactly,' I agreed, 'like a talisman.'

A few minutes later, Helena sat down next to me and put a thin, silver bracelet around my wrist. 'Richard has a talisman,' she stated simply, 'and now you have one too.' I thanked Helena, but said I couldn't possibly keep it. 'Why not?' Maria intervened. 'Because ...' I paused, trying to think how I could explain it in Russian, '... because it looks much prettier on Helena.'

Maria was unconvinced. 'Nonsense,' she said, shaking her head vigorously. 'When you write about your journey, you can tell people about this present from your Russian friends.' It was, I realised, the least I could do. Again I thanked Helena (who by now couldn't stop smiling) and took a closer look at the bracelet's tiny charms, which included a star, a moon, a heart and a bell. In return, I gave her one of the silver medallions that the Churchill Trust had given me back in the UK, which were intended for people who displayed uncommon kindness on our journey. I wasn't convinced that a coin featuring the bluff old bulldog of British politics would have much appeal for a twelve-year-old, but little Helena was wise beyond her years, and she accepted it graciously.

It was gone eight by the time we wrapped up what was left of the picnic. On the way back, Helena talked so quickly she hardly had time to draw breath, but because she was so young, she talked about things which were easy for me to understand: at school, she said, she played basketball, and at home she liked watching films: 'Fantasies are best,' she decided, 'then comedies, then dramas. Oh, and my favourite names are William for a boy ... and Helen for a girl, of course.' But of course.

Anxious to thank them for their hospitality, Rich and I invited Maria and Natasha to have dinner with us. 'But I haven't got anything to wear,' pleaded Maria predictably. With a sweeping gesture, I indicated our sandals and river shorts. Maria paused. 'OK, OK!' she said at last, handing her bags to Helena, 'let's go.' And so began another night of wanton debauchery.

The order of play went something like this: bread, pork; cucumber, pork; vodka, pork; vodka, vodka. I lost count of how many times this sequence repeated itself, but it lasted all night. Vodka with beer chasers, Maria scoffed, was for kids; the traditional way to drink it, she assured us, was 'however you wanted to', so long as it was neat. But naturally there was a catch: if you didn't down it in one, you had to pour what was left down your shirt. This might sound expensive, but when you bear in mind that a litre of vodka in Siberia costs less than 20p, you begin to realise that the only real cost is to your stomach lining, and – by association – your will to live. Rich and I tried gamely to keep up, but it soon became clear we were way out of our depth. Suffice it to say that before long we were both praying that no one would decide to light a match in our immediate vicinity.

Soon after midnight, we were joined by a middle-aged couple who'd been sitting at a nearby table and who were obviously friends of Maria's. Sascha was all charm and charisma, but 'his woman' (his words, I hasten to point out) was painfully shy. I couldn't work out whether she was his wife or his lover, but he was so affectionate and attentive towards her that I guessed the latter.

Right from the off, Sascha treated us like long-lost brothers: 'Pol! Reeechard!' he declared every few minutes, 'we are great friends. England and Russia, we are great friends!' He'd once worked in Holland, he told us, but he was originally from the Ukraine, which he said was full of beautiful mountains and animals. Warming to his subject, he decided that the next day we should go hunting for moose.

'You will wear their antlers on your heads,' he continued, using his fingers by way of a demonstration, 'and when you fly back to England, all of the girls will love you.' We must have looked unsure, though I can't for the life of me imagine why. 'It's true!' he persevered. 'When I wore my antlers in Amsterdam, all the women loved me!'

He asked about our journey, but as soon as I told him where we'd paddled from, he became very serious. 'Mongolia is dangerous,' he hissed earnestly. 'The people there are very bad.' Ironically, this was exactly how Gal had described the Russians back in Mongolia. I tried to explain that the Mongolians *we'd* met were actually very friendly, but he was unmoved. 'That's just what they want you to think,' he said, 'but the moment you turn your back, they'll rob you!' The Russians and the English, it seemed, were the only people who weren't bandits and brigands.

The whole time he talked, Sascha's arm was clamped around Rich's shoulders. When I decided to get some air, he insisted on going with me, saying that the streets were dangerous. He also insisted that Rich should dance with His Woman while he was gone. His Woman looked mildly embarrassed and Rich was understandably mortified, but before long everyone was dancing with everyone else. We only decided to call it a night when the room started dancing all on its own.

The next morning my head felt more like it had been kicked by a moose than decorated by one. We'd planned to set off first thing, but by midday an early start was looking less and less likely. Our first port of call was Maria's shop, where we bought a cold bottle of water to douse our hangovers. For a while we just sat there, quite still. Only when we started to show signs of oxygenation did Maria announce that she was taking us to lunch. I couldn't speak for Rich, of course, but another generous helping of greasy pig fat was just what my churning stomach needed.

Needless to say, the food was actually delicious, and included all manner of traditional Russian dishes, from *pelmeni* (small pancakes stuffed with meat) to *borsch* (a delicious soup packed with cabbage, beetroot and other wholesome goodies). After a while, I was starting to feel human again. At least, that is, until the champagne appeared. Maria toasted our health and wished us luck on the rest of our journey, but she drank alone.

While we ate, we showed them photographs of our families and friends. Without the distractions of the beach to keep them amused, though, it wasn't long before the youngsters started sulking. 'They've obviously had enough of our boring photographs!' I joked, to no one in particular. 'No,' Maria sighed sadly, 'they just want to go back home, to Samara.'

It was late afternoon by the time we picked up our boats. There was no sign of Kolya, so we left a postcard with the girl behind the counter, before continuing down to the beach. Our adopted family walked down with us, and Helen was once again in full flow: 'I'm going to travel for ten years before I get married,' she said excitedly. 'First I'm going to go to England to see Big Ben, then to Europe, then to Africa and America, and then to China and Mongolia.'

I laughed. 'That sounds like the whole world!' I said.

'Yes,' she nodded with a smile, 'the whole world!' I smiled too: for this little girl of twelve going on twenty, there were no robbers and thieves, just exotic-sounding names and far-away places. It was, I felt certain, the best way to be.

As we made our last-minute preparations at the water's edge, Zhena, Natasha's youngest, started playing with Rich's paddle. When Rich lifted him into the cockpit of his canoe, his little arms could barely reach over the sides. Zhena was clearly undeterred. 'I'm paddling to England,' he announced matter-of-factly, waving the paddles around and bouncing up and down in the boat.

Before we left, Helen gave us a good-luck card. On the outside was a big, grinning sun, with the words 'Your smile makes the world light up!' Inside, she'd written: 'It was nice to meet you – you're good friends! Please come and see us again. So Long! Helen x.'

When we finally pushed off, the current was so swift that by the time we looked back, we were out of earshot. We gave one last wave, dropped our rudders into the water, and pointed our boats towards the Pacific.

7 THE BLACK CAT OF SRETENSK

On the beach I'd joked with Maria that we'd only manage a kilometre before falling asleep, but thanks to the current we actually managed about ten. It felt good to be back on the river, but I was exhausted, and I was glad when we found a secluded beach to call home for the night. It seemed like a week since we'd been sent packing by Blondie, and so much had happened in the meantime that it was hard to take it all in. Wearing my new talisman, and with more memories than I knew what to do with, I fell asleep with a smile on my face. I'd come to Siberia expecting the river to be the highlight of our journey, but our quest for food and shelter had led to something equally worthwhile, and infinitely more rewarding.

The next morning I struggled to find any sort of rhythm on the river, so I spent most of the day mulling over our experiences in Olovannaya. On the plus side, this meant that for the first time since we'd set off, I was thinking more about the people we'd met on the river than friends and family back in the UK; on the minus side, it meant that my head was spinning with half-remembered conversations in Russian, and as a result I found it very difficult to switch off.

Perhaps realising that I might be in need of a bit of light relief, that evening Rich dug out his mini *SAS Survival Guide* and brought me up to speed on current wilderness wisdom: I was surprised to learn, for example, that mosses and lichens can be soaked in water overnight and added to stews. The book also contained the following requisite words of wisdom: 'When throwing a rope, be sure to hang on to the other end,' and 'If you hear a weather warning for a tsunami, don't go looking for it.' Frankly, I couldn't understand how we'd got this far without it.

During the night, I dreamed that I was being swept towards the top of Murchison's Falls in my canoe. At Murchison's – for those who don't know it – the River Nile plunges over a long, sloping drop barely 15 feet wide and over 80 feet high. Every second, millions of gallons of water explode through this gap with unimaginable force. It's probably fair to say that anyone getting gobbled up at the top might not be spat out at the bottom for days, so I was understandably piqued at the thought of having to paddle through its guts. I managed to break into an eddy just behind a concrete pillar near the top, but it was too small and, try as I might, I couldn't stay in it. The dream ended with me surfing a huge standing wave just above the lip, not getting swept over the drop, but not able to paddle upstream either. What, I wondered, would Freud have made of that?

Three days downstream of Olovannaya, we reached the confluence of the Ingoda, which was smaller than the Onon, but colder and murkier. Beyond this junction, the landscape underwent a gradual change, from low-slung valley to high, forested hill – on one rare day of rain we could just as easily have been in the heart of the Scottish Highlands as in the depths of southern Siberia.

This was also the point where the much-fêted Trans-Siberian railway joined the river, following it for about 100km before heading northeast into the Shilkinski Mountains. For much of this stretch it came to within yards of the river, and the impressively long goods trains that screeched and rumbled back and forth provided a welcome distraction from the monotony of our daily routine.

What was even more impressive, though, was the railway itself. Started at the end of the nineteenth century and finished less than 25 years later, to this day it remains an astonishing feat of engineering. The first 5,000km, from Moscow to Lake Baikal, took just seven years to complete, despite the fact that workers – many of them exiles and convicts – had to hack their way across Siberia using little more than hand tools. The landscape they crossed was unimaginably harsh, with temperatures regularly dropping below –40°C in the winter and soaring to +40°C in the summer. Floods and landslides were common, and disease also took its toll.

When war broke out with Japan in 1904, temporary rails were laid across the frozen Lake Baikal, to speed the supply of troops and weapons to the front (up until then a pair of ice-breaking steamers had carried the train across the lake). The first locomotive to cross simply plunged through the ice, gashing a hole twenty kilometres long. In short, conditions for those working on the railway were nothing short of horrendous.

Before it was built, travelling overland across Siberia could take up to a year; for those who could afford it, it was quicker to travel via North America and the Pacific. Once the railway was completed, however, the same journey could be made in less than two weeks. Today, the Trans-Siberian takes just six and a half days to travel a mind-boggling 9,289km. In that time, it goes through no fewer than eight different time zones. It remains a miracle of human endeavour, and a testament to the vision – and sacrifice – of those who built it.

The day after we reached the Trans-Siberian, we stopped in a sizeable town called Shilka; we didn't need to resupply for another week, but it was now the middle of June, so we decided to drop Dmitry a line, to find out if he was having any luck with our permissions to paddle along the imminent border section.

The town itself was set back from the river, and was much bigger and more sprawling than Olovannaya. It even had metalled roads, but they were peppered with potholes the size of dumper trucks. 'The health and safety boys wouldn't be very happy about that,' Rich said helpfully, wheeling his boat around one particularly cavernous crater. 'It's an unshored excavation greater than 1.2 metres in depth and there's no prominent public information notice.' Ah, the joys of having an environmental scientist along for the ride.

Again we had the problem of finding somewhere to stay, but after towing our boats across town for two hours, we eventually found ourselves at the train station. The station guard told us we could lock our boats in a freight shed, before showing us to a room overlooking the arrivals hall. It was clean and tidy, with brand new beds and crisp, clean sheets. It even boasted a flushing toilet and an electric socket, although he was quick to inform us that the latter didn't work because there'd been a power cut earlier in the day. Once we'd had a chance to clean up, we wandered to the station café, where he joined us for a quick beer between arrivals. When we got up to leave – a few minutes after he'd hurried back to the platform – the waitress told us there was nothing to pay. 'What do you mean?' I asked, confused. 'The gentleman has taken care of it,' she said simply. We never did find him again to say thanks.

And he wasn't our only saviour in Shilka: because of the power cut, the bank was closed, which meant we couldn't get hold of any roubles. At the telephone exchange in the post office I asked if we could pay for a call to Moscow in dollars. 'Nyet!' came the curt reply. Given that phone boxes were as rare as flushing facilities on the river, I offered to pay over the odds. '*Nyet*,' the woman behind the counter repeated, the corners of her mouth curling into a smug smile.

Maybe it was the way she said it, maybe I was just tired, or maybe it was a combination of the two, but for a moment I felt inclined to agree with whoever once said: 'One of the most curious things about modern Russia is the startling and universal ugliness of the women.' It wasn't true – if anything, the opposite was the case – but it made me feel better. I was just considering a translation for the teller's benefit when I felt a tap on my shoulder. I looked around to see a young, attractive woman holding out a handful of crumpled notes. I blushed, stammering something about not being able to accept it. She smiled, again proffering her hand, and again I said no. At that, and before I could say anything else, she placed the money carefully on the counter in front of me, wished us luck, and walked out the door.

The news from Dmitry was good. That's not strictly true: it was bloody brilliant. The Chinese authorities, it seemed, had decided that we were more of a danger to ourselves than to national security, and were happy for us to travel along the border section. The details were contained in a fax which began: 'The Ministry of Foreign Affairs of the People's Republic of China is honoured to forward the following notification with respect to the intrepid British explorers ...' Clearly, there had been some kind of mistake – we were waiting for a fax with respect to 'the indolent British loafers'.

There was, however, a proviso: we were not to set foot on Chinese territory or paddle in Chinese waters unless we found ourselves in 'extreme major circumstances'. In many ways, this came as something of a blow, because it meant that we would only be able to experience life on one side of the river, but it was a start, and – for now at least – it was probably the best we could hope for.

The next morning, we wheeled our canoes out of the railway station with renewed resolve, anxious to get to the border as soon as possible. Someone, though, had other ideas. 'Who are you?' demanded a man in civilian clothes, barring our way. 'Who are you?' I asked in return, in no mood for hostility. 'Police,' he said testily, puffing out his chest a little, as if to prove it. 'Give me your papers.' Since we'd already been seen by countless local policemen, with and without our boats, I decided to stand my ground – I'd been through this too many times to be intimidated. '*Nyet*,' I said, brushing past him. As I did so, I could practically hear him deflating. I knew he was just throwing his weight about, and so did he. Needless to say, he didn't utter another word.

The day after we left Shilka, we had trouble of a different sort. After weeks of wheezing and spluttering, our stove finally coughed its last cough and died. This was not good. In fact, it was really rather bad: assuming we'd be allowed to paddle as far as the Pacific, we still had at least two months to go. We could have survived without cooked food but it would have been pretty dismal. Whether we could have survived without tea was another matter entirely. Still, we could hardly complain: the petrol we'd been using was dirtier than a chimney sweep's fingernails, and had completely clogged up the stove's sensitive innards. Our only option was to strip these innards out and use what remained as a kind of makeshift flame-thrower. On the upside, this meant our food now cooked in no time; on the downside, it meant everything within a twenty-foot radius was coated in a fine layer of soot. More alarmingly, it also meant we now had to wash as often as once a day if we wanted to avoid losing our suntans.

The extra carbon in our diet, however, soon started to take its toll – either that, or the salami we'd bought back in Olovannaya was well past its prime. The morning after our first culinary cremation, I woke up feeling queasy and lethargic. After a shaky start, I spent the best part of the day doubled-up on a beach. Somehow, between these bouts of nausea, we managed to cover 30km, but all I could think about was lying down and sleeping. By the time we made camp, it was all I could do to stop my intestines from melting in the fierce heat of the afternoon. In a vain attempt to cool off, I soaked my clothes and my sleeping mattress in the river and lay in the shade of the tent, feeling blissfully sorry for myself.

Consulting his health guide, Rich confidently reported that my symptoms were consistent with half a dozen different diseases, three of them fatal. How very reassuring. To cheer me up, he also told me about guinea worms, which apparently develop deep inside the body and devour their host from the inside out. I tried to throw up on him, truly I did, but alas, I had nothing left to give.

By first light of the following day I was relieved to find that the nausea and cramps had gone, but I still felt hot and clammy. Mercifully, though, the early morning mist helped to keep the temperature at bay, shrouding the sun like a thin layer of muslin.

Our destination that day was a ramshackle, log-cabin village called Sretensk, an isolated outpost of the Trans-Siberian and the last significant settlement before the border. Wheeling our canoes conspicuously along the waterfront, we were approached by an old biker in torn leathers and a ruby-red helmet. 'I,' he said proudly, 'am Victor,' as if somehow we should know the name.

He didn't believe us when we told him we'd come from Mongolia, but when we said we were on our way to the border he became positively enraged. It took me a few minutes to realise that he wasn't angry with us, but with the border guards, who he promised would shoot us on sight. 'They will be made heroes, with medals from Moscow,' he thundered, slapping his chest, 'but you will be dead.' And with that, he moulded his hands around an imaginary machine gun and sprayed our chests with an impressive salvo of spittle.

As a confidence booster, Victor's approach clearly needed some work, but we assured him that we had permission to paddle as far as the border from military HQ in Moscow. I even showed him our permits, but he was no longer listening. 'They don't care about papers, only medals!' he urged, slapping his chest again. 'The army, the KGB, they're all the same!' he added, before letting loose a final, contemptuous volley of phlegm and careering off up the road in a plume of dust.

Victor's anger, it seemed, was catching. The babushka who owned the town's only hotel (and I use that word very loosely) wasn't happy about having canoes in her lobby, or – for that matter – Englishmen in her rooms. I gleaned from the torrent of abuse she was hurling at us that we had to report to the town's passport-control office immediately. Unwilling to take us on our word, she marched us there herself, taking great care to stay five paces ahead of us at all times. Thankfully, the customs ladies were less suspicious, and – more to show willing than to follow protocol – they made copies of all our documents and asked us where we'd come from and where we were going.

Apparently satisfied, our self-appointed chaperone was suddenly all smiles, happily giving us directions to the local shops. In Siberia, I was beginning to realise, old habits die hard: after decades of being made to report the movements of foreigners, an entire generation of Russians still lived in the shadow of Cold War paranoia. What I'd mistaken for hostility was actually a kind of fear: fear of us, and fear of what the authorities might do if we weren't accounted for. Once we were, we were someone else's problem, and – just like that – our bristling babushka was no longer a fearsome bully at all, but a frail, and probably very kindly, old granny.

Victor, too, turned out to be a lot less formidable than he'd first seemed. He tracked us down later that afternoon and invited us back to his house, a half-derelict cabin on the waterfront. He seemed to live in just two rooms: a kitchen, with a cooker, a table and a couple of rickety wooden chairs; and a lounge, containing a dog-eared armchair and a simple wooden bed. 'This,' he said proudly, 'is my home. They wanted me to leave,' he added, 'so that they could build a new house, a communist house, but I said no. This is my home,' he repeated. 'Why should I give it to them?'

The mention of 'them' seemed to open the floodgates, and once again Victor railed against the authorities. Communism, he said, had all but killed Siberia, and Putin was finishing the job: 'When Tony Blair comes to Moscow, Putin shows him everything that's good about Russia and hides everything that's bad. The people in Moscow have everything,' he declared, 'while the people of Siberia have nothing.'

He also lamented the demise of a radio station called Voice of America, which he said used to broadcast the truth about what was happening in Russia. 'It gave us our fresh air, our freedom,' he said sadly. 'Now, we hear nothing but lies.' I later learned that Voice of America is still broadcasting, but it's obviously no longer available in Sretensk.

By this stage he was getting quite agitated, so to lighten the mood I asked him if he ever took his helmet off. 'Never,' he said proudly. 'Not even in bed?' I asked. 'Not even in bed!' he laughed, tilting his head slightly and putting his hands together against its side. When he smiled, I thought, he looked like a different person, but it wasn't something he did very often.

While we were talking, he produced a loaf of bread from an otherwise empty cupboard, cutting it into three equal chunks. 'You are hungry sportsmen,' he urged, 'eat, eat!' It was clear that this was his only food, so we refused politely, explaining that we'd already eaten, but he insisted. 'The English are my friends,' he said, by way of persuasion. 'In 1945,' he continued, 'when I was just a year old, life here was very bad. We had no bread, no food, nothing. But the King of England sent food in planes and trucks so that we could eat. Today, I love him with all my heart,' he concluded, clutching his hands to his chest, 'and I love the English, too. Now, at last, I can thank you for the first time.'

It was an impassioned speech, and I felt honoured and humbled in equal measure. When we eventually got up to leave, he pressed what was left of the bread into our hands, again insisting that our need was greater than his. This time, we accepted it gratefully.

The next morning, he took us to see a local English teacher who he said might be able to help us with our border problem. As far as we were concerned, we didn't have a border problem, but after everything Victor had done for us, we didn't feel we could say no.

When we arrived we were greeted by a pretty little girl in a trendy black T-shirt. 'I'll just get Grandma,' she said, as if she'd been expecting us. When Grandma appeared, I apologised for taking up her time, but she just waved my apology aside. She introduced herself as Galya, adding that she was a teacher of Russian literature. 'I only teach myself English,' she said, explaining Victor's mistake, 'but not very well.' She repeated what Victor had told us about the border, and again we tried to reassure her that everything was in hand. She wasn't convinced, but she could see we weren't just popping there on the off chance.

It was, I realised, not an issue of language, but of perspective: Galya, like Victor and the formidable old babushka at our hotel, had endured a lifetime of fear and uncertainty under the old regime. The fact that we had papers from some of the highest authorities in the land meant nothing; rules were rules, and despite all the evidence to the contrary, she couldn't see it any other way.

'We are simple people,' Galya said at last in hesitant English, 'but would you like to drink some tea with us?' I said that we'd love to. Victor took this as his cue to leave, muttering something about having some telegrams to deliver. 'That's how he makes his money,' Galya explained as he disappeared down the road. 'All day he delivers them, but he is still very poor.'

She led us along a wooden veranda with a sun-soaked view over the town and the river valley. 'I'm sorry it's so dirty,' she said apologetically, ushering us inside. Needless to say, the whole house was immaculate, with an intimate, rural charm that wouldn't have looked out of place in Spain or the South of France. She beckoned us to sit down at the kitchen table, which was laden with bread and iced buns, cottage cheese and sugar, and home-made jam made from locally picked berries.

We waited politely for an invitation to start, but when she realised we weren't eating, she just laughed. 'Englishmen always sit quietly, while Russians always ask. When you're in Russia,' she said, wagging her finger in mock admonishment, 'don't sit quietly!'

The rest of the family soon came in to join us. Lena, the young girl who'd answered the door, was Galya's granddaughter. She was thirteen, Galya told us, and lived in Khabarovsk (Khabarovsk, we knew, was also on the Amur, at the eastern end of the Russia–China border). She was staying with her grandma while her mum was in America visiting her boyfriend. Anna, Galya's daughter, lived nearby, but she'd had a fight with her husband and was trying to avoid him. (While we were there, her father-in-law called round, presumably to broker some kind of a peace deal between the two, but as soon as he saw us he made his excuses and scuttled off, much to the amusement of Galya and Anna. 'That'll keep him guessing,' Anna winked with a smile.)

Galya told us that she too lived in Khabarovsk, but that during the summer she came back here to stay in her family home. Life in Khabarovsk was good, she said, but she was less optimistic about Sretensk. 'The mayor here is from Belarus,' she said gravely, 'and he is a bad man, a thief.' Old prejudices, it seemed, were like old habits. 'He doesn't care about this town,' she continued, 'or its people. It used to be a beautiful place, but now it is poor and dirty.'

'Will it be beautiful again?' I asked.

She shook her head. 'Sretensk is dying,' she replied, smiling sadly. 'Last year,' she added thoughtfully 'a princess came here, from England. I don't remember her name, but her great-great-grandfather had built the beautiful street on the riverbank, and she wanted to see it. She came by train, but the mayor wouldn't let her into the town, so she had to turn around and go home.' As if reminded of something, she produced a box full of old letters and photos, which she said were from an English pen friend. The black-and-white images she handed to me were of an attractive brunette with winged glasses and improbably wavy hair. According to the caption on the back, her name was Jane Hackney (how about that for an English-sounding name?) and she was from Middlesbrough.

'In Soviet times,' Galya said, 'Jane would write often, but we were forbidden to write back about life in Russia, so eventually we lost touch; she probably thought I didn't want to write, but I did. I just couldn't.'

By the time we'd finished eating and drinking, it was late afternoon, and we were anxious not to outstay our welcome. As we got up to leave, Galya asked us what we were doing the following evening. I replied that I wasn't sure, but that we'd probably still be in Sretensk. 'In that case,' she said, 'you must come to dinner.' It was more of an order than an invitation, but I resisted the temptation to say 'yes, miss'.

By way of a final word, she also tried to reassure us about Victor. 'Sometimes he is a silly man,' she smiled sympathetically, 'but he is also a kind man.' He was once a great motorbike rider, she said, competing in races all over Siberia, but he was always in trouble with the authorities. 'He used to be known as the Black Cat,' she explained, laughing at the memory. 'He still taunts the police and the KGB, but they don't listen to him any more.'

Apart from this time, it seemed. Victor, in his well-meaning but misguided way, had made himself busy by approaching the authorities on our behalf, and in so doing had alerted them to our presence in Sretensk, and to the fact that we intended to continue as far as the Russia–China border. Later that evening we were in our hotel room having a cup of tea when we heard a knock at the door. Before I even had a chance to stand up, five uniformed men marched in. Their lapels bore an array of badges and letters – police, MVD, FSB and FFGS – and they were all demanding to know who we were and what we were doing in Sretensk. The MVD, I knew, was the latest acronym for the KGB; I had no idea what the other letters stood for, but I was guessing they weren't health inspectors. Taking a deep breath, I forced a smile and made them an offer they couldn't refuse: 'Tea, anyone?'

8 POETRY, PIG FAT & MILK ON TAP

The one who did most of the talking was an MVD officer with a monstrous moustache. He told us that the border section of the river was closed, even to Russians. 'Your papers mean nothing,' chipped in a second MVD man, toying with the pistol that was tucked into his belt. I explained that they'd been organised by the director of a tour company in Moscow, a man called Dmitry Shparo. If they phoned him, I said, he would be able to explain everything. Mr Moustache and his sidekick conferred for a moment and then nodded. 'OK,' the moustache said, 'let's go.'

We expected to be taken to the police station, but instead found ourselves at the post office – apparently, it was the only place in town with a long-distance phone line. It was well past closing time, but Mr Moustache soon found someone to open up and put a call through to Moscow. Thankfully, Dmitry answered. I explained the situation and passed the phone to my abductor. There was pause and then a nod. He asked one of his henchmen for the post commander's phone number. He relayed it to Dmitry (for a good time call Sretensk 91410), thanked him, and hung up. Satisfied that we were at least who we said we were, he drove us back, but he wasn't taking any chances. 'Don't leave the hotel until we come back,' he said sternly. 'When will that be?' I asked. 'Whenever we want,' he said. Dontcha just love a man in uniform?

Not surprisingly, no one came to see us the following morning, so in blatant breach of our curfew, we decided to head to the bank to change some money. On the way back, we were approached by a man with a white beard and a friendly smile. 'Are you the Englishmen travelling on the river?' he asked enthusiastically. My, Victor *had* been busy. I said yes, we were. 'I thought so!' he exclaimed, before introducing himself.

'My name is Igor,' he began. 'I'm a reporter for the local paper.' He went on to ask us a few questions, before saying what a shame it was that we wouldn't be able to continue along the border. 'But we *will* be able to continue along the border,' I exclaimed, exasperated. He just shook his head. 'Just last year two Russians tried to travel the length of the Amur from the source of the Ingoda,' he said genially, 'but they were stopped at Sretensk. They never got any further.'

For the first time since we'd crossed the border into Russia, I was forced to entertain the possibility that we really had reached the end of the road. I wasn't in the mood to argue, though, so to change the subject I asked him what it was like being a reporter in Sretensk. 'Not bad,' he smiled, 'but badly paid, and very quiet.'

Like Galya, he told us Sretensk used to be a busy, thriving town. To illustrate his point, he fished a handful of black-and-white postcards out of his jacket pocket. One showed a drawing of a hot-air balloon filled with smiling passengers; the caption read 'Greetings from Sretensk – The Place to Be!' Another was a grainy photograph of a paddle steamer that looked for all the world like it had been taken on the Mississippi at the turn of the century. Yet another was a picture of the town square filled with Cossacks, taken soon after the 1917 revolution. 'Back then, Sretensk was still a white town,' Igor explained, referring to the regions that were opposed to the communist revolutionaries, or reds.

Every image was superb, and I said as much to Igor. 'If you like them,' he smiled again, 'you should have them.' Once again I found myself refusing politely, and once again my refusal fell on deaf ears. In return, I gave him one of our Henley postcards, although I couldn't help but feel it looked a little trivial in comparison.

The MVD mob never came. We thought about getting back on the river and just hoping for the best, but decided against it. Instead, we phoned Dmitry to ask if he'd heard anything. He told us that he'd arranged for the head of the Border Guard Service to contact the local mayor, and that we were free to continue. When we told Victor the good news later that afternoon, he was oblivious to all the trouble he'd caused. 'You see,' he proclaimed triumphantly, with one last burst of his invisible Bren gun, 'without the help of the Black Cat, you might have been killed!'

That evening, we both donned shirts and trousers for the first time since we'd left London, and walked up the hill to Galya's house. She answered the door wearing a smart black dress and introduced us to her husband, Sergei. Sergei was slightly built, with a ready smile and a firm handshake. He was a PE teacher at the same school as his wife, he told us. Galya added proudly that he was also a musician, and it wasn't long before he was giving us a stirring rendition of a song he'd written about the history of Sretensk. I couldn't really follow the words, but his voice was full of mournful longing, his fingers dancing lightly over the keys of his accordion. It was at once beautiful and haunting, and as Sergei played Galya's eyes sparkled with unabashed pride.

Lena, meanwhile, had also gained in confidence since our first visit. Then, she'd been almost too shy to speak, even in Russian. Now she was talking almost entirely in English, although when she got excited she'd revert back to Russian mid-sentence and blurt out whole stories in twenty seconds flat. She showed us a picture of her mum, who was every bit as striking as her daughter. It turned out that she wasn't actually in America yet, but was leaving in a few days. She was going for a whole year, Lena said, to find a husband. She'd advertised on the Internet, and – not surprisingly – had received dozens of offers. At this, Galya looked slightly worried, perhaps concerned about what we might think, but Lena couldn't have been more excited. As she spoke, I wondered vaguely what I'd have done at her age if two strange, bearded Russians had popped round for afternoon tea. I decided that in all likelihood, I'd have hidden in my room and read.

As it happened, reading was Galya's first love. While we were chatting, she dug out old editions of half a dozen classics – Tolstoy, Dostoyevsky, Pushkin – some of which were over a hundred years old. One of the books she showed us was enticingly entitled *Translating Technical English*, and was full of useful, everyday information on topics like 'building a nuclear reactor' and 'baking suet pudding'. Not surprisingly, it was drier than camel dung in a drought, apart from one incongruous section on limericks and rhymes. There were loads of them to choose from, but the only one I can remember went something like this:

While men have many faults,
Women have only two:
Everything they say,
And everything they do.

There was also a young woman from Russia, who screamed so much none could hush her, but I can't quite remember what became of her. Galya's favourite writer, she told us, was a poet called Yesenin. He'd been persecuted by the Bolsheviks after the 1917 revolution, she said, and had disappeared under suspicious circumstances in 1925. Showing us one of his poems, she added, 'I know you don't have much room in your boats, but I would like to present you with this book, as a reminder of your time in Sretensk.' Taking it in my hands, I guessed it probably didn't weigh much more than a breeze block. Needless to say, it didn't even occur to me to say no.

In return, I presented her with a Churchill medallion. Galya was visibly moved, and Lena kept turning it over and over in her hands, saying how beautiful it was. 'The Queen is beautiful,' I agreed, pointing out her portrait, 'but I'm not so sure about the old boy on the other side.'

After dinner, Sergei retired to watch the football on TV (he lost no time in telling us that England had been royally routed by Romania the day before), while the rest of us escaped to the veranda. In the fading light of dusk, Galya showed us photos taken during her time as headmistress of the local school. Her favourite was a class photo from 1988. I asked her why no one in the picture was smiling, and she said it was because they were all so sad to leave. Again she lamented the decay that – in her eyes at least – was symptomatic of what was happening to towns all over Siberia. I wanted to argue, to tell her that as long as there were still people like her and her family living here, there was still hope, but somehow I lacked the courage – and the grammar – to say it.

We talked until well after midnight. When it finally came time to leave, Sergei, Galya and Lena insisted on walking us back to our hotel. It seemed like a fitting finale to an evening of heartfelt hospitality, and I could only hope that we'd given them more in return than a solitary, silver coin.

The next morning, as if to confirm Galya's pessimistic prognosis, we had to queue for bread for the first time.

Whenever possible, we left bread-buying to the last minute, so that we could enjoy the first loaf while it was still relatively fresh. Given that we had enough room in our boats for four loaves, and that we got through a loaf a day, by the time we got to the fourth it usually resembled a hefty volume of Russian poetry (both in terms of weight *and* texture). There was never any choice about what to buy – bread was just bread. Sometimes it was dark and dense and moist, like walnut bread; at other times it was light and soft and airy; but no matter how it started out, every single loaf we bought followed this irrefutable, four-day rule.

By happy coincidence, Galya was among the gaggle of grannies queuing outside the bakery. As a final kindness, she insisted on buying our bread for us. 'I don't want you to go hungry,' she said. If she was worried about us starving she should have come with us to the shop selling chocolate. Well, I say 'shop' singular, but we bought everything it stocked, so we had to go to two more. In all, we bought 56 bars to add to the 30 we already had. Now, this may sound like a lot, but … aw heck, who am I trying to kid?

The problem (let's give it a whirl anyway) was that chocolate was quite hard to come by and as the main source of sugar in our diet, it was essential when it came to keeping our energy levels up. Although we could be reasonably sure of finding bread every four or five days – or every 200 to 250km – we were never sure when we'd next be able to stock up on chocolate. At this rate – and assuming we'd be allowed to continue along the border – we guessed the nearest Nestlé depot was about twenty days away. Our stockpile of 86 bars thus worked out at just two bars each a day, plus an extra six in case of emergencies (such as running out of chocolate).

Oddly enough, one of the bars we bought – with the words 'I Love You' emblazoned on the wrapper in chintzy Cyrillic – featured the stamp of the Birmingham Torch Awards. Don't get me wrong, I'm sure a Birmingham Torch Award is indeed an accolade to be proud of – I'm just not convinced it would sway Siberian consumers one way or the other: Chocolate, sir? May I suggest Belgian truffles, or perhaps Bendicks of Mayfair? *Nyet, spaseeba* – I'm after something really special. Do you happen to have anything that bears the stamp of the Birmingham Torch Awards?

Galya came down to the river just as we were getting ready to push off. We thanked her again for everything she'd done, and she promised to pass on our best wishes to Victor, who was nowhere to be seen. There was a moment of awkwardness as we said goodbye, and then, quite unexpectedly, she hugged us both and said, 'Go with God.' With these words still ringing in our ears, we gave a final wave, dropped our rudders into the water, and began our last leg to the Russia–China border.

We'd been in Sretensk much longer than expected and we now had just seven days to paddle the remaining 360km to the border. We knew the exact distance because this was the number stencilled on the first of numerous marker posts that we passed as we made our way downstream. Initially it was unclear what these numbers signified, but it soon became apparent that they were counting down the distance to the border.

The posts themselves were made up of white slats arranged horizontally in the shape of a triangle, all supported by a tripod of timber perhaps twelve feet high. The numbers were painted in black on the slats, although they were often too faded to read. When they were nine or ten kilometres apart, they provided a useful gauge of progress, but it wasn't long before we started seeing them every kilometre. On long straights this meant we were often able to see half a dozen at a time, and our progress – or rather, our lack of it – was suddenly all too apparent; it was one thing knowing we had 360km to paddle in a week; it was quite another counting them down one by one.

These marker posts – presumably built by the military – also signalled the appearance of the river's first real traffic, in the form of a small passenger boat crammed with screaming kids. It was hard to tell if they were yelling for us to paddle over, or for the captain to run us down. A short while later we saw an isolated heap of snow hidden in amongst the trees. Given that we'd been experiencing temperatures in the high 80s for almost a month now, this seemed nothing short of miraculous, and provided a timely reminder of what the river must be like for much of the year.

With the traffic, though, came an increase in pollution. Most of the time it wasn't that obvious, but on one occasion we almost paddled right into it: there, in the shallows of a bend in the river, lay a massive steel drum, perhaps ten feet high and fifteen feet long. The metal itself was at least half an inch thick, and it looked as though whatever it had once contained had since been violently sucked out. I glanced around to see where it might have come from, but there was nothing but forest for miles around. Someone, it seemed, had dropped half a power station into the river without even noticing.

Three days after leaving Sretensk, we passed a tiny village called Chasovaya. From the river it looked like a ghost town, but no sooner had we drifted by than we heard the ominous roar of an outboard motor behind us. Before we knew what was happening, we'd been forced into the bank by two MVD men in a battered speedboat. The driver wore a dark, standard-issue moustache, while his partner sported a sharp, no-nonsense crew cut and a bulging holster on his hip.

'Where have you come from?' demanded Pistol Pete. 'From Mongolia,' I replied, wearily. They both laughed. 'No, seriously, where've you come from?' he repeated. 'From Sretensk,' I said finally, realising there was little point in forcing the issue. He demanded to see our documents, and proceeded to pore over our various letters from the Army, the Federal Frontier Guard Service and the Chinese Embassy in Moscow. After a minute or two, he handed the papers back, apparently not satisfied. 'Don't go anywhere,' he barked brusquely, before gunning the speedboat's engine and carving back upstream.

Now, before I go any further, let's consider this for a moment: we were – unless I was very much mistaken – in the heart of Taiga country, surrounded by mile after mile of dense, impenetrable forest (if you cast your mind back a few chapters, you'll recall that Siberia's Taiga is the largest forest on the planet, covering an area roughly the size of mainland America). Furthermore, they were in a supercharged speedboat, while we were paddling barges masquerading as canoes. Where on God's great earth, I wondered, did they expect us to go?

So we sat on the riverbank and waited, cursing the gargantuan imbecility of Pistol Pete and his moustachioed amigo. We cursed their boss, their boss's boss, their grannies (heartless hoteliers to a woman) and even, I'm ashamed to say, their children. Which is ironic, really, because when they returned, that's exactly who they brought with them.

From a distance it was hard to make out who the extra passengers were, although I remember remarking to Rich at the time that the MVD seemed to be getting younger every day. Only when they got closer did it become clear that they were not a pair of border bigwigs, but a little boy and girl of perhaps eight or nine. Clambering cheerfully onto the bank, Pete held out a plastic bag. 'A present,' he smiled, 'from the kids.' Inside was a giant, ice-cold jar of milk and a loaf of warm, freshly baked bread. There wasn't any humble pie in there, but if there had been, I'd have eaten it whole.

I didn't know what to say, and said as much, but Pete just waved it off. The most appropriate way to say thank you, it seemed to me, was to share our bounty with them, but as soon as we'd both taken a long, deep draught of milk (so deliciously cold it made my teeth hurt), they wished us good luck and sped away. 'Hang on!' I shouted after them, 'What are your names?'

'Igor,' said Moustache Man; 'Alexander!' cried Pete. And with that, they gave a final wave, and were gone.

Our new-found love of all things military meant we now had plenty of time to vent our frustrations on something else: namely, insects. Mosquitoes had been a problem for some time, but now that the forest was getting thicker, every bloodsucker from here to Shanghai seemed to be holidaying on the Siberian Riviera.

By far the most voracious were the horseflies (so called because they weren't much bigger than Shetland ponies). Maybe it was the heat, or maybe it was the isolation, but before long I was swatting them indiscriminately with decisive, deadly swipes of my paddle. As they became more frenzied, so too did the killing, until soon I was tearing off their wings and tossing their still-buzzing bodies into the water … On reflection, I can see how such behaviour might be seen as a tad aggressive, but at the time it was all I could do to avoid going completely mental.

It got to the point where I couldn't paddle more than a few yards without slapping my shoulders or taking a manic swipe at some invisible foe. It was bad enough on the water, away from the encroaching forest, but on the banks it was unbearable. Wearing a shirt helped with the smaller insects, but it was no defence against the horseflies, which could – I felt quite sure – happily bite their way through chain mail. Besides, most of the time it was too hot to wear anything other than our birthday best. It wasn't long before we started taking our food breaks on the water, drifting in the current and hoping that things might be better in the evening, when it was cooler.

The problem was that when the sun did go down, the horseflies were simply replaced by mosquitoes, which were now so voracious that our entire campsite routine revolved around staying under cover as much as possible. If it was too warm in the tent – and it often was – something as simple as an evening swim became a logistical nightmare: first, you'd have to take all of your clothes off inside the tent, before making a mad dash for the river; once there, you'd have to submerge yourself to the nostrils, head tilted ever-so-slightly backwards, to keep the area of exposed flesh to the bare minimum (if you'll excuse the pun); finally, you'd have to dash back to the tent and throw yourself headlong inside. The key to the whole operation was the door man, whose job it was to open and close the tent opening at the precise moment of re-entry: too early, and the mosquitoes would swarm in unchecked; too late, and you'd bounce off the tent, fall sprawling to the ground, and lose half a pint of blood from your buttocks.

One evening, Rich got so fed up with being confined to the tent that he decided to go for a walk in the woods. After bathing in insect repellent and donning three or four layers of clothing, he stepped into the breach with the words: 'I'm just popping out, and I might be gone for some time.' Some time later, he duly reappeared, covered in a layer of mosquitoes so thick that it was hard to see what colour his shirt was. It took him a long time to brush them off, and even then we spent the rest of the night hunting – and being hunted by – the ones that made it past the mesh.

This hunting was fast becoming something of a nightly ritual: no matter how careful you were – and no matter how good your doorman – it was impossible to keep the tent mosquito free. Each evening we would decorate the lining of the tent with another smattering of blood-red smears. At one stage, it was getting so colourful that we resorted to using some Russian-made fly spray instead, but we soon knocked this on the head when we realised that it was doing to us exactly what it was supposed to be doing to the mosquitoes.

While we were paddling, our only distraction from this constant barrage of bloodsuckers was each other. Sometimes we'd drift apart, both metaphorically and literally, and it wasn't unusual for Rich to be a mile or more in front. At other times, though, we would talk all day, yarning about everything and nothing (usually nothing). We enjoyed one such afternoon a few days short of the border, when Rich saw fit to outline the basic principles of Einstein's theory of special relativity to me (not just relativity, mind, but *special* relativity).

Not being much of a scientific bod, I followed his enthusiastic explanations only vaguely, although I do recall something about a pole-vaulter running into a barn and having the door shut behind him. According to our man Albert, if the fellow ran fast enough (say, 300,000km per second) the door could be closed before his pole hit the other end of the barn, even if – and here's the clever part – the pole was longer than the barn itself.

In the days that led up to the border, we also spent a long time discussing what we might do if the river remained off-limits in July and August. We estimated that the distance from the start of the border section to the end of the river was 3,000km; if we paddled as hard as we had back in Mongolia (i.e. nine or ten hours a day), this would take us about fifty days, assuming the river's current remained constant (although this was very unlikely, given that we were now less than 500m above sea level). We didn't know when the river would freeze over, but if we resumed paddling on 1 September, there was just a chance that we'd make it to the Pacific in time for tea and medals.

This left us with the question of how we'd fill the inter-vening months. In the end, we came up with two options: we could either hitch a lift to Ulan Ude – some 800km to the west – and spend some time canoeing around Lake Baikal, or we could forget paddling altogether and head 2,000km east, to the Kamchatka Peninsula. Lake Baikal, our guidebook informed us, was over 600km long and 1,637m deep, making it the deepest lake on earth. It also contained one-fifth of the world's fresh water – more than all of America's Great Lakes put together. Kamchatka, meanwhile, was an impossibly remote wilderness full of active volcanoes, raging rivers and hot sulphurous pools. Although both of these options appealed, they also meant compromising the integrity of our source-to-sea journey, something which – after paddling over 1,500km – we were quite keen to avoid. Oddly enough, it never even occurred to us that we might not be allowed back on the river in September.

The day we were hoping to reach the Russia–China border also happened to be Rich's birthday. He got two cards: one that I'd fashioned from the home-made effort he'd given *me* a few weeks before (I basically cut off the front to make an ultra-light camping card), and one from his family, which I'd had hidden in my boat for the best part of two months. Thanks to his mum's weight-saving savvy, it was barely an inch square, but frankly, I was glad to be shot of it.

We didn't know what to expect when we actually got to the border. Alexander had mentioned something about there being a watchtower at the 9km marker post. 'You'd better stop there,' he'd advised, 'otherwise … pop, pop, pop.' He mimed these last three words with the help of an extended arm and an imaginary trigger. It was difficult to know if he was being serious, but we stopped at marker post 13, just to be on the safe side. Beyond this point, we continued with caution, anxious to spot any trigger-happy border guards before they spotted us.

As we got closer, however, the heavens opened and the rain came down in sheets, making it hard to see anything. Somehow the dark, heavy clouds and the mist rising off the river seemed appropriate; I half expected to see a helicopter gunship appear over the horizon, Wagner's *Ride of the Valkyries* blaring over the loudspeakers. In the event, we had to make do with a couple of gunboats and a solitary watchtower, the latter manned by a guard with eyes the size of saucers.

The saucers, I realised as we got closer, were in fact binoculars. Rich and I gave each other a final nod of encouragement and paddled over to the base of the tower. This, I thought ruefully, was it: it was our 43rd day on the river, and in the next few minutes we'd finally learn if it was to be our last.

9 GUNS & GUNBOATS (PART I)

We pulled up alongside a pair of battleship-grey gunboats with long, reedy aerials and enormous, swivelling spotlights mounted on their decks. We later learned that because of a petrol shortage in this neck of the woods they weren't going anywhere, but at the time they looked quite foreboding.

We were greeted by five men, three wearing what looked like naval uniforms and two dressed in camouflaged trousers and – despite the rain – Nike T-shirts. I say 'greeted', but it was more of a grunt really. Then came the inevitable question: 'Where are your documents?' We duly produced everything in our paper arsenal, including the fax from the Chinese Embassy. The two T-shirts scrutinised each document in turn before handing them back. One of them wandered off to radio his boss. Assuming that it might take a while for the boss to arrive, we sat down on our boats to wait.

As the rain got heavier, I asked the remaining T-shirt if there was somewhere we could sit that was a bit more sheltered. With a wary nod, he showed us to a nearby canvas tent that contained two beds, two blankets and a squadron of sheltering mosquitoes. While we waited anxiously inside, he stood guard outside. After a tense half-hour, he asked us if we'd like anything to drink. I thought about saying, 'Does a bear shit in the woods?' in Russian, but decided it might lose something in translation. Earlier, I'd entertained vague hopes of arriving at the border to find a well-stocked bar complete with comely serving wenches, but instead we had to make do with tea in a tent. An hour later, we were on our fourth cup, greedily devouring great doorstops of bread smothered in lashings of condensed milk.

Eventually, though, even tea wasn't enough to take my mind off the job in hand, so – grasping the bear by the bristles – I asked what we were waiting for. 'For the rain?' he suggested, with a shrug. 'And then what?' I said, hoping I'd understood him correctly. 'And then you can continue,' he shrugged again. 'But what about paddling on the river in July and August,' I asked, somewhat stupidly. 'You can continue,' he repeated, matter-of-factly. Somewhere along the line, it seemed, something had indeed got lost in translation – as a result, we'd spent the best part of two hours scoffing his food and drink, and generally making a nuisance of ourselves. I was absolutely mortified, and tried to say as much, but this merely confused the issue, so we just mumbled our apologies, gathered up our things, and skulked self-consciously back to our boats.

It wasn't until we'd left the watchtower and the gunboats far behind that we realised quite what this meant: we were free to continue not just along the Russia–China border, but all the way to the Pacific Ocean. For the first time since we'd dreamed up the idea of travelling the Amur River from source to sea, our goal finally seemed within reach. Well, give or take the odd 3,000km, anyway.

In fact, it was precisely this distance that dominated my thoughts when we made camp later that evening. The overwhelming sense of relief that I'd experienced soon after leaving the border post had quickly been replaced by an equally overwhelming feeling of exhaustion. Up until now, we'd had some deadline to work to, some new border to aim for, and at each stage there'd always been a chance that we wouldn't be allowed to continue. Ironically, it was this uncertainty that had kept us going. Now that all of the major hurdles were behind us, it felt as though the battle was won, and that our journey was all over bar the paddling. In reality, it had only just begun.

In the event, a good night's sleep was all that was required to restore my mood of general blissdom. With nothing to hurry us the next morning (other than the small matter of the river freezing over at some point in the not too distant future) we were at last able to relax and enjoy the paddling, safe in the knowledge that we'd no longer be sent home prematurely. I say *paddling*, but – as is the wont of loafers at large – the first hour involved much buffing of fingernails and adjusting of shirtsleeves.

Alas, any feeling of resolve soon evaporated when we got close enough to read the number '889' on the white slats of the border's first marker post. We didn't know it yet, but this was the distance to Blagoveschensk, a major town about halfway along the border (what we also had no way of knowing was that when this sequence reached zero, another one would start, counting down not only the thousand kilometres to the end of the border, but the additional thousand to the Pacific Ocean. Had we known this, we would almost certainly have cried like babies).

To start with, the Chinese side didn't look any different from the Russian side: in both cases, forest was the landscape of choice. As we made our way down a long straight that morning, however, our view was interrupted by something glinting at us from the far end. We soon discovered that the source of this staccato light display was the window of a Chinese river barge moored downstream. Although there was no sign of life, it was piled high with huge logs. A little further on, we passed a tiny village called Luoguhe. On the Russian side, almost directly opposite, was a watchtower. It was hard to tell if it was manned, but the dark shadow between the roof and the sentry box seemed to keep a watchful eye on us as we paddled cautiously past.

As I shifted my gaze from village to shadow and back again, the reality of being confined to the Russian side of the river hit home for the first time. I wanted to stop at Luoguhe, to have a look around and say hello to some of the locals, but because of red tape and Red paranoia, we had to make do with a frustratingly one-sided view of river life. From where we were, I could just make out the distant silhouettes of people waving at us from the far bank, but all I could do was wave ineffectually back.

Not that the Russians were unfriendly, mind: a short while later we saw a couple of gunboats bedecked with sunbathing recruits. As we slid past, one of them shouted out 'I love you!' in near-perfect English. I wanted to believe him, really I did, but he doesn't write, he doesn't phone …

That afternoon, perhaps by way of consolation, I went for my first foray into the woods with Rich. We wanted to take some photographs of a heron's nest in the trees near our campsite, and decided to climb the grassy bluff behind to get a bird's-eye view. As it turned out, the bluff was much steeper than we'd anticipated, and we had to clutch tussocks of grass most of the way up to prevent a long – and probably very painful – slide back down. Sweating streams in the fierce heat of the afternoon, we finally crested the brow of the hill to discover that we were now hundreds of feet above our heron. Still, it gave us a great view of the river: this was the first time we'd seen it from anywhere other than our boats, and it looked majestic. Taking it all in from so high up also helped to put everything in perspective, and made the distances involved seem much less daunting.

To avoid the precipitous slopes we'd scrambled up, we skirted the hill and descended a densely wooded valley filled with ferns and flowers, and brightly coloured butterflies. From the river, the Taiga had always looked like little more than a vast cordon of conifers, with nothing but pine needles to carpet the forest floor, so I was amazed – and not a little surprised – to discover that it was so lush and colourful. It was also very still, and refreshingly cool, and – at this time of the day at least – mercifully free of mosquitoes.

When we got back to our campsite, Rich noticed with alarm that our tent had been moved a few feet closer to the water. It took us both a moment to realise that it wasn't the tent that had moved, but the river. We weren't sure if we were imagining it, so we poked a long stick into the sand right at the water's edge and waited to see what would happen. About an hour later, the stick was marooned a foot away from the beach, which – by implication – meant that our tent was now a foot closer to the water, and getting closer all the time. After a brief discussion, we agreed that a river this wide couldn't possibly rise more than a few inches overnight, so we decided to stay put.

This was mistake number one. Mistake number two was deciding to move our entire campsite – including our boats – only *after* we'd undressed and crawled into our sleeping bags for the night.

Because there were trees right behind our tent, we had to carry everything a few hundred feet along the beach to find a suitable alternative. I couldn't be bothered to put any of my clothes back on, so to minimise my exposure to mosquitoes, I threw all of my gear into my sleeping bag and ran – Santa-style – across the beach. I was so fast on the outward leg that the bastards didn't even get a look-in. It was only when I returned to retrieve the tent that my bum was bitten clean off.

The next morning, the beach where our original campsite had been was under a foot of water. In all, the river had risen about two feet since we'd made camp the day before. Now, it had a deep, swollen feel to it, and for the first time since we'd set off from the source it looked very, very big. It was also fast – in the half-hour it took us to fill our water bottles and perform all of the other little jobs that had become part of our early morning routine, we drifted the best part of two kilometres. If things carried on like this, I thought excitedly, we'd never have to paddle again.

That afternoon, we passed Mohe, a neat, modern-looking village featuring rows of colourful houses marching down to the riverbank. The houses themselves were all manner of shapes and sizes, and contrasted starkly with the rickety log cabins on the Russian side. A group of young Chinese girls were having a heated discussion with someone bathing in the river, and the harsh, atonal sounds of their banter only served to emphasise the differences between the two countries. As I listened, it occurred to me that whenever I'd crossed a border by road, I'd never really noticed much of a change from one country to the next. Sure, the languages may have been different, but there was almost always some degree of similarity, a vague sense of overlapping cultures.

A natural boundary like a river, on the other hand, only seemed to accentuate the *differences*, particularly when you were steering a plumb line straight down the middle. Here, a sliver of water barely wider than the Thames had resulted in the evolution of two entirely different races: the people to the north were essentially descendants of Europeans who had emigrated – or been deported – east; they had Caucasoid eyes and hair of all different colours; they wrote in Cyrillic and worshipped God (often in secret, during Soviet times); and they ate stewed potatoes and cabbage soup with knives, forks and spoons. Those to the south meanwhile, all had black hair and Asiatic eyes; they wrote in Chinese characters and worshipped Buddha (again, when it wasn't forbidden); and they ate rice and noodles with chopsticks. Geography had kept them apart as they'd migrated and evolved, and history had conspired to keep them apart ever since.

That night, we camped on an idyllic, Robinson Crusoe island in the middle of the river. To our delight, we discovered that we had twice as many noodles as we needed to last until our next resupply, so we ordered the galley to double the men's rations, effective immediately. Less delightful was having to get up in the middle of the night to put the outer on our tent (it rained so rarely that we hardly ever put it up in advance). There wasn't enough time to throw on any clothes, so we just leapt naked into the night and fumbled around with the guy ropes for a few minutes, before diving clumsily back inside. Predictably, it stopped raining the moment we lay down.

In the days that followed, we re-established our daily routine of paddling, swimming, eating and sleeping. To help pass the time when we were on the water, I spent the first few hours of each morning working on my Russian vocabulary, and it wasn't long before I could say that Rich was an environmental scientist (*oochonoy okrazhenaya*) and that I was a travel writer (*zhornaleest na pootyeshestveye*), although I still didn't know my dog (*sobaka*) from my sausage (*kolbasa*). Somewhat more troubling, I realised, leafing through my dictionary, was that for the last month I'd been introducing myself as *Pol* (for some reason, Russians couldn't get the hang of the 'au' in Paul, so I'd decided to simplify it). Needless to say, it is to the lasting credit of everyone we'd met that none of them had so much as batted an eyelid when I'd told them my name was Sex Grogan.

I also spent some time trying to learn a few words of Mandarin, just in case we ever found ourselves in 'extreme major circumstances', but although our pocket phrase book presented a comprehensive list of characters, it was hard to know what they actually sounded like. In fact, with over 50,000 to choose from (each a masterpiece in its own right) it's a wonder the Chinese have time to write anything other than shopping lists. Still, after some judicious study, I felt reasonably confident that I could say the words hello, thank you, and – perhaps most importantly – I love you.

As it turned out, this confidence was hopelessly misplaced. Early one morning we heard someone shouting at us from a small boat on the Chinese side of the river (it's a curious law of acoustics that anything yelled over a distance of more than 200 metres sounds like 'Oi!' almost regardless of the language used to do the yelling). We were no strangers to being heckled by strangers, but this 'oi' sounded quite aggressive, so we chose to ignore it, safe in the knowledge that we were deep in Russian territory, and that no one in their right mind would dare to come anywhere near us. And we were right: the people who *did* dare to come anywhere near us were completely mental.

There were three of them in the boat, all young lads in their late teens or early twenties. When they got close, the yelling stopped abruptly, as if they'd suddenly lost heart, and for a moment there was an awkward silence. '*Nee how,*' I greeted them, in the best Mandarin accent I could muster. They stared at me blankly. 'Hello!' I tried again, this time in English. More blank looks.

By and by, one of them held up a bottle and tilted it to his mouth. I shrugged, not sure what he was trying to say. He handed the bottle over, indicating with his thumb and forefinger that I should only drink a little at a time. I thought that perhaps he was just being churlish, but as soon as the first drops passed my lips, I realised that he had nothing but my best interests at heart. It tasted vaguely fruity and utterly toxic, and for a brief moment I thought that my throat was actually going to melt. I only started to relax when it went to work on my ravaged stomach lining instead.

Rich declined my offer of a quick tipple (he'd never felt quite the same since our big night out in Olovannaya almost a month before), so I handed the bottle back to our hosts. Shaking their heads, they indicated that we should keep it. They also gave us a packet of cigarettes, despite our insistence that neither of us smoked. I tried to thank them in Chinese, but they still didn't have a clue what I was talking about. I wasn't sure what else to say, but they saved us any embarrassment by starting up their motor, singing 'bye bye' in English, and chugging back the way they'd come.

As the spluttering of the little outboard faded behind us, I took a proper look at our gifts. The bottle boasted a red-and-white label bearing the legend 'Beijing Ming' in English above a dense collection of Chinese characters. The cigarettes, meanwhile, bore the words '*Hei-lung Jiang*', or Black Dragon River (the Chinese name for the Amur). As I stowed them both inside my boat, in the space by my feet, I couldn't help but remember Natasha's sentiments back in Olovannaya, that the Chinese were all thieves; the fact that the first Chinese people we'd met had given us a bottle of melon-flavoured fire-starter and a packet of souvenir cigarettes seemed to tell its own story.

It was during our fourth day on the border that we came across an abandoned watchtower. Like all of the watchtowers we'd seen so far, it was about 100ft high, comprising a small wooden hut atop a flimsy-looking scaffold. The scaffold itself was made out of steel struts, with a metal ladder zigzagging its way up the middle. This particular example creaked and swayed alarmingly in the wind, and it looked like it hadn't seen service since the Cold War, but if it had stayed standing that long, we reasoned, an extra couple of visitors wouldn't hurt. We had to take care on the way up to avoid the missing steps and the broken floorboards, but the view from the top was superb.

The watchtower was positioned right on the water's edge in the middle of a long straight, and we could see four or five kilometres in either direction. Across on the Chinese side there was nothing but forest as far as the eye could see, and it seemed hard to believe that this whole region once bristled with guns and missiles, faced off across a few hundred feet of water. We knew from experience that the Russians still maintained a sizeable military force in the area, but so far we hadn't seen a single Chinese border guard, let alone a gunboat or watchtower. We also knew that the border between Russia and China had been disputed on and off since the Russians first rolled into Siberia in search of fur in the seventeenth century. More recently, it had formed one of the longest fronts of the Cold War, a border so sensitive that it was off limits even to Russians. One of the problems (apart from the obvious threat of invasion and/or nuclear attack) had been a question of ownership: there were some 3,000 islands along the section of river that made up the border, and many of them had long been claimed by both countries. In 1969, Soviet forces had seized Damansky Island (actually on the Ussuri River – one of the Amur's major tributaries) and the military build-up that ensued had lasted the best part of twenty years.

Tensions had undoubtedly eased since the collapse of communism, however, and luckily for us, ownership of the river's islands had finally been ratified in a treaty signed just over a year before. In fact, as far as we were aware, there hadn't been a gun fired in anger on the Amur since the late 80s, so it came as something of a surprise when – later that afternoon – we were shot at.

10 BORDER GUARD BLUES

The noise was as loud as it was startling. Only when I saw a bright red flare arc across my bow did my heart start beating again. Not surprisingly, the flare had come from the Russian side of the river, so we pulled obediently over to the left bank and waited. Before long an armed soldier came running down the beach towards us, but any remaining concerns I may have had were soon dispelled when he slipped on a stone and fell flat on his face, sending his gun clattering to the ground. When he eventually reached us he was clearly flustered, but he managed a ragged salute before offering each of us a sandy hand. Following close behind was a cool-looking character in a blue shell suit and white plimsolls, who frowned paternally at his clumsy companion before introducing himself as Dennis.

Before we had a chance to reply, Dennis launched into a series of questions about our journey: how far had we travelled, how much did we paddle each day, how long would it take us to reach the ocean? 'Don't you want to see our documents,' I asked, a little incredulous. 'No, no,' he said, waving my question aside, 'that won't be necessary.' I was amazed: given the regularity and rigour with which our documents had been inspected so far, I had just assumed that the question 'where are your documents?' was hard-wired into the brains of border guards at birth.

Once we'd answered all of his questions, we showed him our maps and some of our kit, including our can of bear spray, which was now permanently mounted on the deck of Rich's boat. 'Is this for mosquitoes?' Dennis asked. 'No, it's for bears,' I replied, trying to explain how it worked. 'That's no use!' he laughed, shaking his head scornfully. 'What you need is a big stick!' He went on to explain that the best way to defend yourself against a bear attack was to take a large, forked stick and thrust it up under the bear's arms. Thus incapacitated, the bear could then be stabbed at leisure with a small penknife (although he neglected to provide any additional insight as to how said penknife might be opened when one hand was otherwise engaged with 300 kilos of snarling rage). Convinced he was trying to wind us up, I waited for his earnest expression to break into a knowing smile, but when the smile failed to materialise, I realised he was quite serious and – perhaps more to the point – quite mad.

As a parting gesture he sent his sidekick off to fetch some bread for us. We offered to go with him to save him having to make the return journey, but Dennis just shook his head. 'Not allowed,' he smiled, before adding in thickly accented English: 'Top Secret!'

The morning after we were shot at by Dennis, we met Alexei, who was equally entertaining, if slightly better dressed. We were paddling past a small village called Zhalinda, debating whether or not to stop and buy more bread, when we spotted a border guard on the beach. Not wanting to take any chances, we paddled over to say hello.

'Good morning, gentlemen!' the guard exclaimed in English, when we finally beached our boats at his feet. I replied in

Russian, guessing that this was probably one of only two phrases he knew (the second being 'I love you'), but as I was about to find out, I could hardly have been more wrong.

With a salute, he introduced himself as Major Something-or-other, Commandant of the Zhalinda Border Garrison, 'but you can call me Alexei,' he added, with a wry smile. Like Dennis, he seemed more intent on talking to us than seeing our documents. Speaking English the whole time, he told us he had a wife and a daughter, and that he was originally from a small town in central Russia. He'd learned English at school, he said, but he hadn't had a chance to use it in over ten years. He asked us if there was anything we needed. When I said we'd like to buy some bread, he insisted on taking us to the shop himself, ordering his henchman to keep an eye on our boats. We hadn't gone far on foot when he waved down a passing jeep to take us the rest of the way. From the outside it looked like any other army vehicle, but inside it boasted floor-to-ceiling shag-pile carpeting. The Siberian military, I was beginning to realise, was something of a law unto itself.

Alexei was so determined to use his English that he practically did our shopping for us – we didn't really need that much, but he was so excited that we didn't want to burst his bubble. On the way back, he asked if we were planning to stop at Albazino, about 20km downstream. I told him I wasn't sure. 'You should,' he said. 'There's a good museum there. Perhaps you'd like to see it?'

Needless to say, it seemed unlikely to me that a tiny village in the middle of nowhere boasted a good museum, but I was quite happy to humour him. 'We'd love to,' I replied, with as much enthusiasm as I could conjure. 'In that case,' Alexei beamed boyishly, 'I'll come with you.' He asked how long it would take us to paddle there. 'About two hours,' I replied. 'OK,' he said, 'see you there in two and a half.' And with that he turned on his heel, and vanished into the village.

On the way there, Alexei pulled up alongside us in his speedboat. He didn't look happy. 'You must not violate the border,' he said, jabbing his finger at us angrily. 'If you do not paddle on the Russian side, you might be arrested by the Chinese.' What he didn't realise was that we were getting fed up with being restricted to one side of the river, and that being arrested by the Chinese would've livened things up nicely, but I didn't say as much.

The real problem was going where the water went: it was all very well staying close to the left bank, but more often than not the main flow of the river was in the middle or to the right. To battle this current just so that we could stay on the left would have been extremely difficult, if not impossible. This was hard for someone in a speedboat to really appreciate, so I just nodded earnestly and did my best to look contrite. Satisfied that we'd learned our lesson, Alexei softened, and smiled paternally. 'See you there,' he winked, before spinning the wheel of his boat and disappearing in a plume of water.

A short while later, we passed a Chinese village with a long, tiled embankment running all the way down to the water's edge. It looked like an artificial beach at a leisure centre. There were steps at intervals, and Chinese characters spelled out in the tiles. The contrast with Albazino couldn't have been more acute: instead of gleaming tiles, it boasted a steep, muddy bank with crumbling concrete stanchions. Set back from the river was the usual collection of log cabins and tiny, one-room shops. There was also a watchtower, and, just as Alexei had promised, a small museum.

The latter, I was stunned to discover, was nothing short of superb. It was housed in a traditionally built wooden building that looked like it had gone up that morning – in fact, the garden at the front was still unfinished, and was busy with people digging, weeding and planting. The doors and window shutters were intricately carved, and the whole place had a quaint, *Swiss*

Family Robinson feel to it. The curator, a learned-looking man with a deep scar across his balding scalp, was clearly thrilled to have two English visitors, and he insisted on giving us a guided tour. While he talked, Alexei translated, and as we went from display to display, the history of the Amur unfolded in front of our eyes.

Until the Russians opened the region up in the late seventeenth century, he explained, the Amur was under the control of Manchuria, then a province of China. In 1650, a Cossack merchant named Yerofey Khabarov was commissioned by Tsar Alexei to explore the Amur region. Albazino was the first town he founded, but it soon became the focus of cat-and-mouse fighting between the Cossacks to the north and the Chinese to the south. At various times the village was torched, blockaded, razed and rebuilt, and he described each episode in great detail, with the help of models, relics and dramatic panoramas which brought the whole period vividly to life (many historians have compared the conquest of the East by the Russians to the taming of the West by the Americans, but instead of it being driven by a search for gold, it was propelled by the hunt for fur, which for centuries was Russia's most important export).

The second section of the museum documented life on the river in the nineteenth century, and the Cossack reacquisition of the north bank from the Manchurians. Among the relics were some enormous samovars (traditional Russian tea urns) and some original black-and-white photographs of Cossack soldiers and local schoolchildren.

The third part, meanwhile, was dedicated to the Second World War, and in particular to a local hero who had twice been awarded the Order of Lenin (the Soviet equivalent of the Victoria Cross), not to mention a dozen other medals. The names of those who'd lost their lives were also listed, and – considering the size of the village – they made daunting reading. Mind you, given that 26 million Russians died during WWII (recent estimates put the number at closer to 40 million, but even based on the lower figure, it's still only a couple of million shy of every single male in Britain today), perhaps it shouldn't have been all that surprising.

The final part of the museum was set aside for displays of local flora and fauna, including a stuffed bear cub which looked more like a mangy dog. But the tour wasn't over yet: the adjacent building was a lovingly crafted replica of a seventeenth-century log cabin, complete with a mill for grinding flour, an oven made of bricks, and a cot suspended from the ceiling. There was also a wonderfully cool and spacious summer room, with an icon of the Virgin Mary in one corner (such icons were – and indeed still are – considered an important part of the Russian Orthodox Church). Throughout it all, Alexei's animated translation was nothing short of brilliant, and it amazed me that he'd even learned words like 'battle', 'hero', and 'cot', let alone that he could remember them.

On our way out the curator gave us a badge as a souvenir: on it was an impressive, stylised drawing of the original village bearing the legend 'Albazino, 350 Years' in Russian. Before we really had a chance to thank him, however, Alexei was ushering us out the door and hurrying us back to our boats. On the way he gave us another fatherly pep talk on the dangers of straying into Chinese waters and then – as if to show us that he wasn't a complete stick in the mud – he invited us to join him for a quick aperitif. Stowed beneath the wheel of his speedboat was a small cucumber, half a loaf of bread and a big bottle of vodka. He poured the vodka into three large tumblers and toasted our journey, before wishing us luck and bidding us a fond farewell.

Despite the overwhelming heat and the heavy drinking, we added another twenty-odd kilometres to our tally before setting up camp on a broad shingle bank. Later that night, for the second time in less than a week, we were outwitted by something that moves at less than six inches per hour.

My bladder alarm woke me at around 2 a.m. and – peering out through the mesh of the mosquito net – I saw a thin, smooth layer of fog covering the pebbles all around the tent. I gave this some sleepy, early morning consideration before deciding that it probably wasn't fog at all, but water. In the few hours since we'd fallen asleep, the river had risen about two feet, and was now lapping lasciviously at the bottom of our tent. The moment I tried to sit up, the groundsheet sloshed like a waterbed.

'Rich,' I whispered, as calmly as I could manage under the circumstances, 'I think you might want to look outside, and then I think we might want to move our tent.' At this stage everything inside was still dry, and the whole thing was mildly amusing. The moment we lifted the heavy items out of the back of the tent, however, it floated up, lowering the front lip of the ground sheet and letting the water flood in. It was at this stage that we learned flood-evacuation lesson one: always take your sleeping bag out of the tent first. We hauled everything a few feet higher up, and pitched the tent on a slope below a steep mud embankment. It wasn't ideal, but there was nowhere else to go – if the river rose any higher than this, we realised, we'd be in trouble.

Not surprisingly, it took me a while to get back to sleep, partly because I was looking anxiously at the river every three minutes, but mostly because my sleeping bag was sopping wet. I must have dozed off eventually, though, because I had a dream that we woke up the following morning to find two gun barrels thrust through the mosquito net; having already been woken up once in the middle of the night, Rich was in no mood to have his beauty sleep interrupted a second time. 'Will you just fuck off!' he shouted indignantly, before rolling onto his back and making a sound like a pig snorting a mud milkshake through a straw.

The next morning (in real life that is, not in the dream) the spot where our tent had been was now under three feet of water, and the shingle bed we'd originally camped on was now a fast-flowing channel about 50ft across. The river, too, had taken on a whole new character: it was wider and swifter, and seemed to be pulsing with energy. That morning, we covered the first 15km in a little over an hour, by far the fastest we'd travelled on the river so far. But what we gained in terms of speed, we lost in terms of space: each day the banks seemed to be getting lower and lower, and the beaches were fast disappearing; we just had to hope that they wouldn't disappear altogether.

We made camp that night on the highest shingle bank we could find, but following some careful probing at the water's edge, I was relieved to discover that the river had stopped rising – for now. It was the 'for now' bit that worried me, and I spent most of the night checking and rechecking the river level.

We woke soon after dawn to find the river cloaked in a dense pall of fog. It was so thick that once we were under way, it was impossible to tell where the water ended and the sky began. The first thing I noticed was what a colourless world it created; the second was how still everything was – usually, the forest provided little more than background noise, but today the chirping and chattering of the birds sounded like a symphony. With visibility down to just a few paddle strokes, it was easy to get disorientated, and at one point I was convinced that we were paddling upstream. A little while later, I completely lost sight of Rich, and it was only by chance that we bumped into one another again half an hour later. 'Mr Boddington, I presume?' I quipped, as he emerged from the mist. 'The very same,' he replied with measured nonchalance. 'And you are …?'

The mist reminded Rich of a summer he'd spent in Canada teaching canoeing to the British Army. Each course, he said, had more or less revolved around the same gag: after covering basic skills on a small lake, the squaddies were driven to Athabasca Falls, one of the most tortuous – not to mention dangerous – waterfalls in the country. A quick glance would have been enough to tell anyone with an ounce of white-water experience that attempting the falls was death on a stick.

After wandering down to get a good look, the squaddies were then told that they'd be starting their day's paddling by running the falls. The sane ones, of course, started to wet themselves, torn between losing face in front of their mates on the one hand, and dying a cold, watery death on the other. Those with previous white-water experience simply said no. The majority, though, could hardly wait to get on the water, and were even disappointed when they were told that they couldn't do it. Such are the benefits, I mused, of having your fear glands removed at birth.

I also couldn't help thinking that the odd waterfall or two wouldn't have gone amiss here on the Amur, just to liven things up a bit. Still, I couldn't really complain: before we'd left the UK I'd expected there to be little or no discernible current after the first few hundred kilometres, so the fact that it was still racing along after over 2,000km was nothing short of miraculous.

Not that we didn't have our own fair share of hazards to contend with though: that evening, we discovered that our water filter was no longer working properly, which meant that we now had to sterilise our drinking water with iodine until the end of our journey; we knew it wasn't safe to use iodine for more than a few weeks at a time because of its possible side effects, but luckily we had no idea what these side effects were, so there didn't seem to be much point in worrying about them.

Maybe it was the three diseases I'd contracted overnight, or maybe I was just suffering from a severe case of hypochondria, but the day after the filter fiasco was a real struggle. A strong headwind was whipping up a fair amount of chop, and no matter how hard I paddled, I couldn't keep up with Rich. By the end of the second session I'd completely lost sight of him. I tried to spur myself on by yodelling a few sing-along favourites ('American Pie', 'The Boxer', that sort of the thing), but it didn't help. When we finally made camp that afternoon, I was exhausted – all I wanted to do was lie down, close my eyes, and let Robbie Williams entertain me on my Walkman.

Just before I turned in for the night, I saw a dark, furry creature scurry across the beach barely a stone's throw from the tent. It was about the size of a small dog, with white markings on its rump. Rich didn't see it, but we guessed it was some sort of pine marten or mink. It was the first wild animal we'd seen since Mongolia, and – perhaps not surprisingly – it got me thinking about other wild animals. The Amur, we knew, was home to a number of large mammals, including moose, wild boar, brown bear, the elusive Amur leopard, and even an endangered species of tiger, *Panthera tigris altaica*. The latter was highly prized in China for its bones and skin, and when the Russian border guards weren't tracking and arresting illegal immigrants, they were kept busy by poachers crossing the border in search of game. As for us, we had hoped that the river's wildlife would be one of the highlights of our journey, so we were quite disappointed that we'd seen so little.

The following morning, we drifted into a small village called Chernayevo and beached our boats below the watchtower, half expecting – given recent encounters with the military – to be presented with manna from heaven. Instead, the good Lord sent us a surly youth with the metabolism of a three-toed sloth (if I tell you that a sloth sleeps for twenty hours a day, and that – on average – it walks at just five metres per hour, you'll get the idea). In fact, for the first five minutes, he didn't even come down from his perch. We would have given up and paddled off if we hadn't been so fixated on finding bread and milk. When he at last came down, I told him we were looking for a bakery. In a voice as ponderous as his plod, he radioed through our request to his boss.

When he came off the radio, I asked him what he'd found out, but he just shrugged in slow motion. Realising we weren't getting anywhere, we set off into town, at which point our sloth became a cheetah, pouncing in front of us and barring our way. 'Nyet!' he said, shaking his head. I was indignant. 'Why not?' I demanded, a little tetchily. 'You must wait for the commandant,' he said with surprising authority. 'Well why didn't you say so?' I wanted to shout, but I didn't. I just smiled stiffly and went back down to the beach to wait.

After almost an hour, a plain-clothes border guard finally pulled up in a big black sedan and told us to get in. I had visions of being bundled to a KGB safe house with a bag over my head. What actually happened was almost as scary: because we hadn't been in a modern car since we'd left Mongolia almost two months before, everything felt new and exciting and – more to the point – very, very fast. I don't know if it was the potholed roads or the erratic driving, but I was soon clutching the door handle and bracing with my feet like my life depended on it.

When we finally got to a shop, we discovered we'd risked life and limb for nothing: there was no bread, and there wouldn't be any until five o'clock that evening. The plain-clothes man told us that if we were happy to wait, he'd bring some down to the river for us. It was now early afternoon, which meant another long delay, but if we wanted bread we didn't have much choice – the next village was three days away, and we could hardly live on chocolate in the meantime.

Still, at least this time we knew how long he'd be – or so we thought. We settled down near our boats to wait, right at the base of the watchtower. Not surprisingly, we attracted a fair amount of interest from the local villagers, but to start with they kept their distance, perhaps wary of what the sloth might do if he became agitated.

The first to brave coming closer was a very slim and very attractive woman who we'd seen on the riverbank when we'd first arrived. She seemed to be in her mid-thirties, with warm eyes and a shy smile, and up close she looked even prettier than she had from a distance. When she came over, she hardly said a word, instead handing us a small parcel wrapped in clingfilm. Inside was a stack of freshly made pancakes. Stunned, I stammered a thank you, but she just smiled. 'Be careful,' she said kindly, 'they're still quite hot.' Before I could say another word, she walked away. I wanted to stop her, to invite her to join us and thank her properly, but I couldn't get the words out. We never saw her again, and – to my lasting regret – we never did discover her name.

Her visit opened the floodgates, as one onlooker after another came down to see the crazy English canoeists for themselves. Many were still wary of venturing too close, preferring to just sit and watch from a distance. One young woman though, had no such reservations: she marched straight up and introduced herself as Valya. She could hardly have been more different from our Pancake Princess: despite the fact that it was still the middle of the afternoon, she wore a satin dressing gown and pink slippers. Her blonde hair was short and spiky, and she had a knowing, slightly cynical smile. The little boy she was holding – who looked to be about three or four – had the same sea-blue eyes and wild blond hair as his mother. 'This is Zhena,' she said, following my gaze. 'Zhena, say hello to the nice Englishmen.' Zhena clearly had more sense than to talk to a couple of hairy foreigners, but he was fascinated by Rich's boat, and wasted no time in crawling into it. He was so small he could practically walk around inside, but for the most part he just sat facing the wrong way, moving his body back and forth to try and get the thing moving.

Needless to say, Valya thought this was hilarious, and she couldn't stop laughing and clapping. The more she laughed and clapped, the more animated Zhena became, and pretty soon he was literally giddy with excitement, falling over whenever he tried to stand up. While he performed, Valya flicked her fingers against her throat with a wink, and asked us if we'd like some vodka. I must have grimaced, because she added: 'Not now, but later. I'll bring some down to the beach this evening, after I've put Zhena to bed.' We were reluctant to camp so close to the watchtower, but we felt it wasn't an offer we could refuse, so – for better or worse – we accepted.

In the event, it was probably no bad thing. The bread didn't arrive until ten o'clock, by which time it was too late to paddle anyway. Alas, Valya never returned, so instead we befriended the two young guards who'd delivered our bread, inviting them over to our tent for a cup of coffee. They were grateful for the drink, but they weren't very talkative, so we just sat on the beach to watch the sunset, listening out for the occasional movements of the three-toed sloth lurking high above us.

11 SUN, SAUNAS & HOMEMADE WHISKY

Unfortunately for us, sloths are nocturnal, and can often be heard radioing a report to HQ every hour on the hour, throughout the night. In the morning I woke to find a dead cat on the beach a few yards upstream of our tent and wondered if – despite the weight of scientific evidence to the contrary – sloths might also be carnivorous. It seemed odd that I hadn't noticed it the afternoon before, until I realised that the wind was now coming from upstream, and that the only reason I'd spotted it now was the rank smell of rotting flesh being wafted in our direction. Suffice it to say that when we finally said farewell to cheery Chernayevo, there wasn't a heavy heart in the house.

Our spirits were soon lifted, however, when shortly after leaving the village we were passed by a huge barge blaring out music that sounded like Chinese opera. The singing was very loud and very rousing, and despite the unorthodox nature of the broadcast, it somehow seemed appropriate in the valley of the Black Dragon River. Not for the first time, waving was the only way to communicate with those on board, all of whom looked as stunned to see us as we were to see them.

Thus inspired, we spent much of the day trying to remember – and sing – the words to all of Simon and Garfunkel's hits. 'Homeward Bound' and 'The Boxer' weren't too tricky, but 'Hazy Shade of Winter' and 'The Zoo' were another matter entirely, and we never did get the verses in the right order. When Rich had had enough of S&G (really rather quickly, as it happened) he busied himself with the maps, worrying about the huge, 30km loops we were paddling that weren't taking us any closer to the Pacific (because I didn't have any maps, I remained blissfully ignorant of what direction we were travelling in – as long as we were going downstream, I couldn't have cared less).

During the final session of the day, a big thunderstorm kicked off behind us and chased us downriver, eventually overtaking our boats on a long straight that was hemmed in on either side by some vertiginous rock pillars. The worst of the storm passed us by, which was probably just as well, as for the next two hours we were treated to a display of electrical energy on the horizon that was as intense as it was humbling. When we finally made camp that evening, the sky overhead was a deep, bruised blue, threatening to wash us away with its first clap of thunder.

The next day dawned much the same, but this time the storm didn't hit us until we'd made camp that evening, on a small shingle island opposite some sandstone cliffs: one minute we were sitting in the tent, writing our diaries, the next we were bracing our shoulders against the poles, hoping they wouldn't snap in the battering wind. Unfortunately, the tent was at right angles to the onslaught, so rather than being streamlined, it acted like a huge sail, lifting one side of the tent off the ground and threatening to collapse the other. The combined noise of the wind and rain was deafening, and the river was being whipped into such a frenzy that at one stage I thought it might flood our tiny island. It was the most intense storm I'd ever been in, and it was strangely exhilarating being in the midst of it all. And then, just as suddenly as it had started, it was over. The rain stopped as if a tap had been turned off and the wind died to nothing in a matter of minutes. In the stillness that followed, the cliffs glowed gold in the amber light of the setting sun.

The effect of the storm on the weather was dramatic. The next morning the air was pristine; it was as if the clouds had been gathering moisture for months and had now spent themselves completely. By midday, the bottomless blue of the sky was so intense that it looked almost black, and the sun was blisteringly hot, with temperatures approaching the sizzling side of 30°C. But impressive though the weather was, it was nothing compared to what the next twelve hours had in store: soaking in saunas; touring a piggery; grappling with a bear's claw; and, last but not least, drinking home-made whisky with the local border guards.

It all began harmlessly enough. That afternoon, we drifted past a watchtower just upstream of Novovaskresenovka (hereafter known simply as 'the village', for obvious reasons), trying to decide where to begin our quest for supplies. We couldn't see the village from the river, so we pulled up at a small beach, hoping that we might be able to see more from the bank. Finding little more than a track, a tractor and some fields, we decided to keep going upriver, and were heading back to our boats when we noticed a plume of dust billowing down the track towards us. Twenty seconds later, a car skidded to a stop at the end of this track and two armed guards piled out. They looked like they meant business. Compared to the chaps at Chernayevo, I thought, these boys were practically Special Forces.

The first man – stocky build, dark hair, bushy moustache – looked like he'd stepped straight out of a military training manual; the second was the spitting image of Robbie Williams, entertainer extraordinaire and purveyor of the finest teenage fantasies. 'Hello!' the man with the moustache greeted us cheerfully. 'Do you have any maps?' I pointed to the waterproof sleeve mounted on the deck of Rich's boat. 'Show me where you camped last night,' he continued, innocently. Little suspecting that there might be a catch, I gladly pointed out the island where we'd sat out the storm.

'Aha!' he cried out, as if he'd caught me with my hand in the sweetie jar. 'Why did you camp on a Chinese island?' he demanded. 'We thought it was Russian,' I stammered truthfully, although even as I said it I realised how lame it sounded. 'It was much closer to Russia,' I tried to explain, 'and there was no way of telling from our maps if it was Russian or Chinese.'

He thought about this for a moment, and then nodded. 'OK,' he said, 'but you must stay on the Russian side from now on. How far do you paddle each day?' he continued. 'About forty kilometres,' I said. 'In that case, tomorrow night you must camp here,' he insisted, marking the spot with a cross, 'and the next night here.' I couldn't help but notice that each cross was next to a village, which meant there'd almost certainly be a watchtower nearby.

'And what about tonight?' I asked. 'Tonight,' he exclaimed, with an ominous flick of his throat, 'you're drinking home-made whisky with us!'

Thus enrolled in another night of heavy hooning, we stowed our boats at the base of the nearby watchtower, jumped into the car with our captors, and headed off in the direction of the village. On the way, the man with the moustache introduced himself as Valera. 'And this is my good friend Vladimir,' he added, jerking his thumb at Robbie. Robbie just grinned amiably.

When we got close to the village, Valera asked us if we wanted any milk. It seemed like a slightly odd question, but milk sounded more promising than whisky, so I nodded enthusiastically. 'In that case,' he declared dramatically, 'you shall *have* milk.' A minute later, he pulled up outside a traditional wooden house boasting a white picket fence and a well-kept garden. He led us through the garden and beckoned us into a small cabin to the left of the main house. Inside, two women were busy preparing food: one of them had long, dark hair and attractive aquiline features, and was about the same age as us. The other one was older – maybe in her mid-forties – and wore her hair in a fashionable bob. She greeted us fondly, as if she'd been expecting us. 'My name is Zuma,' she smiled, 'and this is my daughter, Helena. Please, come in and make yourself at home.'

The room we were in was more like a studio flat, with a long table opposite the door and a small bed tucked up against the wall on the far side. To the right of the table was a kitchen area with a big, wood-burning stove, and above the bed was an impressive wall-hanging of a deer in a forest. It wasn't as spotless as Galya's place had been back in Sretensk, but it had the same cosy feel to it.

Before we even had a chance to sit down, however, Valera asked us if we'd like a shower. I wasn't sure if this was a polite way of saying we smelled as bad as a touring paddler's pants, but we hadn't had a shower since we'd left the UK, so I didn't hesitate to take the plunge.

'Let me show you where it is,' Valera said, leading us outside and across the garden to a wooden outbuilding. For a fleeting moment I had visions of standing under a rusty old bucket with holes drilled into the bottom, but when Valera opened the door, I realised it wasn't a shower at all, but a sauna. In the middle was a big, black stove with a giant pot of steaming water on top, while on the floor was a vast, metal tub full of ice-cold water. Along the far wall was a wooden bench with two smaller basins for washing. Valera handed us each a towel, and left us to it.

Uncharacteristically thrilled at the prospect of being clean, I slipped into my birthday best before you could say 'pass the soap'. The sauna was breathtakingly hot, and it wasn't long before I was glistening with pearls of sweat. Using a small basin to mix hot water from the pot with cold water from the tub, I washed every nook and cranny I could find. When there was nothing left to scrub, I filled my basin with ice masquerading as water, and – holding my breath – tipped the whole lot over my head. I gasped involuntarily, clenching my eyes shut and jumping up and down on the spot. It was – and I want to be completely clear about this – absolutely freezing. We both repeated the entire process twice more, before emerging into the garden looking like a couple of baked beetroots.

Physically and spiritually cleansed, we made our way back to the kitchen to find the table laden with salad, bread and bowls of steaming stew. Valera told us it was venison – the meat, he said, came from a deer he and Vladimir had bagged the day before. Warming to the subject of hunting, he showed me a keyring made out of a bear's tooth: it was about two inches long, with a white tip and a brightly polished surface. 'Where can you buy these?' I asked, slightly concerned for the local bear population. 'You can't just buy them,' Valera laughed. 'You have to hunt for them!'

Lunch began – as seems to be customary in these parts – with three shots of vodka. Or so we thought. It was actually home-made whisky, made from nothing but yeast, sugar and water, and was – Valera reliably informed us – 45% proof. Oh goody. The first and second shots weren't too bad, but by the third every tube between my nose and my belly was ablaze (it was at this stage that Helena went from being shy and reserved to being whammed and wonderful, entertaining everyone with jokes and antics that were only hilarious because we were all as merry as she was).

Once the stew had been seen to, the table was cleared to make way for bread, milk and bowls of small, white sweets. To start with we just drank the fabled milk, unsure what the bread and sweets were for, but Zuma showed us how to chomp down on the soft, sugary *confeti* while simultaneously chewing a piece of bread and taking a swig of milk. I must have looked sceptical, because she insisted it was nicer than it sounded. She was right – it was delicious.

While we were eating, Zuma disappeared for a few minutes, returning with an armful of goodies. 'You must take some of these sweets back home to your girlfriends,' she insisted, 'and here's a packet of cigarettes for you. They're Russian,' she laughed, by way of an apology, 'but they're better than nothing.' She also gave us each a single bar of peach soap, although I couldn't for the life of me imagine why.

After the milk and sweets, it was time for a grand tour. Zuma was clearly embarrassed, insisting there was no need to show us around, but Robbie was adamant, taking us to see the pigs and their piglets, the chickens and their chicks, and row after row of potatoes, cabbages and sunflowers. The scene was much the same in the garden next door, and the garden after that. In the face of an uncertain future, it seemed, people all across Siberia were returning to their roots, and to the only thing they really could trust: their land.

And so it continued. As afternoon turned to evening, we simply went from one meal to the next, pausing only to carry the table outside into the garden when the sun went down. For dinner, we slurped our way through bowl after bowl of fish soup, all mopped up with chunks of dark bread, while the whisky flowed unchecked. As we ate, we were joined by more and more people: Zuma's son, Pavel, who was just three years old; her two daughters, Anna and Katalina, who were both fifteen going on twenty; and finally Zuma's mother, who at almost 84 seemed utterly confused about who we were and what we were doing there (I never did work out where Zuma's husband was, and I didn't like to ask).

The whole night became a blur of eating and drinking. I even have vague memories of launching into a Russian song that I'd once learned in evening class; I was convinced it would go down like a lead balloon, but I'd hardly got as far as the second word before my voice was drowned out by a raucous and rousing rendition of 'The Little Christmas Tree'.

As we talked, Valera asked me why we'd decided to travel on the Amur. 'It was because we didn't know anything about it,' I explained. At this he launched into a toast: 'In Moscow no one knows about Siberia either,' he laughed. 'They don't know about real life!' He pointed to the garden, with its huts full of chickens and pigs. 'This,' he beamed, 'is real life. This is the real Russia.'

At around eleven, after a final toast to our health and happiness, Valera and Robbie rose to leave. They said they had to get home to their families, who lived about 100km away. As a parting gesture, Valera took the bear tooth off his keyring and handed it to me. 'A talisman for your journey,' he said soberly. 'It's my present to you.' I didn't know what to say, so I just took his hand in mine and shook it warmly. Robbie, meanwhile, flashed his last cheeky grin of the evening. And with that, they climbed into their car and sped off into the darkness.

Soon after midnight, everyone adjourned to the kitchen. We showed Zuma photos of friends and family back in the UK, and in return she passed around a few albums of her own. Many of the people featured in the albums were sat all around us: there was a whole series of them picnicking by the river, and another set of Zuma and her friends in China, in the modern-looking border town across the river from Blagoveschensk; most of these were of people buying food, eating in restaurants and having a good time, and the whole place seemed to have a fun, inviting feel to it.

When I asked Zuma if it was as nice as it looked, however, she could barely suppress her scorn. 'It's dirty,' she said crossly, 'and the locals aren't very nice.' As with many people we'd met, from Mongolia to Mangut, she seemed to be inherently suspicious of her nearest neighbours: Gal, our Mongolian driver, hadn't thought much of the Russians; Sascha, in Olovannaya, had nothing but bad things to say about Mongolia; and, not for the first time, someone had it in for the Chinese. Given that most of the Mongolians and Russians we'd met were invariably warm-hearted and welcoming, it seemed more than likely the Chinese were getting a bad press, but without going to China ourselves, it was hard to know why this was the case – I just hoped that we'd get a chance to find out before we reached the end of the border.

It was gone one by the time Zuma showed us to our room. It reminded me of the lovingly restored cabin we'd seen in the museum at Albazino. The difference here, of course, was that it was somebody's home. While I was getting ready for bed, something Robbie had said earlier reminded me that this was our fiftieth day on the river, and that we'd now covered almost exactly 2,200km, the halfway point of our journey; staying the night in a traditional Siberian cabin was, I thought fondly, a very fitting way to celebrate. As I slid gently into a coma after our day of scorching sun, steaming saunas and venison stew, I could hardly believe that we'd come to Siberia expecting nothing but pouring rain, empty wilderness, and 'the occasional bits of sheep'.

Breakfast the next day consisted of a bowl of soup and a pile of noodles, the likes of which we hadn't seen since Mongolia. As soon as we'd eaten, we all made our way down to the river. Rich and I collected our boats from beneath the watchtower and said our farewells. I didn't know how to thank Zuma, and I said as much, but she just shook her head. 'It's not you who should be thanking us,' she replied sincerely, 'but us who should be thanking you.' It was the nicest thing she could possibly have said. As for the rest of that day, I can honestly say it was a bit of a blur, and Rich apparently felt the same: his diary for 13 July simply reads: 'Another long paddle, and I can't remember anything about it.'

What happened that evening, however, was much harder to forget. We camped on the Russian side of the river opposite a big, shiny-looking Chinese town called Huma. Mercifully, there was no sign of any border guards, despite the fact that this was where Valera had told us to spend the night.

Rich spent the first part of the evening performing open-heart surgery on his camping mat. A few weeks before, a small bubble had appeared between the nylon outer and the foam inner. To start with it hadn't been much of a problem, but after a while it had started to grow, and it soon became clear that if this growth went unchecked, Rich would eventually have to sleep on a long, inflatable sausage. His only option was to lance the offending boil, slice it down the middle, paste the outer back down, and patch the whole thing up. Like all major surgery, it was a team effort, and after completing the operation, we both sat down on the patient to share a quick fag.

Yes, that's right, a fag. I know I've already mentioned that neither of us smoke, but in the last week two different groups of people had given us cigarettes, and it somehow seemed churlish not to at least try them. Being the goody-two-shoes that I am, the closest that I'd ever come to smoking was setting fire to a rolled-up strip of newspaper in the woods behind school at the tender age of ten. Rich, however, was something of an expert, having once absconded from school for a whole week to sit around a campsite with his mates drinking beer and smoking two packs a day, although as far as I knew he hadn't touched a cigarette since.

We decided to try the Chinese ones first, mainly because they had a filter, and generally looked a lot less nasty. Rich got the thing going, took a long drag and handed it over. I puffed away a couple of times, but couldn't really see what all the fuss was about. 'It might help if you inhale,' Rich pointed out politely. In reply I took not one, but two deep drags. That did the trick. If I'd been standing up, there's no doubt in my mind that I'd have fallen over. As it was, I simply keeled over onto my back. I thought it might be funnier if I tried to stand up, and sure enough, it was.

The Russian Prima cigarettes weren't as strong, and took longer to kick in, but they did the trick eventually. I vaguely considered taking up smoking until the end of the trip, or at least until we'd finished both packs. I had half a mind to smoke them all there and then, just for kicks, but Richard the Wise counselled against it, and I was glad he did; a few minutes later, I started feeling quite queasy, and decided that if I never smoked another cigarette in my life, it would be too soon.

The next morning – perhaps as a reminder of more innocent times – Rich recited 'Albert and The Lion', a poem so full of wit and whimsy that I felt aggrieved my parents hadn't acquainted me with it sooner. I can't quite remember the plot, but basically it was about a little boy called Albert, and a big lion, and how – after an amusing sequence of events – one of them eats the other.

We stopped for lunch below an imposing cliff face. Perched on top of the cliff was a watchtower manned by a couple of guards, who were no doubt making a careful note of all our border violations. The thought that we were now being watched all the time and that we had to camp where we were told seemed to go against everything our journey stood for. We'd got this far without anyone else telling us what to do, we reasoned resentfully, so why should now be any different? The more we discussed it, the more agitated we became, and by the time we made camp that evening, we'd somehow managed to talk ourselves into a night paddle.

Paddling at night, we decided, would kill a number of birds with one, well-aimed stone. For a start it would be much cooler at night, which would be a welcome relief from the oppressive heat of late morning and early afternoon. It would also be fun: with the sky clear and the moon on our side, it was the perfect night for an impromptu adventure. And finally – but perhaps most importantly – it would mean paddling without being seen by any border guards or having to stop at any watchtowers. For some reason, it never even occurred to us that paddling at night along one of the world's most sensitive border zones might not actually have been such a good idea.

We pushed off into the inky blackness soon after midnight, bound for the rising moon, which lit a shimmering path down the middle of the river. In many ways the moon was a godsend because it meant we could see where we were going, but even hundreds of yards from the bank it felt like a spotlight; trying to adjust our eyes to the darkness, we slipped past trees that were watchtowers and watchtowers that were trees, holding our breath and hardly daring to put our paddles in the water. Only when mist started to rise off the river did we begin to relax, taking care not to run into any of the Chinese barges moored midstream.

Today, I have a snapshot memory of that night, of Rich slicing through the water beside me, half shrouded in mist and silhouetted by the moon. Every second was a thrill, and it was without doubt the most memorable night of the entire trip. Of course, at the time I had no idea that it was very nearly the *last* night of the entire trip.

12 PRESIDENT PUTIN & THE GOOD NEWS GIRLS

We paddled for five hours before making camp on a steep, shingle beach in the half-light of dawn. All told, we'd now been on the go for nearly 24 hours, and I couldn't wait to slide into my sleeping bag. I didn't stir again until mid-morning, and even then I only got up because the sun was starting to microwave everything inside the tent. After a swim to cool down, we had breakfast on the beach, and began packing our boats in preparation for the first session of the day.

We were just hoisting the tent over our heads (to shake out any nocturnal visitors) when I heard a strange throbbing sound coming from upstream. Seconds later, two gunboats roared into view, trailing vast rooster-tails of spray. After the tranquillity of the last twelve hours, the noise was deafening. As the boats thundered towards us – aiming for a point roughly between my left and right eyes – I could just make out the death's-head decals emblazoned on their bows. They were, I felt quite certain, the two gunboats of the apocalypse, come to exact penance for a lifetime of loafing (under normal circumstances, I'd have expected four, but times were obviously hard in hell, and I could only assume that there wasn't enough petrol for the full complement).

Mercifully, the beach we were on was too steep for the gunboats, so they pulled into an eddy downstream and waited for us to paddle down. We packed up our tent as slowly as we could, frantically trying to come up with a plausible explanation for how we'd managed to cover forty kilometres without being seen by a single border guard. There wasn't one. The more we discussed it, the more improbable our excuses became: we were avoiding the heat of the afternoon; we were practising our celestial navigation; goodness, is that the time? We had no idea it was getting so late …

I had visions of being sent home in disgrace, never to set foot in Siberia again. After months of battling bureaucracy and border guards, it seemed ironic – not to mention a little galling – that our entire journey was now at risk because of something *we'd* done. For the first time since setting off almost two months before, I felt sick with worry.

When we finally pushed off, I still didn't know what I was going to say, and the knot in my stomach was fast becoming a noose. In the end, I decided there was only one thing for it: I would play the mindless optimism card and hope for the best. As we paddled past, I chirped a cheerful hello, acting as if this was the third apocalyptic encounter we'd had that morning. In reply, the men on the boats just waved back, clearly a little stunned. I held my breath, waiting for a shout or a gunshot to break the spell, but it never came. Once we were a few metres downstream, I tried to look relaxed, resisting the urge to paddle like a lunatic. As a few metres became a few hundred, I breathed a long sigh of relief and flashed Rich a knowing grin. The end of our journey, it seemed, was no longer nigh, and I promised myself there and then that I'd never do anything naughty again.

Appropriately enough, 'naughty things I've done' became that morning's topic of conversation. Rich told me about the time he put a small electric motor in a toaster just to see what would happen (it exploded), and the time he stuck a compass in a car tyre to find out how fast it would go down (very fast indeed).

In return, I told him a story that continues to haunt me to this day: when I was about four years old, I decided my dad's car needed a wash, but because I didn't know how to use a hose, I opted to use gravel instead (at this stage, it's probably worth mentioning that the car in question was brand new, and had been coveted by my father – on and off – since the dawn of time). Holding my tiny palms together, I scooped a handful of stones from the driveway and hoisted them onto the roof. I was just reaching for a second handful when my mum ran screaming from the house, swept me off my feet, and hugged me as if my life depended on it. Only when I was much older did I realise that, in fact, it had done: if my dad had ever found out what I'd been doing that sunny spring morning, he would almost certainly have come after me sporting a long black cloak and a crescent-shaped farming implement.

That night we set up camp on the only stretch of beach we could find. On the Chinese side was a busy industrial centre with neat, square-windowed administrative buildings and bright, shiny factories. On the Russian side – where we were camped – was a small slagheap. After we'd eaten, a border guard appeared and asked us when we'd be leaving the next morning and where we were planning to camp the following night. Adopting a suitably deferential tone, I told him everything he wanted to know. Our days of freedom, I realised, were over, and we had only ourselves to blame.

Over the next few days, we played some games to pass the time. We spent an entire afternoon naming 49 of America's 50 states (Wisconsin was never going to be easy) and another two days playing 'Guess the Girl'. This was basically our own version of 'Twenty Questions', in which only famous females were permitted, but what started as a bit of harmless fun soon turned to desperation when I spent two hours trying to identify Mrs Tiggywinkle. Less traumatic, although no less tricky, was coming up with our Top Five (by which I mean the top five girls we'd most like to have breakfast with). For the sake of argument we ruled that girlfriends were inadmissible, partly because they were already a given, but mostly because we didn't want to limit our options. My, but these were exciting times.

As luck would have it, excitement was only just around the corner. On 18 July we reached Blagoveschensk, the first big town we'd seen since leaving Ulaan Baatar over two months before. Significantly, it was also the first town we'd come across that was mentioned – albeit briefly – in our guidebook, thanks largely to the fact that it was on a branch line of the Trans-Siberian railway. Most of the entry was devoted to its history: like many towns in the region, Blagoveschensk was founded as a Russian military outpost in the middle of the seventeenth century, but was later seized by the Manchurians. In 1856 it was recaptured by the Russians and given its present name, which literally means 'Good News'. The name seemed appropriate: thanks to booming cross-border trade, Blagoveschensk soon became the most important city in Eastern Siberia. In 1900, however, the good news turned to bad when the Russians slaughtered every Chinese in the city, to avenge the deaths of Europeans caught up in China's Boxer Rebellion (the Chinese, apparently, weren't too keen on their country being carved up by European colonialists). Later, during the Cultural Revolution, China broadcast 24-hour propaganda across the river using massive loudspeakers. On the morning that we drifted into town, however, all *we* could hear was the faint warble of Chinese music emanating from a floating restaurant moored to the riverbank.

Heihe – where the music was coming from – featured an impressive, high-rise waterfront that looked as though it had sprung up in the last twelve months. Shiny new skyscrapers gleamed in the bright sunlight, pirouetting cranes danced across the skyline, and the water's edge was white-tiled and spotless. On the Russian side, meanwhile, we could see nothing but mud, trees and the occasional smokestack. It was only when we rounded a bend in the river that the forest finally gave way to a procession of impressive-looking buildings, marching along a promenade high above the water's edge. It didn't look as bright and shiny as Heihe, but the beaches and bars that lined the waterfront were bustling with bathers and drinkers, and the whole town had a relaxed, resort-like atmosphere that was as unexpected as it was welcome.

We pulled up below a wide staircase near the centre of the promenade. Skipping to the top of the steps, we found ourselves on the edge of a large square enclosed by an amphitheatre of imposing administrative buildings. In the middle of the square was a fully functioning fountain, its pools overflowing with giggling children, and on the far side was a busy, four-lane street. Finally, right in front of us, there was an open-air café complete with Coca-Cola parasols. The thought of an ice-cold Coke after months of drinking fetid river water was too tempting to pass up, so we hauled our canoes up the steps, parked them alongside one of the tables and sat down to watch the world go by.

And by 'world', of course, I mean girls. Everywhere we looked there were women – young and not so young, pretty and not so pretty – all dressed in tight, tight tops and even tighter bottoms; they tottered along the promenade like it was a catwalk, doing their level best to burst their seams. It was enough – to borrow a line from Chandler – to make a bishop kick a hole in a stained-glass window.

We tried to remember how girls dressed back in the UK, but even allowing for the fact that we'd been in the woods for far too long, we felt sure they didn't look anything like this. While we ogled, Rich came up with a theory for why this might be the case: Siberian girls, he suggested, spent so long wrapped up in the winter that they went crazy in the summer, exposing as much flesh as they could, as often as they could. For my part, I thought they probably dressed like this because *they could*: after decades of conservatism under communist rule, young people could finally wear – and say, and do – whatever they wanted.

After we'd had our fill of the golden elixir (Coke, that is, not girls) we went in search of a hotel. The first place we tried was right on the square. It was full. The second place, near the end of the promenade, was also full. I was absolutely stunned: I couldn't believe that in a town as big as Blagoveschensk we couldn't find a room for the night. By the time we'd wheeled our boats to the third hotel (an unprepossessing place on a backstreet about 500m from the square) I was beginning to get a bit anxious. The woman at the reception desk was in her mid-fifties, with a big bouffant hairdo and wide, gold-rimmed glasses. When I asked her if she had any rooms, she shook her head apologetically. 'But you must have something,' I said, trying to sound as desperate as I felt. 'There is nothing,' she insisted. 'In fact, you'll be lucky to find a room anywhere in town.'

'Why is everywhere so busy?' I asked, still hoping that I might be able to win her over. 'There's a big delegation in town,' she replied. 'President Putin is here for a summit on cross-border relations.' Ah. That explained it. Suffice it to say, the irony of the situation wasn't lost on me: while Big Vlad had booked up every hotel in town, the two people who epitomised the very spirit of cross-border relations couldn't find so much as a broom cupboard to call their own.

Or so I thought. When I told Ms Bouffant how we'd got to Blagoveschensk, she asked where our boats were. 'They're outside,' I replied. 'Show me,' she said, beckoning me across the lobby. Gazing at them from the hotel door, she let out a long, soft whistle. 'Here's what I'll do,' she said finally. 'The director's office has a bed in it. If you want, you can stay there.' I could have kissed her purple lips and ruffled her hivelike hair.

The room in question boasted a desk, a sofa bed, a small fridge and an *en suite* bathroom. Ms Bouffant apologised that it was so small, but by that stage we'd have rather slept in a bathtub than resume our traipse around town. She even agreed to let us store our boats under the stairs in the lobby, much to the amusement of the other guests.

The first thing we had to do was shave: out in the Taiga our beards had looked bushy and splendid; here in the big city, they looked bushy and ridiculous. Much as I liked my mutton chops, I was quite glad to see my face again, even if I wasn't as handsome as I'd remembered. Rich, meanwhile, went from wild-eyed woodsman to baby-faced crooner in a matter of minutes.

Thus groomed, we hit the town, intent on mounting an all-out charm offensive. Our first port of call was the café we'd visited a few hours before. It was a balmy evening, and the whole town seem to be out on the promenade, drinking in the open-air bars or wandering along the waterfront. It wasn't long before we were joined by a blonde in a tight-fitting dress and a man in equally tight-fitting trousers. She was a student at the local university, she told us, and her boyfriend was a policeman. Because she was speaking Russian, it took me a while to realise she was slurring her words – my suspicions were only confirmed when she got up to leave and careered gracefully into a nearby table.

A short while later, her boyfriend returned. 'The woman is waiting,' he whispered, looking furtively over his shoulder. I wasn't sure I'd understood him correctly. 'The woman is waiting,' he repeated, this time with a knowing nod. Call me a little wet behind the ears if you will, but I was a bit taken aback. I wasn't sure what to say, so in the end I decided to play it dumb: 'The woman is waiting for what?' I asked innocently.

BARBED WIRE & BABUSHKAS

Clearly exasperated, the boyfriend shook his head, spat something suitably obscene in Russian, and wandered off to find his friend.

Our next encounter was much more civilised. A girl with thick dark hair and a broad smile came over to our table. 'May I join you?' she asked in English. '*Konyeshna,*' I replied in Russian – of course. She introduced herself as Julia. 'I'm studying to be a teacher at the local university,' she said modestly, 'but my English is very bad.' In fact, she spoke English better than anyone else we'd met in Russia, and we both enjoyed being able to talk to someone without having to concentrate on every single word that was being said. We told her about our journey, while she told us about her course, her friends and her family.

After we'd been chatting for about half an hour, she reached into her purse and pulled out a hundred-rouble note (worth about £2). She wrote something on one side and handed it to me. 'If you're here for a few days and want to go out, give me a call,' she beamed, and with that she waved coyly and disappeared into the parade of people that was spilling past the café. It was only when I looked more closely at the note that I realised it had a portrait of Mulder and Scully from the *X Files* on one side and a pair of skulls on the other. Next to Scully, Julia had written: 'For Paul and Richard to remember Julia and Russia. Good luck!'

The final highlight of the evening was provided by someone we didn't even meet. It was getting on for late o'clock when we noticed a girl with big, frizzy hair bopping in the square. She wasn't the only one dancing, but she was certainly the only one groping herself and grinding her crotch up against the back of a chair. The raunchier her dancing got, the more people cheered, and the more people cheered, the raunchier it got. Just when I thought she was going to tear off her dress, two men walked up behind her, picked her up by the arms and carried her into a waiting police van; she was still dancing when they slammed the doors shut and carted her off to the nearest nick.

The next morning, feeling slightly the worse for wear, we decided a tour of the town was in order, and soon found ourselves in a vast fairground near the waterfront. Everything looked a bit tatty and run-down, but all of the rides were overrun by screaming children having the time of their lives.

Unable to resist our own inner children, we had a go on the Ferris wheel, only to be told off by a spotty teenager for going round twice. Equally entertaining was a display dedicated to military hardware: for five roubles (about 10p) we could sit in – and have a guided tour of – a stunt plane, a transport plane, or a helicopter. Given our unhealthy obsession with helicopter gunships, we opted for the latter, but the guide's description was so detailed I couldn't follow most of it. Had my Russian been slightly better, I felt sure we could have flown the thing by the time he'd finished.

That afternoon, we met President Putin (by which I mean we saw him drive past in a big black car with tinted windows). We couldn't be sure which of the eight big black cars with tinted windows he was in, but my money was on the third one along. The roads around the town square had been closed all day, and the streets were thronged with people, despite an incessant downpour that had started a few hours before. Other than what I'd read in the papers back home, I didn't know much about Putin, but the fact that he wouldn't even show his face to his supporters seemed like a pretty poor show to me. I couldn't help remembering Victor's words back in Sretensk: 'When Tony Blair comes to Moscow, Putin shows him everything that's good and hides everything that's bad. The people in Moscow have everything, while the people of Siberia have nothing.'

On the way back to our hotel we passed what looked like an outdoor-equipment shop. Inside was an array of fishing tackle, tents and – most pertinently – camping stoves. The smallest one we could find was a squat cylinder about the size of a biscuit tin. The instruction booklet was printed in dense Cyrillic, and the whole thing must have weighed about two kilos, but as long as it didn't cover everything in soot, I couldn't have cared less. 'How much?' I asked. 'Three hundred roubles,' the owner replied. That was about six pounds. 'We'll take it,' I said. On the way out, I had another quick look at the instructions. 'How hard can it be?' I asked Rich with a shrug. Of course, the question I should have been asking was: 'What are the chances that this thing will blow up in our faces and kill us both?'

Back at the hotel we phoned Julia and arranged to meet her in the square later that evening. In the meantime, we exposed ourselves to an unhealthy dose of Russian MTV. My favourite video was about a guy at a car wash (bear with me here), which just happened to be staffed entirely by beautiful girls. While he was waiting for them to start scrubbing, he closed his eyes and fell asleep. The next thing he knew, said girls were writhing about on top of his car wearing nothing but g-strings and soap bubbles – fancy! Another gem was simply called 'Beer', which had a catchy chorus that went something like: 'Beer, beer, beer, beer is good, Beer, beer, beer, beer is great.'

Finally, at number one in the charm charts was the brilliant and memorably titled 'Girls', which included the immortal line: 'Black, white, yellow or red, all girls are great in bed.' Well, quite.

With these words still disturbingly fresh in our minds, we went to meet Julia. She took us to a Chinese restaurant, where we were joined by one of her friends from university. 'This is Ksenia,' she said. 'Ksenia, meet the boys.' Ksenia had big brown eyes and a vaguely horsey smile; her nickname, she told us, was 'The Smiling Horse'. As nicknames go, I thought, it sounded a bit harsh, but she didn't seem to mind. As we talked, it soon became apparent that she was something of a drama queen: when I asked her to pose for a photo she said (in English), 'I am not a circus clown,' before adding 'Where is my script? Where is my make-up?' Despite that, however, she was every bit as entertaining as Julia, even if her jokes did lose a certain something in translation: the only one I can remember was about a little girl standing in a playground with a bloody kidney in one hand and a still-beating heart in the other. 'Oops,' says the little girl, 'what a sneeze!'

Ksenia also enlightened us on the origins of throat-flicking: once upon a time, she explained, there was a messenger in the Russian army who was extremely brave and fleet of foot, but who was also partial to the odd drop of vodka. During a particularly ferocious battle, the army's general sent the messenger to request reinforcements, but to make sure he wouldn't forget the message, he had it burned onto his neck with a branding iron – hence the flicking of the throat.

As well as jokes and anecdotes, Ksenia also taught us some Russian slang. Again, I don't remember most of the expressions she came out with, but the one that sticks in my mind is 'C peevom tretyem', which roughly translated meant: 'It's OK with beer'. This, Julia told us, could be used in reference to almost anything. What's she like? She's OK with beer. Do you like your boyfriend? He's OK with beer. Does my bum look big in this? It's OK with beer. You get the idea. Our own contribution to the linguistic melting pot included 'top banana', 'brass monkeys' and 'pear-shaped' (I thought about 'tits up' but decided, on balance, that pear-shaped was easier to explain).

While we were chatting, I asked them both what they thought of China. Julia had never been – she didn't have the right papers – but Ksenia was obviously quite well travelled. 'I like the big cities like Beijing and Harbin,' she said, sounding a bit showy, 'but Heihe is dirty, and the people there aren't very friendly.' This was, I couldn't help recalling, almost exactly what Zuma had said back in Novovaskresenovka. I couldn't understand it: from the river, Heihe had looked far cleaner than Blagoveschensk, with its gleaming tiled promenade and its bright, shiny hotels. There was only one thing for it, I decided: we'd just have to go there and find out for ourselves.

13 CHICKEN FEET & OTHER TEMPTING TREATS

The very next morning, we wandered down to the east end of the promenade and jumped on the daily ferry to Heihe (although we didn't have permission to paddle in Chinese waters or land our canoes on Chinese territory, we saw no reason why we couldn't visit China through traditional channels using the standard tourist visas we'd been given back in the UK). It was packed with Russians carrying armfuls of empty bags and boxes, presumably to be filled with cheap Chinese goods. The journey itself took about ten minutes – the river was only a few hundred metres across, but the ferry had to point almost straight upstream to make any headway against the strong current. Getting through customs on the far side was a whole new experience, but we emerged unscathed after being questioned by a tiny Chinese girl who looked almost as confused as we did.

The moment we walked outside we were accosted by a taxi driver. 'Gastinitsa nada?' he asked, in ropey Russian. 'He wants to know if we need a hotel,' I translated. 'He'll probably just take us to the most expensive hotel in town,' Rich said doubtfully. I agreed, but as neither of us spoke more than a few words of Chinese, I didn't see that we had much choice. After a brief discussion, we decided to chance it. On the drive into town, our driver gave us a quick guided tour. He pointed out the brand new Trade Centre (built specifically for cross-border commerce), the athletics track, and the local food market. 'Heihe is changing fast,' he said. 'It used to be a small town, but now there are over 60,000 people here, with another 60,000 expected in the next two years. Everything is being knocked down and rebuilt,' he added, waving his hand at the cranes and buildings that towered overhead. Cross-border commerce, it seemed, was booming in Heihe.

As expected, the hotel he took us to was the biggest on the waterfront, boasting acres of tinted glass and a glitzy lobby complete with chrome fittings and crystal chandeliers. It was ten times more expensive than any of the hotels in Blagoveschensk, but even then it only came to about £15 a head, so we booked a room, dumped our bags and headed straight back out, anxious not to waste a minute of our short stay in China.

The first thing I noticed was how quiet everything was – it was nearly eleven o'clock, and the streets were almost completely devoid of people. It was only when we spotted a clock outside a bank that I realised Heihe was two hours behind Blagoveschensk, and that most of the town's shops and market stalls hadn't even opened yet. The second thing I noticed – much to my surprise – was that it was every bit as dirty as we'd been led to believe; the shiny new waterfront, it seemed, was little more than window-dressing for streets that were strewn with trampled litter and pockmarked with murky puddles.

While we waited for the town to wake up, we wandered into a nearby café. We had no idea how to order, so we just pointed to a few of the goodies piled high on the counter and hoped for the best. We ended up with two generous platters of cold meat and two chicken dumplings the size of croquet balls. We ate with chopsticks, much to the amusement of the girls behind the counter. They must have assumed we were Russian, and the sight of a Russian using chopsticks was clearly too much for them. When we said 'thank you' in Chinese, they practically fell about laughing.

By the time we got outside, Heihe was heaving. Compared to the wide, tree-lined avenues of Blagoveschensk, the streets here were narrow, crowded and noisy. Cars honked and screeched incessantly, and the pavements were packed with traders selling everything from cantaloupes to car parts. Again, they assumed we were Siberian: 'Need melons?' they sang urgently in Russian. 'You must need melons! How about spark plugs? I can give you a good price on spark plugs!'

The litter I'd noticed earlier, I now realised, wasn't a sign of squalor, but of success: the stall-holders and shop-owners were simply too busy making money to worry about half-eaten honeydew slices or hastily discarded cardboard boxes. It also occurred to me that it wasn't Heihe's litter that Siberians found distasteful, but the prosperity that produced it. Their scorn was a symptom of jealousy: if the Chinese can make money, they thought reasonably, then why can't we?

Part of the answer, I knew, lay in the fact that China produced the sorts of goods that both the Siberians and the Chinese wanted to buy, and as such any profits went straight into the pockets of local traders. With no equivalent production industry of its own, Siberia's only exports to China were limited to less tangible commodities like timber, arms and electricity, with profits going straight to the government, or to the shadowy wheeler-dealers who brokered deals from afar.

When we'd had enough of the hustle and bustle of the town centre, we escaped to the promenade. Scattered along the waterfront were half a dozen large boats and a series of shingle beaches littered with bathers and fishermen. We stopped for a drink at one of the floating bars overlooking the river and watched people washing their cars or their clothes down by the water's edge. For lunch we bought a whole cooked chicken, complete with crispy feet. Now, call me Mr Fussy, but I wasn't too keen on the idea of gristle'n'claws, however tasty. Mr Greedy, on the other hand, couldn't get enough of the stuff, and practically swallowed his whole.

Surprisingly enough, neither of us felt very hungry that evening, so we decided to head back to the bar on the river for a quick drink. Wandering in, we found ourselves in the middle of a private party. We were just about to wander back out when one of the guests beckoned us over and thrust a couple of sizzling kebabs into our hands. I'd have been less surprised if he'd slapped me in the face with a wet kipper and called me Mary. All I could do was grin and say *Shee Shee*. Before long, everyone in the bar was beaming at us and chattering excitedly in Chinese. None of them spoke a word of Russian, so we had no way of explaining that we were English, but they couldn't have cared less – as far as they were concerned, we were just two lads looking for a drink. Anxious not to outstay our welcome, we finished our kebabs, downed a quick beer, and sidled back outside, the sounds of sing-song farewells ringing in our ears.

But that was by no means the last of the night's big surprises. Back at the hotel, I spent a few minutes gazing out across the town from our fifth-floor window. On the other side of the street I noticed a young girl in a shiny blue dress sitting on the steps of a shop. Behind her was an old woman sweeping the floor. Before I closed the window, I sneezed once, quite loudly, and thought no more about it.

A few minutes later, I heard a knock at the door. It was almost midnight, so we decided to ignore it. Whoever it was didn't get the message, and knocked again. I was just getting up to answer it when the door opened and two women barged in. The first was the old crone from the shop and the second – to my lasting surprise – was the girl in the shimmery dress. Before I could say anything, the old crone pushed the girl towards me, said something in Chinese and turned to leave. I paused just long enough to notice that Shimmery Dress Girl was really rather pretty. 'There must be some mistake,' I said, in Russian. 'I didn't mean to sneeze. Please, you must leave now.' In reply, the old crone gave the girl another encouraging shove and leered lecherously at me. It was my turn to push now: as gently and politely as I could, I corralled them both back across the room, ushered them out into the hallway, and closed the door behind them.

The next morning, we had a few hours to kill before catching our ferry back to Blagoveschensk, so after a breakfast of soup and noodles at the hotel, we went in search of the local market. When we got close to the centre of town, we made the mistake of asking someone for directions. Unbeknownst to us, it was something that was to colour our view of China for the rest of our trip.

The market itself was housed in a vast building with a glass roof. Inside, goods were laid out on trestle tables with edge-to-edge efficiency, and piled as high as gravity would allow. Vendors were clamouring for attention, selling every kind of food you could imagine: fresh fruit and veg, dozens of different teas, octopus by the bucket load, and sackfuls of chilli powder in every shade of red and yellow imaginable. Together, the combination of colours and aromas was intoxicating.

I was just about to sample some squid when I was approached by someone wearing a crumpled suit and a sly smile. After a moment I realised it was the man who'd given us directions to the market a short while before. 'You must give me five roubles,' he said in Russian. I couldn't help feeling that I'd heard this somewhere before. 'Why?' I asked, as politely as I could. 'All visitors to the market must pay five roubles,' he replied, his smile still intact. This all sounded very unlikely, but rather than risk antagonising him, I just returned his smile and walked away. Not surprisingly, he followed me. 'But you must pay five roubles,' he insisted. Again I ignored him, and for the next five minutes he followed me around like a lapdog, hoping that I'd eventually give in and toss him a bone. To start with it was all quite amusing, but when he followed us outside, I knew it wasn't going to end well.

'Give me the money!' he snarled, grabbing my arm. I shook him off – I'd been away from home far too long to be intimidated. Taking a deep breath, I held my face six inches from his, looked him straight in the eyes and said, 'Nyet,' as tersely and clearly as I could. To my surprise, he just shrugged, smiled his waxwork smile, and disappeared into the crowd.

As we made our way back to our hotel, I realised there was another reason why so many of the Siberians we'd met were so wary of their nearest neighbours: our little run-in at the market, I felt sure, was typical of what Russian visitors to Heihe – and doubtless Chinese visitors to Blagoveschensk – faced on a daily basis, while the welcome we'd received at the riverside bar less than twelve hours previously was almost certainly atypical. But I couldn't help thinking there was something else, something more fundamental: it wasn't just that the Chinese were prosperous, or that they were aggressive, but that they were so very *different*; they were loud, energetic and excitable; they spoke in a harsh, atonal tongue; and they ate battered chicken feet for lunch. They were, quite literally, a race apart, an unknown entity that was easier to despise than to understand.

Back on the ferry, the bags that we'd seen people carrying on the way out were now filled to bursting. In addition, most of the men on board were wearing four or five leather jackets, one on top of the other, presumably to avoid paying import tax. Some of them were even wearing two or three pairs of jeans, each a size smaller than the next. It was a graphic lesson in free enterprise, but it seemed to me that these overdressed Michelin men were getting the rough end of the deal.

Returning to our hotel that evening, we were delighted to discover that we'd been promoted from the manager's office to a twin room on the third floor. We were just unpacking some of our stuff when we heard a knock at the door. I couldn't believe it – surely the old crone hadn't followed us across the river? To my immense relief, she hadn't. Instead of the old crone, I found Julia standing out in the corridor looking distinctly pleased with herself. 'What, what!' she chirped in English. 'Surprised to see me?' I smiled gratefully. 'Surprised, and delighted,' I said. She seemed to like that. 'How was China?' she asked. 'It was OK with beer,' I replied, waving my hand uncertainly. She laughed. 'And what are you doing this evening?' she continued. 'We're going out with you,' I said matter-of-factly. 'Good!' she said. 'Where would you like to go?'

As it turned out, we didn't have much choice. After a drink at one of the open-air bars down on the promenade, Julia took us to the imaginatively named Russia Night Club. Outside on the steps, we were joined by two of her university friends, Dennis and Nastia. Dennis had short blond hair and a cheeky grin, and looked young enough to be my son; Nastia, meanwhile, had long, dark hair and a serene smile, and looked old enough to be my girlfriend. The club itself didn't seem like much from the outside, but inside it was a glass-and-chrome explosion that wouldn't have looked out of place in Clapham. At one end of the room was a stage with a glitzy silver curtain, while at the other was a retro-looking bar complete with black-tie bartenders.

After finding a table near the bar, we ordered a bottle of vodka and five shot glasses. This – I couldn't help thinking – was going to get messy. Dennis, Julia told us, was 'crazy for dancing', and it wasn't long before he was leading us all onto the dance floor. I couldn't speak for anyone else, but I hadn't drunk nearly enough to start strutting my own peculiar brand of stuff. The truth is, I've always had a bit of a problem with dancing: it's not so much that I'm bad at it (although I am), but that I'm physically incapable of moving any limb more than an inch without at least a litre of alcohol inside me (curiously, once this quota has been reached, my arms and legs will happily move as far as space will allow). And so it was on this occasion: try as I might, I could do little more than cock my legs and nod my head like a stork standing on a hot tin roof.

Eventually though, the vodka started to work its magic, and I was soon flailing my arms and legs around with the best of them. I was just starting to get warmed up when the dance floor cleared and a man in a penguin suit sauntered out. 'Ladies and gentlemen,' he began, before launching into a stream of unintelligible syllables. Julia could hardly contain her excitement, but instead of telling me what he'd said, she just smiled coyly, and nodded her head in the direction of the stage.

Seconds later, it was filled with naked people grinding up against each other to a soundtrack of hardcore dance music (all in the name of art, naturally). I was stunned, and – I have to confess – not a little mesmerised. Julia rescued me from my stupor: 'They're all university students,' she yelled over the music. 'They work here during the summer to help pay for their courses.' Apparently, that wasn't the only thing they paid for. 'Getting good grades can also be expensive,' she added. 'Do you mean people can pay for good grades?' I asked, not sure I'd heard her correctly. 'It's not common,' she admitted, 'but it's easy enough to arrange.' I asked her what it might cost for an A grade. 'Perhaps 5,000 roubles per subject,' she shrugged casually. That was about £100. Here in Siberia, it seemed, free enterprise wasn't just limited to leather and Levis.

We eventually staggered back to our hotel at 4 a.m., and the next morning we paid for our foolishness in spades. We'd planned to get back on the river that morning, but we didn't even make it out of bed until midday. We spent the afternoon doing all of the things we'd neglected to do over the last few days, like phoning Dmitry, filling our fuel bottles, and stocking up on supplies. It was gone seven o'clock by the time we marched back to the hotel to retrieve our boats. Alas, Ms Bouffant was nowhere to be seen, so we passed our thanks and farewells onto the concierge, before wheeling our mobile homes across the lobby and out into the street.

Before we left, we met Julia down on the waterfront for one last drink. While we were chatting, I gave her one of my Churchill medallions. In return she presented me with a Robbie Williams cassette; all of the song titles were in English, but the small print was in Russian. It was a perfect souvenir. 'Thank you,' I said sincerely. 'This is top banana!'

By the time we'd taken our boats off our trolleys and carried them down to the water's edge, we'd managed to attract quite a crowd. Just as we were pushing off, I heard someone say, 'They're only foreigners – they don't know what they're doing.' Two months ago, I thought, he might have been right, but not now: we were loafers at large, and nothing – but nothing – could stop us.

Well, apart from the gunboat we ran into about half a kilometre downstream. We pulled obediently alongside it and handed over our papers. 'Are you the Englishmen?' asked one of the crew. I wanted to say, 'No, we're the Chinese,' but I just kept my trap shut and nodded. 'OK,' he said, 'sorry to bother you.' And with that, he wished us luck and gave us a friendly push downstream.

Before we go any further, I want to be absolutely clear about something: it was *great* to be back on the river. Not that we hadn't had a good time in Blagoveschensk – we had. It was just nice to be on our own again, in our boats, paddling wherever the current happened to take us. That night, we camped on a secluded beach just a few kilometres downstream of the town, and watched as the dying rays of the day set fire to the sky. I was asleep before the sun slipped below the horizon.

To celebrate our first full day back on the water, I plugged into Robbie Williams, and was just losing myself in 'Life Thru a Lens' ('... wake up on Sunday morning, everything seems so boring, is that where it ends, with your life through a lens?') when Rich – paddling in front and also listening to his radio – turned around and pointed frantically behind me. Looking over my shoulder, I was surprised to see a large passenger ship bearing down on my tiny canoe at an alarming rate of knots. I hadn't heard a thing, and neither – apparently – had Rich. The only reason he'd turned around, he told me with a slightly manic grin once we were out of harm's way, was because he thought he'd heard *me* shouting at *him*. As we continued downstream in the ferry's wake, I made a mental note to myself: keep a better look out for passenger ships the size of small villages.

Significantly, this was the first Russian boat we'd seen without spotlights since leaving Sretensk almost a month before. It seemed odd that there were so few Russians using the river when there were so many Chinese barges ploughing back and forth, but the authorities were clearly so paranoid about policing the border that it probably shouldn't have surprised me that much. It did occur to me that the proximity of the Trans-Siberian railway might have had something to do with it, as it obviously made long-distance river transport redundant, but that didn't explain the absence of fishing boats on the river, or the lack of local ferries for people and provisions.

As for the rest of that day, I remember very little about it. At some point we passed a marker post that revealed we were now a mere 900km from Khabarovsk (the town at the end of the border), but for the most part I just enjoyed being back on the water, with the sun in my eyes and the wind in my hair. One thing I did notice, however, was that the river we were on now was very different from the one we'd been on a week before: it was so wide that from the middle it was often difficult to make out the banks, and the steep, forested valleys that we were accustomed to had also gone, to be replaced by a vast, open flood plain. We often couldn't see much more than water in every direction, which created a feeling of isolation that was as exhilarating as it was daunting.

We camped – after failing to find a single watchtower – on a wide, sandy island in the middle of the river. With time and light to spare, Rich got out our new petrol bomb – sorry, I mean stove – and tried to get the thing going, first by looking at the instructions, then by guesswork. Needless to say, neither approach proved very fruitful, despite a few promising fireballs. In fact, after an hour of twiddling and tinkering, the only thing that hadn't caught fire was the bit that was supposed to.

But the stove was the least of our worries: while Rich was setting fire to things, I couldn't help noticing that the river was rising, but by the time we'd actually cooked dinner (on the old stove) we were too tired to do anything about it. There was a short sand step between us and the river, and I estimated that it would have to rise at least a foot during the night to get anywhere near the tent. In fairness, it *really* didn't look like it was coming up that quickly, but just to be on the safe side, I set my alarm to go off every two hours. My diary for that the rest of that night reads as follows:

1 a.m.: Wake up a minute before the alarm goes off. Water still rising but nowhere near boats or tent. 3 a.m.: Wake up 30 seconds before alarm goes off. Water now over step. Rich suggests holding off until it reaches our boats. Too asleep to realise that if the water reaches our boats, they'll float off. 5 a.m.: Dream that water is seeping underneath the tent and that we have to evacuate the whole campsite. Wake up a few seconds later to find that water is seeping underneath the tent and that we have to evacuate the whole campsite. Our boats are bobbing gently up and down beside the tent. 10 a.m.: Wake up to find our evacuation site is also under

threat. There's nowhere else to go. Have to forego breakfast to pack up our boats in time. Seriously consider cancelling the whole trip.

In all, the river rose three feet in a little under twelve hours. To cheer ourselves up we spent the rest of the morning listing – and discussing – ex-girlfriends in chronological order. Well, that's not quite true: I listed my girlfriends; Rich listed as many as he could remember. Where pertinent, we included background information and ratings in a variety of different categories. A tenuous link in our train of thought then led on to a conversation about female border guards, and – more specifically – why we hadn't seen more of them on the river. In the animated discussion which followed, we even came up with a suitable uniform, which included fluffy fur hats, camouflaged miniskirts, and felt-lined, knee-length booties. Not that we were bored, you understand.

After calling it a day that evening, we camped on the highest shingle beach we could find, on an island about four feet higher than the river. Even then the water came to within half a foot of the tent during the night. And, as if that wasn't enough, the very next day we were shot at. Again.

14 GUNS & GUNBOATS (PART II)

The day started innocently enough. The night had been clear and starry – as starry, in fact, as any we'd seen since Mongolia – and, despite the prospect of another early-morning evacuation, we'd both slept well. We pushed off from our fast-disappearing island soon after nine, and spent the first session thinking about what it might be like to repeat our journey in winter ('cold' seemed to be the general consensus). The flooding had made a marked difference to the water's surface, which was now pockmarked with a flotsam of floating scum, logs and bottles – while this made it look depressingly dirty, it also meant the current was sweeping us downstream like a mile-wide waterslide. From the middle of the river (we'd long since given up trying to stick to the Russian side) it was often hard to tell if we were looking at the banks on either side, or just a series of islands. We were passing just such an island when I first heard the shot ring out across the river. I'd like to say that I was more prepared for it this time, but I wasn't. When the whiplike crack tore through the still morning air, my first, god-given instinct was to duck. My second instinct, based more on experience than divine intervention, was to look up, hold my breath and hope – really rather earnestly – that I'd see a bright red flare fizzing overhead in the next nine milliseconds.

The thing about flares, of course, is that they're a lot slower than bullets, so when a shooting star did finally arc across the morning sky, it didn't arrive a moment too soon. Following its trajectory, we spotted a gunboat and a handful of uniformed men on the shore of an island to our right. They were waving us over, but the current was so strong there was no way we could reach them. Even when we pointed our bows straight upstream and paddled like lunatics, we were still swept well past, much to their exasperation. We pulled into an eddy a few hundred yards downstream, but it wasn't long before the gunboat roared into view, almost ramming us into the bank in the process.

The skipper demanded that we paddle back upstream to where the other guards were waiting. 'It's not possible,' I said, with as much finality as I could muster. 'Why not?' he snapped. I rolled my eyes indignantly and swept my arm downstream to indicate the speed of the current. The penny dropped, but only after sinking through a few inches of cerebral cement first. 'In that case,' he continued, 'you must put your canoes on the deck of my boat and I will ferry you back.' This was equally ridiculous – it would have been much easier for us to just walk back along the shoreline – but I was in no mood to argue and neither, it seemed, was he. After much heaving and scraping, we finally slid both canoes across the deck of the gunboat, positioned them so that the ends were sticking out on either side, and clambered up after them.

Gingerly, the skipper eased out of the eddy and ploughed stubbornly back upstream. After all of our run-ins with gunboats over the last few weeks, it was actually quite exhilarating to be sat on the prow of one, and by the time we'd pulled up to where the rest of the guards were waiting, my mood had all but evaporated. Treading cautiously across a long wooden gangplank balanced precariously between the boat and the bank, we were greeted by a well-dressed officer with narrow features and a sharp-looking haircut. He introduced himself as Alexei, and told us that he was the commandant of the border post in Poyakovo, which was just a few kilometres downstream.

Formalities over with, he led us to an incongruous picnic table in the shade of a tree set back from the river. We were joined by another officer with heavy jowls and a moustache the size of a small badger; he produced a large, leather-bound book and opened it on the table in front of us. Each page was twice as wide as it was high, and each folded out to create a strip that was perhaps a metre long. On each strip was a beautifully presented map of a short section of river, complete with islands, watchtowers and villages, and information on depth, distance and flow. Running roughly down the middle of each section was an erratic red line that indicated the precise location of the Russia–China border. The scale was 1:25,000, which meant that the book contained about forty metre-long maps, all of them drawn by hand. It was, quite simply, a work of art.

After asking us how far we paddled each day, Alexei pointed out where he wanted us to camp for the next week. He insisted that we stay at villages from now on, and so that there was no ambiguity, he numbered each overnight stop on our own maps with a pencil, and made a note of the names and dates in a little notebook. The message was clear: camp where you're told, or suffer the consequences. The idea of being told where to camp was anathema to us, but this time it was so explicit that there didn't seem to be much we could do about it. We just had to resign ourselves to the fact that we were no longer in charge. If we couldn't beat them, I thought, we'd just have to join them.

So we did – for a slap-up picnic of tinned meat and fish, bread and honey, and sweet, milky tea. While we ate, Alexei told us to expect rain for the next few days and pointed to a section of river on our maps that was three or four days downstream. 'Here,' he began enthusiastically, 'the river narrows and flows between steep cliffs. If it continues to rise, you should be able to paddle a hundred kilometres in a single day.' I asked him if there were any rapids to speak of. 'No,' he laughed, 'it's just deep and fast. You won't even have to use your paddles!' It sounded like our kind of river.

Once business had been taken care of, Alexei gave us a handful of tiny cucumbers, a bagful of wild onions and a small clutch of eggs. Needless to say, the eggs didn't make it as far as the next village without cracking, but the cucumbers were mouth-wateringly crisp, and for the next few days the wild onions provided some much-needed bite to our otherwise bland evening meals.

Before we got up to leave, I asked Alexei if there was somewhere in Poyakovo where we could buy a few provisions. 'Of course,' he said amiably, 'let me take you there.' He walked us back to the gunboat and beckoned us on board, but I had to explain that we couldn't accept a lift – we'd paddled almost 3,000 kilometres to get this far, and I wasn't about to miss out a section in the middle, even if it was only a few kilometres. Alexei seemed to understand what I was trying to say, but he still insisted on providing us with an escort as we drifted downstream. He must have spent the time brushing up on his *bons mots*, because when we finally arrived, he was ready for us: 'Friends!' he exclaimed in English, as if he hadn't seen us for weeks. 'How are you?'

While we were shopping I asked Alexei if there was a hotel in the village. He seemed to think we'd be better off camping under a watchtower, but I managed to persuade him that we wouldn't do a runner. The good news was that there was a hotel just a few hundred yards from the river. The bad news was that the manageress was clearly aggrieved at the thought of two (admittedly malodorous) foreigners staying in her fine, upstanding establishment. As she argued with Alexei, her tremulous tones echoed along the cavernous corridors, but after much stamping of feet and shaking of fists, she finally showed us to our room, which boasted an *en suite* shower *and* a sitting room. The strange thing was, the moment Alexei had gone, she was all smiles.

We spent the afternoon wandering along the waterfront, and soon realised that there wasn't much more to Poyakovo than the street we were staying on. The waterfront itself was dominated by a vast mill, which had long since ground its last bushel of grain. From the river it had seemed sleek and impressive, but from up close it looked like little more than a relic, a stark reminder of more prosperous times. Poyakovo, I couldn't help thinking, was a village on the verge of extinction.

The next morning dawned dark and foreboding. We made our way to the town's only café for breakfast, and ordered two rounds of bangers and mash. I had visions of a meaty casserole drowned in a delicious sweet-pepper sauce, but instead found myself forcing down a single scoop of instant mash and two tepid hot dogs on a styrofoam plate.

By the time we'd emerged from the café it was absolutely pissing it down, and the thought of spending the next seven hours getting wet filled me with a due sense of exhaustion and dread. Had I known that it was going to be more like 27, I think I might well have wept into my coffee.

We rolled our boats down to the beach and de-wheeled in front of the usual crowd of onlookers, who cheerfully waved us on our way. There was a strong headwind blowing upstream and, because the river was so wide and open, it was whipping up a fair amount of chop. It wasn't rough enough to capsize our canoes, but it was more than rough enough to slow our progress, and it made it almost impossible for us to establish any kind of rhythm. All we could really do was put our heads down, set our upper lips to stiff, and bash our way through the oncoming waves.

We'd only been going for a few minutes when we heard a gunboat thumping through the swell behind us. We looked round to see Alexei standing on the front deck and pointing towards the bank. What, I wondered despondently, had we done now? We paddled obediently over to the nearest beach and clambered out of our boats. When the gunboat pulled up a few seconds later, Alexei leapt lithely from the prow and marched purposefully over. 'Gentlemen,' he began, 'you cannot leave yet.' Before I could ask why not, he stood stiffly to attention, saluted us both, and presented us with two gold pins. Each bore the legend 'Old Border' in Russian, below which was a picture of a uniformed guard carrying an AK47, and – in the background – an outline of the USSR. They were a great souvenir, and I tried to say as much, but he just shrugged and grinned. 'I'd give you my hat, too,' he laughed, 'but I'm not sure you've got enough room in your canoes!'

Once we were out in the middle of the river, the white-capped waves were so big and the river so wide that it was often difficult to see the banks; but for the wind in our faces, we wouldn't have known which way was downstream. After only a few hours, every single muscle in my body was aching; this, I reasoned, was partly due to the onset of cold weather, but mostly due to lack of use. Although on paper we'd paddled six hours a day, every day, for the last ten weeks, we hadn't done an honest day's work since our dash to the Russian border in the first ten days. In the meantime, our arm muscles had atrophied, our leg muscles had all but disappeared, and our potbellies looked like they were due any day now.

After the first session, we stopped for lunch beneath a watchtower, not out of any sense of duty, but because it was the only place which offered any shelter from the rain. We were just settling down to eat when a damp-looking soldier appeared from the woods and asked us if we'd like to go somewhere warmer. We did. For some time now, the rain had been lashing through the opening of my paddling jacket and soaking inexorably southwards. This front of moisture was already dampening the hem of my river shorts, and as any man who spends a lot of time in the outdoors will tell you, once the old walnuts get wet, you might as well strip to your birthday best and dance naked in the rain. There is nothing – but nothing – worse than a wet willy in a rainstorm.

Our guardian angel led us – quite literally – down a garden path to a sprawling complex of buildings. The whole compound was surrounded by an impressive barbed-wire fence, and to one side was a large, puddled parade ground. We slipped through a gate in the fence and continued along a narrow track hemmed in by neat little lines of cabbages, carrots and potatoes. Once inside the main building, we were shown to the office of the camp commandant, a weaselly-looking man with neatly parted hair and a small rectangular moustache. He introduced himself as Victor. 'You must be hungry,' he said warmly, 'but before you eat, let's get you out of these wet clothes.' Victor, I thought gratefully, was clearly a man who appreciated the importance of a dry scrotum. He led us to a large drying room where we hung our jackets and spray-decks alongside row after row of camouflaged clothes.

Back in his spartan office, a young recruit served us thick chunks of buttered bread, cherry jam, and sweet, milky tea served in dainty china cups. It was really rather civilised, but for all his hospitality, Victor was clearly at a loss about what to say, so after a few half-hearted questions about our journey he started showing us his small collection of archaeological artefacts. It included arrow- and spearheads, which he said dated from the seventeenth century, and coins and notes dating from the eighteenth and nineteenth centuries. He also showed us an enormous fish-hook, which he said was used to catch sturgeon.

'Fifty of these hooks are suspended in a line across the river and held down by weights,' he said, by way of explanation. I asked him why they were so big. 'Because the fish are so big!' he exclaimed. 'There are millions of sturgeon in the Amur, and some of them weigh as much as six hundred kilos.'

Once he'd exhausted this line of conversation, he moved on to the next. 'Do you have flares?' he asked excitedly. At the time, I didn't know the word for 'flare' in Russian, so I just shrugged uncertainly. 'You know, flares?' he repeated, pointing an imaginary gun at the ceiling. When I said no, he reached into a drawer and pulled out a short pistol with a big fat barrel. For a fleeting moment I thought he was going to give it to us as a present. I was just beginning to wonder how we'd explain it to HM Customs at Heathrow when he stood up, beckoned us out of his office, and led us outside. Taking a flare from his pocket, he loaded the gun and handed it to me, holding his arm up to indicate the safest trajectory. The bang, when it came, was much more deafening – and oddly more thrilling – than I'd ever have imagined, and my ears were ringing for minutes afterwards. He loaded a second round for Rich, and then fired one off himself, just for good measure.

As a parting gesture, he gave us a guided tour. In addition to the drying room, a kitchen and a handful of offices, the main building housed a 50-bed dormitory, a corridor of classrooms (complete with chemical-warfare suits) and a weights room (with barbells made from train axles). The smaller buildings, he told us, contained more dorms and classrooms. By the time we'd seen all we were allowed to see, our clothes were so dry they felt almost brittle.

Once we'd rustled them back on, Victor walked us back down to the river in the rain. As we slid into our boats, he presented us with a pair of slender wooden arrowheads and a single coin. On one side of the coin was a wreath of wheat, while on the other was the number '3', with the word 'Kopek' written in Cyrillic, and the date '1923' inscribed below it. It was dark and bowed, and had clearly passed through a few palms before reaching ours. In return, I gave him a postcard with a message of thanks on the back. He took off his hat, slid the postcard inside and popped it back on his head. 'Good luck,' he said, pumping our hands energetically, 'and I hope the weather gets better soon!'

It didn't. In fact, it got worse, and with the river still rising, it was getting harder and harder to find somewhere to camp. On many of the islands, even some of the trees and bushes were barely managing to tread water, so when we arrived at our designated campsite later that afternoon, we were relieved to find that it was well clear of the current. Behind the campsite was a long, barbed-wire fence stretching as far as the eye could see in either direction. On one side there was a narrow, no-man's land of trampled soil, while on the other was an abandoned watchtower. On closer inspection, the fence looked badly neglected, and was overrun with enormous sunflowers. On the World Service that morning we'd heard that Putin had recently announced unlimited defence spending, but it seemed to me that fixing a few fences was the least of Siberia's worries.

The following day, the wind continued to rage with a vengeance. We were supposed to paddle to Innokentovo, a village about 85km downstream, but even in perfect weather this would have taken us eight or nine hours, so we decided to allow ourselves two days to get there instead of one. This clearly contravened Alexei's strict instructions about where and when we should camp, but under the circumstances we didn't think anyone would mind. Needless to say, we were wrong.

When we made camp early that afternoon, we were approached by a young-looking officer who was as anxious as he was confused. 'Who are you?' he demanded, without any sort of preamble. I was obviously too used to being greeted by border guards at every turn, because I could hardly contain my indignation. 'Who are we?' I exclaimed, sounding more than a little pompous. 'Why, we're the Englishmen of course!'

He just looked at me blankly. 'Have you got any documents?' he asked, after careful consideration. No, we tiptoed the last 2,000km without so much as a scrap of toilet paper to our name … 'Of course,' I said eventually, realising that I was being a little unfair. 'Would you like to see them?' He nodded curtly. He pored over every single piece of paper in our possession before he was satisfied. And then, without so much as another word, he left. A short while later, a radio operator pulled up to our tent on a motorbike. 'Good day,' he said quietly. 'Do you know you're not supposed to be on the border?'

Once again we went through the rigmarole of showing our papers and visas, but he didn't seem that interested. He started asking us about our journey, and then, apropos of nothing at all, he handed me a ten-rouble note. On it he'd written, 'To the Englishmen, from Sascha.' It somehow seemed inappropriate to accept it, but he insisted. For a while he just stood there, as if waiting for something to happen, but after a while he clambered back on his bike, waved goodbye and sped off along the riverbank.

It was only when we were slipping into our sleeping bags a few hours later that we heard him pull up again outside the tent. Crouching down in front of the mosquito net he asked us if we had a light, and then, in the same breath, he added: 'Do you have any postcards of England?' I was slightly stunned, partly because it was such an odd question, but mostly because I was completely naked. Covering my modesty, I passed him a lighter and reached into my map case for a postcard. I had no idea how he knew about them. All I could think was that word had been passed from one border post to the next as we'd made our way downstream. I entertained vague notions of them becoming a source of myth and legend, traded like hard currency for antique coins, officers' hats and crisp, ten-rouble notes. When I finally gave him one, he nodded his thanks, wished us luck, and vanished in a swirl of cigarette smoke.

Mercifully, the wind had blown itself out by the following morning, but the rain continued to lash down for most of the day. The river was now racing downstream with renewed vigour, and occasionally we paddled past floating trees, logs and other bits of debris. In five hours we covered 55km, by far our fastest rate of progress so far. While we paddled, I thought back to our first few days in Mongolia, when the river had been clean and clear, and barely a boat-length wide. So much had happened since then that it seemed hard to believe we were even on the same river.

Other than that, I don't remember thinking about much more than how wet my testicles were getting. Somehow, the little bottle-holder moulded into the plastic between my legs kept filling up with water, even though I was sealed into the canoe's cockpit by a spray-deck that was tighter than a kettledrum. The lining of my shorts, meanwhile, was acting like litmus paper, soaking up the water and channelling it with alarming efficiency into the reservoir around my groin, which was kept nicely chilled by the ice-cold river water flowing just a few inches below the hull.

The campsite options at Innokentovo were limited, but we eventually found a spot that was high enough above the river to avoid being flooded, and far enough from the village to avoid being disturbed. Or so we thought. Soon after sundown, half a dozen kids of assorted shapes and sizes came down to pay us a visit. To start with they just sat on top of the bank, too shy to come any closer. Eventually, though, they sent down an emissary, who discovered – no doubt to his considerable relief – that we didn't eat little boys, and that we were, in fact, quite friendly.

Pretty soon, the entire gang was arranged in a semicircle around the front of our tent, but only when they were all sitting comfortably did they turn to the subject uppermost on their minds: namely, swear words. I tried to pretend that I didn't know what 'fuck off' meant, but when the smallest little boy yelled out, 'Kiss my penis!' in English, it was all I could do to stop myself from laughing out loud. No one, it seemed, could top this, and one by one the kids lost interest and drifted away.

It rained most of the night, and the next morning we woke to find a small cow sheltering in the porch of our tent. By the time we were ready to push off, however, the skies had cleared completely, and we were blessed with blazing sunshine for the rest of the morning. Thanks to the oil-slick stillness of the water, the hours raced by as fast as the current, and before we knew it we were approaching Kasatkino, the next small settlement marked on our maps. We stopped just upstream of the village and asked an old fisherman if there was anywhere we could buy bread. He told us we needed to continue a little further downstream.

Eventually pulling up where he'd suggested, we got out of our boats to have a look around. At the top of the bank was a substantial barbed-wire fence punctuated by a small, open doorway. There wasn't another soul in sight, so we pulled our boats up the beach, ambled through the opening and went in search of the local bakery. Not long after that, we were locked out of the village and placed under armed guard.

15 FONZIE & BLONDIE

In Siberia, trouble wears an unkempt camouflaged uniform and a vague, vodka-stewed expression. 'Who are you?' barked the border guard from inside his battered car. I told him. 'Where are your documents?' he demanded (at least, I think that was what he said – it was hard to tell, what with all the slurring). I said they were in our boats, which were down at the river.

He thought about this for a fraction less than three minutes. 'Get in the car,' he said finally, opening the passenger door from the inside. It was only a hundred yards back to the river, so I said we'd walk. 'Get in the car!' he growled. 'OK, OK,' I replied, thinking, 'no need to get your moustache in a twist.' Actually, I didn't say this out loud – I had no idea how to say the word 'twist' in Russian.

He drove us back down to the beach, followed us to our boats, and pored over our papers, his eyes swimming erratically across every page. Eventually, he shuffled off in search of his boss, ordering us not to go anywhere in the meantime. While we were waiting, we were joined by two young lads who were enjoying a quick Monday afternoon tipple down on the beach. They were intrigued by our boats and our journey, but they didn't seem to understand how far we'd come. In fact, this was consistent with what we'd found all along the border: if we told people we'd paddled from Mongolia and that we'd been on the go for ten weeks, they just nodded politely; if, on the other hand, we told them we'd come from the last big town we'd passed, they were often agog with amazement. 'But that's miles away,' they'd say incredulously. 'You must be crazy.'

The same was true for where we were going: if we said the Pacific, they just stared at us blankly; if we told them we were on our way to Khabarovsk (now just a few days' distant), they'd pat us on the back and say what fine fellows we were for even attempting such a long and arduous journey.

We were well into our second round of vodka and cucumber when the camp commandant arrived, bristling with self-importance. He had a narrow, ratlike face, and perched on his nose was the biggest pair of aviator sunglasses I had ever seen. If he'd been standing next to a jukebox wearing a white T-shirt and a leather jacket, he might have looked like the Fonz; as it was, he was standing on a beach in the middle of Siberia wearing a pressed shirt with a button-down collar, and he looked faintly ridiculous.

'I am the commander-in-chief of the border post of Kasatkino,' he said haughtily, snapping to attention, 'and you must be the English canoeists.' He was sharp, this one. 'You may camp on the bank,' he continued tersely, 'but you must not go into the village, you must not speak to anyone, and you must not let anyone speak to you. Do I make myself clear?'

To start with I thought he was joking, but he soon showed us that he meant business by ordering our new-found friends off the beach. Judging by their boyish grins, they must have thought the whole thing was hilarious, and as they got up to leave they flashed us a look that said 'we'll be back'. The Fonz, though, clearly wasn't as dim as he looked. 'And don't even think about coming back,' he snapped testily. 'There will be guards patrolling this beach all night.'

To my surprise he went on to round up everyone else on the beach, including a family who were picnicking down by the water's edge. Once the beach had been cleared, all the gates in the fence were bolted, effectively locking *us* out of the village, and everyone else in. I was amazed – I just couldn't believe we posed that much of a threat.

The only place flat enough for our tent was at the top of the steep bank directly opposite the barbed-wire fence. Between the tent and the fence was a strip of no-man's land protected by a tripwire, and just a few yards beyond the fence were the neat wooden houses of the village itself. While we were unloading our boats, Fonzie came down to check up on us one last time. 'I'll be watching you,' he said slyly, 'so don't go anywhere.' And with that he gave a final salute, darted through a nearby gate in the fence, and locked it demonstratively behind him.

In due course, two armed guards appeared, pacing back and forth along the length of the fence. Every so often, people would approach the barbed wire, only to be moved on by the guards. Occasionally, though, someone would appear when the guards were out of sight, at the far end of their patrol. The first to take advantage of this loophole in security was a man on a motorbike, who asked us if we needed any milk, meat or potatoes. I said thank you, but assured him we were OK. 'Not even milk?' he asked, as if we couldn't possibly survive the night without it. 'If it's not too much trouble,' I replied uncertainly. 'No trouble at all,' he beamed, and with that he reached into his knapsack, pulled out an enormous jar of milk, and slid it between the barbed wire at the base of the nearby gate. I ran over to retrieve it, nodded my thanks, and scurried back to the tent, just in time to see the guards reappear around a bend in the fence a few dozen yards downstream.

We were also visited by a group of young lads who wanted to know where we were from and what we were doing on the river. To start with, the guards ignored them, but when they realised that we were talking to them, they became quite agitated and waved them on with the muzzles of their guns. The self-appointed spokesman for the boys – the one who'd asked all of the questions – protested, arguing that he was only trying to practise his English, but the guards were unmoved. For my part, I wanted to be able to voice my frustration, to tell the guards how petty and narrow-minded they were being, but my Russian wasn't up to it. Instead I just shook my head and said, 'What a shame,' as meaningfully as I could – not surprisingly, the guards didn't bat an eyelid.

And so we were left once more to our own devices. We ate pilchards and noodles, we drank chilled milk straight from the jar, and we waited for the sun to set on the wooden cottages and sunflower gardens that glowed warm and welcoming behind their bleak, barbed-wire barricade.

The guards continued to wander back and forth past the front of our tent all night. The next morning, we asked one of them if we could buy some bread and butter before we left. Reluctantly, he agreed to unlock the gate. And then – presumably addled by lack of sleep – he made a vital error: he let us wander freely around the village. While Rich roamed the streets sowing the seeds of capitalism, I went in search of the smallest little boy I could find and ate him for breakfast.

The first shop we came to was owned by a middle-aged, middle-weight shot-putter who was as hostile as she was unhelpful – I was surprised news of my child-eating had travelled so fast. 'Do you have any bread?' I asked politely. 'Nyet!' she snapped. 'How about butter?' I continued, undeterred. 'Nyet,' she repeated. 'I see,' I said with a smile that could have melted all the margarine in Kasatkino, 'and do you know where else we might be able to buy these items?' 'Nyet,' she replied without a moment's hesitation. 'Well, thanks anyway,' I chirped, 'you've really been most kind.' And may your beard grow to be as splendid and bushy as mine …

The next shop was much more welcoming, and before long we were back at our boats, stocked up and ready to go. Before pushing off, however, we slid the now empty milk jar back through the barbed wire, opposite where our tent had been, and placed a signed postcard underneath, by way of a final farewell to sunny Kasatkino, and the not-so-happy days of our very own Arthur Fonzarelli.

When we finally got under way, we spent most of the first session discussing the events of the last 24 hours, and trying to decide who was to blame. Rich seemed to be quite sympathetic to Fonzie's cause, arguing that he'd only been following orders, but I wasn't so sure. It wasn't so much the orders that had annoyed me, as the way they'd been carried out. I couldn't help but feel that out here in the back of beyond, a modicum of discretion wouldn't have gone amiss. The thing that saddened me most was that we'd been forbidden from talking to any of the children – what possible harm, I wondered, could have come from telling them about our journey?

During our second session, however, something happened that once again restored my faith in human nature. Rich and I were paddling a short distance apart when I heard the now familiar throb of an outboard motor behind us. Looking round, I saw a sizeable barge bearing down on Rich at alarming speed. Rich realised what was happening and moved left to avoid being run down, but to my surprise (and his, for that matter) the boat followed suit and continued straight towards him.

From where I was sitting, it looked like it was going to hit him, but just when I thought I might inherit Rich's radio after all, it slid to his right. Moments later, unidentified objects began arcing out from the deck towards Rich's boat. Oh great, I thought: not content with scaring him witless, they're now going to finish him off with depth charges. But the explosions never came, and now that they were closer, I could see that the Chinese crew didn't look in the least bit hostile; in fact, they looked giddy with excitement. It was only after they'd sped past that I realised what they'd been throwing at us: bobbing up and down in the water around Rich's boat were packets of instant noodles, and a lapful of big, juicy tomatoes. 'They almost heaved a watermelon at me,' he said matter-of-factly, 'but I waved them off because I was worried it might land on my head.'

After a week of paddling through the vast, open flood plains to the east of Blagoveschensk, we finished the day heading for the hills above Pashkovo, and the gateway to the 'Canyon of Doom', the name we'd given to the long corridor of fast water that Alexei had told us about back in Poyakovo.

In contrast to the steep banks and barbed wire of Kasatkino, Pashkovo boasted an inviting waterfront with a gently sloping shoreline and an impressive backdrop of emerald-green hills. As we slid our boats up the grassy verge near the village, we were greeted by a British holiday-maker. Actually, that's not strictly true – he just looked like one. He was wearing garish shorts, a white T-shirt and flip-flops, and his beaming face was the colour of pink grapefruit.

'I'm the border-post commander in Pashkovo,' he said carelessly, 'but you can call me Yevgeni.' When he asked to see our passports, I thought we were in for the usual grilling, but instead he just wrote down our visa numbers in a little notebook and handed them back.

While he was writing, a moustachioed man in a sky-blue tracksuit staggered over and held out a big, beefy hand. '*Kak maladyetz!*' he exclaimed, shaking our hands vigorously: 'What fine fellows!' Yevgeni just laughed. 'This is Andrei,' he said, introducing him, before adding in a whisper: 'He's a good friend of mine, but he's had too much to drink.'

As if to prove it, Andrei promptly challenged Rich to an arm wrestle. Rich suspected, as I did, that Andrei was something of a local legend when it came to arm wrestling, and prepared to be duly drubbed, but after just thirty seconds of half-hearted flexing and straining, Andrei's arm trembled momentarily, and then collapsed. I wasn't sure if this was altogether diplomatic of Rich, but Yevgeni thought it was hilarious, and even Andrei took it on the chin. '*Kak maladyetz!*' he repeated good-naturedly, before shaking our hands again and stumbling back the way he'd come.

Once he'd taken care of business, Yevgeni invited me up to his house on the edge of the village while Rich set up camp. Inside, in the living room, sat the most beautiful girl I had ever seen. She was perhaps 21 or 22, with tumbling blonde hair and the sort of deep blue eyes you could happily drown in. Yevgeni motioned me to sit down, invited me to help myself to anything that I liked the look of, and then promptly left the room.

The girl smiled coyly. I smiled back nervously. Despite myself, I couldn't help thinking about a story I'd once read in *Danziger's Travels* (the very same *Danziger's Travels*, in fact, that had featured a bulging Churchill Trust envelope). Invited to stay the night in someone's home, the author was asked by his host what he thought of the exotic Iranian beauty who'd joined them for dinner. He blushed politely and forgot all about it. Later that night, however, while he was lying back and dreaming of England, she slipped into his bed and initiated a night of intimate cross-cultural relations.

Suffice it to say that I wasn't quite sure how to handle the same situation in broad daylight, but just as I was starting to think that I should do more than just sit there, Yevgeni burst back into the room carrying what looked like a huge animal carcass. 'A souvenir!' he announced with a grin, before rolling a vast, bearskin rug onto the floor with a triumphant flourish. I didn't know whether to feel relieved or robbed.

Once I'd got over my initial disappointment at Yevgeni's untimely interruption, I considered his offer more carefully. For a fleeting moment I thought that a bearskin rug might make a nice addition to the bottom of our tent, but decided – on balance – that we didn't really have room for twenty square feet of fur. When I tried to explain this, Yevgeni was nothing if not understanding.

'Of course,' he nodded, 'perhaps you would like something smaller?' Before I could answer he reached across to a shelf and pulled out a book that couldn't have been much bigger than the complete works of Shakespeare … in Braille. It was a hardback copy of Tolstoy's *Peter I*, which was, he told us, his favourite book. Inside he wrote: 'Richard and Paul: to remember for a long time the friendship between us.' As he passed it to me, he said the word 'present' in English, with the stress on the second syllable. I thanked him earnestly, cradling the hefty tome in my arms and made a mental note to dig out a Churchill Medallion when we got back to the boats.

There were more surprises as he led me back outside. On a windowsill in the porch was a half-finished painting of a buxom brunette riding a grizzly bear across a starry sky. The figure and some of the sky were painted in, but the bear was only outlined in pencil. It was really rather accomplished, and I gave Yevgeni an exaggerated nod to say as much. 'I taught myself,' he said proudly. 'I write stories, too,' he added, passing me a clutch of A4 sheets. 'It's a fantasy,' he explained, 'to go with the painting.' It was all meticulously handwritten in elegant, flowing Cyrillic. Yevgeni, it seemed, was a man of many talents.

Before we left, he insisted on a quick shot of vodka. By now, I was getting used to mid-afternoon drinking, but I was no match for Yevgeni, who downed his generously filled tumbler without so much as a wince.

On the way back to the beach, he pointed out a figure lying curled up beneath a tree. 'Good for nothing,' he said in English, before launching into a long and rambling diatribe in Russian. From what I could make out, the objects of his scorn were Asians. 'And by Asians,' he said, stabbing his chest proudly, 'I mean people who aren't European like you or me. They come here without any money, they don't do any work, and then they drink themselves silly in the sun.'

Soon after that, he lost me completely, and I couldn't do much more than nod or shake my head in time with his own nodding and shaking. Yevgeni's rant, I suspected, belied a deeper fear that was shared by many of the Siberians we'd met, not that the Chinese worked too little, but that they worked too much: with up to a million migrants already living on the Russian side of the river (many of them illegally), it seemed that it was only a matter of time before they began to hijack Siberia's entire economy.

The moment we arrived at the water's edge, he asked to see our maps, and repeated everything he'd said about half an hour before. The more he talked, the more rambling and incoherent he became, until eventually I couldn't understand a word he was saying. He was, I realised with surprise, completely stocious. Up until now, he'd hidden it quite well, but the quick snifter back at his house had clearly been one too many. I decided that he probably needed to get out of the sun, so I presented him with his Medallion and indicated that we needed to rest. 'OK,' he agreed, giving a lolling nod, 'but if you need anything, you know where I live.' And with that, he shuffled slowly home, where he no doubt slid straight into the warm, welcoming arms of oblivion.

Later that evening we went for a walk along the waterfront, just to have a look around. At the far end, just a few hundred yards from our campsite, was a mechanical digger attacking a vast mound of coal on the beach and dumping it into the back of a waiting truck. The digger operator was the only one who seemed to be doing any work – in the cab of the truck, two young men were necking vodka and entertaining a couple of beaming blondes. At one point, the man in the digger forgot to lower his shovel and brought down an overhead electricity cable, but he didn't seem to notice, and the men in the truck just carried on drinking.

We were just about to turn around and head back to our campsite when the door of the truck opened and one of the men staggered up the bank towards us; it was only when he got closer that I realised it was Yevgeni. 'These guys get paid ten dollars for four days' work,' he said, shaking his head, 'and all they do is sit around and get drunk.' This seemed a little harsh, given that he'd just been bouncing one of the girls up and down on his knee, but I didn't say as much.

'Would you like to go for a beer?' he asked. 'Where?' I replied, still harbouring hopes of an illicit liaison. 'In the bar of course,' he answered with a shrug. 'There's a bar in Pashkovo?' I asked, a little incredulous. 'There's always a bar if you know where to look,' he laughed knowingly.

The bar – if it could be called that – was very quiet, and doubled as a late-night shop and cigarette dispensary. On the left, as we walked in, was a counter, and on the right was a row of dimly lit tables. Yevgeni bought the first round and toasted our health and our journey. We told him about our lives back home, and in return he told us about his ten years of military service in Afghanistan, Chechnya, and now Siberia. I asked him if he'd served in these places during wartime, but all he would say was that he'd seen things he never wanted to see again.

Whatever these things were, they'd clearly taken their toll: he told us he was 31, but he didn't look a day younger than 40. He had a seven-year-old daughter in Birobidzhan, he said, a hundred kilometres to the north, but he was separated from his wife, so he didn't get to see her that often. He was fed up with his job, with the border, and with the Chinese, and was hoping to retire in a year, to write fantasy books. In the meantime, I couldn't help thinking, he was finding his fantasies at the bottom of a bottle.

After just a couple of beers, Yevgeni looked liked he was on his way out again, so we walked him home. Before we left, he shook us both firmly by the hand. 'Paul, Richard!' he said fondly, 'if I don't see you in the morning, good luck with the rest of your journey, and the rest of your lives.'

At dawn the next day, we pushed off into a dense pall of fog and headed into the Canyon of Doom. Visibility was down to just a few dozen yards, which only helped to heighten our sense of anticipation. Gradually, though, the fog dissolved to reveal an impressive, steep-sided valley that was just a few hundred yards across. Its slopes were shrouded in swathes of impenetrable forest, broken only by the occasional outcrop of rock. All day the scenery was like this, as we doglegged gently from one section of canyon to the next, swept along by a current that was every bit as fast as we'd hoped it would be. The landscape made a welcome change from the monotony of the last few weeks, while the speed of the water provided the perfect opportunity for a spot of loafing. Our so-called Canyon of Doom, it seemed, wasn't that scary after all.

Well, at least not compared to the sound of AK47s being cocked outside our tent later that night.

16 THE CANYON OF DOOM

Perhaps I should explain: that day, we'd ended up paddling over 80km (easily our best stint of the trip so far) before pulling up at the tiny village of Pompeyevka. In fact, it was so tiny we couldn't see it; all we *could* see was dense forest in every direction. We couldn't even see a watchtower, but we'd been told by Yevgeni that there was a border post nearby, so we just set up camp and waited for the cavalry to arrive. No one came. We went for a swim and cooked some supper. Still no one came. Eventually, just as it was getting dark, we gave up waiting and dropped off to sleep, which was more or less when we were surrounded at gunpoint.

For those who've never had the pleasure, the sound of half a dozen semiautomatic weapons being cocked outside a tent while you're inside is very loud indeed. One of the guards barked something in Russian. I miaowed something back in English (it might have been 'Mummy', but I couldn't be sure). In the silence that followed, I decided that the safest thing to do was to show my face, so I unzipped the tent and stepped out into the darkness. It was hard to know which was more distressing, the armed guards or the mosquitoes, but my money was on the mosquitoes: by the time I'd stood upright, I'd already been bitten a dozen times, while I hadn't been shot at once.

'Good evening,' a shadowy figure said stiffly in Russian. 'Are you the English canoeists?'

I found it hard to believe that six armed guards had been deployed around our tent just on the off chance that we might be Belgian canoeists, but I bit my tongue. 'Yes,' I said, as calmly as I could. Apparently satisfied, he went on to say that he'd been expecting us a few hundred metres downstream, but that if we'd like to stay where we were (we did) he'd be happy to post a couple of guards near our tent to keep an eye out for bears. I told him it wasn't necessary, but he insisted. And with that, he swatted a mosquito on the back of his neck, wished us luck, and left us to it.

My diary for the rest of that night reads as follows:

12pm – still recovering from a combination of post-traumatic stress and massive blood-loss. Nursing mosquito bites by torchlight, am alarmed to discover curious rash on chest. Consulting health guide, learn that skin is cultivating some sort of festering fungus. Alas, don't have any festering fungus cream to hand, so instead make do with a combination of Mycil foot powder [see Chapter 3 for details of Mycil's miraculous, cure-all properties] and fusidic acid; to be honest, I have no idea what fusidic acid is, but Rich assures me it once worked wonders for him on some sores he picked up in the Congo ...

After a fitful night's sleep, we woke to find that the river was once again shrouded in mist. The air was also miraculously still, which meant we could make out every gurgle and ripple coming from the water's surface.

While we were making breakfast, these gurgles and ripples were interrupted by an unnerving, mechanical clanking coming from somewhere downstream. As we listened, the clanking got louder, and was soon joined by a deeper, more natural-sounding thud. Peering uncertainly into the gloom, we eventually saw a rowing boat emerge from the mist. A man was standing tall on the prow, looking for all the world like an errant knight, while a second figure, hunched in the body of the boat, was heaving on a giant oar. Despite this quixotic image, however, it soon became clear that the chap at the stern was having enormous difficulty just keeping the boat in a straight line, much to the frustration of the fellow at the bow.

When at last they got close, the man at the prow stepped deftly onto the bank and marched over to where we were standing. As he approached he held out his hand and flashed us an embarrassed grin, as if to apologise for the erratic performance of his hapless oarsman. It was only when he spoke that I realised he was the guard who'd been in charge of our little ambush the night before.

'Do you like fish?' he asked, as if it was the most natural question in the world at eight in the morning. I told him we did. He nodded, clicked his fingers, and waved to his companion, who duly arrived carrying four fine-looking fish. 'We caught them this morning,' he said, handing one to me. It was about a foot long, with a pale, slender body. Its scales were very slippery, and it was still bleeding at the gills.

'Do they taste good?' I asked. 'They're great with salt,' he replied, returning my smile. I tried to give them both a postcard, to say thanks, but they just shook their heads as if to say that wasn't necessary, before wishing us luck and wandering back to their boat.

When we pushed off half an hour later, we were immediately swept towards the thick bank of fog near the middle of the river. We were still in the Canyon of Doom, but because visibility was down to just a few metres, we could hardly see each other, let alone the canyon sides. When the fog finally lifted an hour or so later, we were surprised to find ourselves within spitting distance of the Chinese bank. Like the Russian bank, it was steep and forested, but as we paddled, we began to notice occasional signs of life in the form of tiny, riverside shrines. Typically, these shrines were signified by three Chinese characters, each about a foot high and made out of wood. The characters were invariably bright red, which made them easy to spot in amongst the trees. The shrines themselves usually featured some sort of miniature pagoda, and one of them even boasted a short flight of steps leading up from the river. As they became more frequent, I began to wonder what they meant and if they each said something different: 'Big Waterfall Ahead – Stop Soon'; 'Only 100 Metres to Go – Last Chance to Stop'; 'Big Waterfall Here – Why Didn't You Stop?'

Thankfully, there were no waterfalls, but that's not to say the rest of the day was without interest. Later that morning, we heard a bear crashing about in the woods on the Russian side of the river. Given that we hadn't seen anything much bigger than a rat in the last 3,000km, we were quite keen to catch a glimpse of it, so we paddled over and peered into the shadows.

As we got closer, the noise got louder, but still we couldn't see anything. Finally, after we'd drifted as close as we dared, the noise stopped abruptly and a voice hissed, 'Go away!' in Russian. Needless to say, I froze. 'Go away!' the voice repeated, this time sounding quite miffed. The cacophony coming from the trees, it seemed, hadn't been produced by a bear at all, but by the stealthy footfalls of a top-secret border patrol. Sure enough, when I looked around to see who or what they were tracking, I noticed a small fishing boat in the middle of the river. A short while later, a shot rang out and a flare arced across the water, sending the fishing boat scuttling back to the Chinese bank.

It was a much longer day than expected, but we managed a stately 12kph, despite some serious slacking in the second session. Our destination that afternoon was a village called Yekaterina, which was heralded by a squat little watchtower perched on a steep bank high above the river. The commander of the local border post was waiting for us when we arrived. He suggested that we camp near the watchtower, away from the village, which meant lugging all of our gear up thirty-odd feet of steep, unstable sand. We soon realised our canoes were too heavy to haul up fully loaded, so we emptied them onto the narrow beach below the bank and carried everything up, bit by bit. All told, we had to slide up and down the shifting slope four or five times, and – given that this was the first proper exercise we'd had in months – the sweat was soon streaming off us in salty rivulets, spattering the sand as we stumbled clumsily back and forth.

On the plus side, being so high gave us a better view than we were used to, and once we'd been for a swim in the river to cool off we took stock of our surroundings. To our right (as we faced the river) was the watchtower, while to our left, on the far side of a small gully, was the village proper. Once again, it was completely fenced off, but that didn't stop people waving and smiling at us as they passed by. On the far side of the river, meanwhile, directly opposite the village, was a watchtower so tall and impressive that it made ours look like a treehouse. It resembled an air-traffic control tower, with long antennae sprouting from the roof and vast windows staring back at us across the water. It was the first watchtower we'd seen on the Chinese side, and it made me realise just how cold and uncomfortable the rickety wooden huts on the Russian side must be in the depths of a harsh Siberian winter (or any Siberian winter, come to that).

We positioned our tent so that it was overlooking the river and settled down to cook some dinner. Rich gutted the largest of the four fish we'd been given that morning, popped it in a pot, and boiled it up with some noodles. Now, I'd love to be able to say that the resulting concoction was delicious, but I can't: all I can say is that it tasted vaguely fishy, although I suspect this had more to do with the salt Rich added at the last minute than any subtle flavour afforded by the fish itself.

After we'd eaten, we were joined by a young border guard with a broad smile and a long, sloping forehead. His name, he told us, was Yevgeni. He was 21 years old, and was nearing the end of his two-year posting in Yekaterina. After that, he said, he wanted to return home to Svobodny (a small town just to the north of Blagoveschensk) to become a mechanic.

He asked us about life back in England, and more specifically about the cost of everyday items like bread and beer. When I told him, he whistled softly. 'How about a whore?' he asked with a grin. Naturally, I had no idea what the going rate for a prostitute was, but I guessed about 2,500 roubles (£50). Yevgeni just laughed. 'All you need in Siberia,' he said, 'is a spare half-hour and a cheap bottle of vodka!'

While we talked, half a dozen Chinese barges chugged upstream, some of them passing within a stone's throw of our campsite (Yekaterina was on the inside of a bend, so I assumed they were straying into Russian waters to avoid the stronger current on the far side). Yevgeni didn't seem to take much notice of them, but just as it was beginning to get dark, he reached into his satchel and pulled out a flare gun. 'Would you like to take a photo?' he asked mischievously. More often than not we were forbidden to take photographs along the border, so I was more than happy to take him up on his invitation. He waited until a long barge laden with logs slid past, directly opposite the tent, before launching a bright red flare across its bow. Almost immediately, the barge began to change course, and it was soon out in the middle of the river, obviously straining against the faster flow. I'd had no idea that a flare would have such a dramatic effect, and while the smoke billowing from the gun had certainly made for an impressive photo, I couldn't help but feel slightly guilty about the trouble it had caused the unsuspecting Chinese skipper.

Later that night – at about 1 a.m. – Yevgeni returned to give us a photo of himself posing in his barracks with a table-tennis bat. On the back he'd written: 'Paul & Richard, from the Russian soldier.' Rich was understandably annoyed at him for waking us up, but not nearly as annoyed as he was the next morning when he discovered that a tin of condensed milk had been stolen from outside our tent. I felt sure it was nothing to do with Yevgeni (he'd already refused repeated offers of chocolate the night before), and I didn't really care about the missing milk, but I couldn't help but feel aggrieved that one of his colleagues had taken advantage of us. It was the first thing we'd had stolen on the entire trip, but, as we were about to find out, it wasn't to be the last.

The paddle to Amurzet, our next overnight stop, was short but punishing: it was easily the hottest day of our journey so far, with temperatures on the mind-melting side of 35, and by the time we'd reached the upstream end of town, we were exhausted. Yevgeni had told us there was a hotel near the river, and all day we'd been looking forward to a cold shower and an afternoon kip. As usual, we had no way of knowing where to beach our boats, so we just pulled up at the first watchtower we came to, confident that one of the border guards would be able to point us in the right direction. Given our experience in Kasatkino, however, we should have known better. Dispensing with the usual formalities, the two guards at the tower ordered us to stay where we were until an officer arrived. I asked how long he would be and they just shrugged. I also asked if we could wander a short way along the beach to find some shade, but they simply shook their heads in unison.

So we settled down to wait, hoping we wouldn't have to endure the hellish heat of the afternoon for too much longer; out on the river, the water had helped to moderate the temperature, but here on the beach we felt like we were being baked from the ground up. In the end, we had to wait three gruelling hours. By the time the Big Cheese finally arrived, I was fuming, but he was too busy trying to ignore us to notice. Even when he led us back along the beach to the hotel, he made a point of walking ten yards in front of us at all times, presumably so he wouldn't have to talk to us.

Still, he seemed happy enough for us to leave our boats below the watchtower so we wouldn't have to haul them around town, and he did eventually show us to the door of the hotel. Inside, it was surprisingly dark and dingy, and despite the hot weather, the manageress wore a long, velvet dressing gown. She spent three days filling out a series of forms in triplicate, before showing us to a simple room with two narrow beds and a small sink. To our immense disappointment, there was no shower, but the room was mercifully cool, and the sheets on the beds were clean and crisp.

After a much-needed nap, we went in search of somewhere to eat, and soon stumbled upon a canteen just around the corner from the hotel. We walked in to find ourselves in the middle of a private party, but we were soon shepherded to a back room and lavished with bowl after bowl of borsch, and peppers stuffed with garlic and lamb.

Thus replete, we went for a walk around the town. The whole place was laid out in a grid, and – unlike most of the villages we'd visited in the last few months – it boasted wide, open spaces and leafy, tree-lined boulevards. There was no promenade to speak of, but at the town's centre, not far from the hotel, was an impressive whitewashed square, presided over by a statue of Lenin. The most noticeable thing about the whole town, however, was that it was almost completely devoid of *people*. To start with, we thought this might have had something to do with the oppressive heat, but even when we ventured back to the *stalovaya* for seconds later that evening, we hardly saw a soul –

it was as if everyone in Amurzet had gone into hiding. Well, almost everyone: that night, while we were sleeping, there was at least one person down at the beach, busy rifling through our belongings.

When we wandered back down to the river the following morning, we found our boats exactly as we'd left them, upside down underneath the watchtower, with their holds tightly sealed. It was only when Rich opened one of his hold's hatches to get his buoyancy aid out that he realised his sunglasses and his compact camera were missing (luckily, he'd taken his SLR camera and most of his other valuables with him to the hotel). Whoever was responsible had obviously taken great care to leave everything exactly as they'd found it, in the hope that we wouldn't notice anything was amiss until it was too late. More disturbingly, the fact that the watchtower was completely fenced off from the rest of the town meant the culprit was almost certainly one of the border guards.

The guard manning the watchtower looked like a teenage version of Elmer Fudd. When I told him that some of our stuff had gone missing, he didn't seem in the least bit concerned. It was only when I pressed the issue that he finally deigned to call his boss on a battered old field telephone, but the line from the tower to the nearby border post was at best temperamental, and at worst completely useless. Even when he did finally get through to someone, he seemed singularly incapable of relating what they'd said. 'Is your boss coming?' I asked. Elmer shrugged. 'When is he coming?' I said, trying a different tack. Another shrug. 'How long will he be?' I persisted, ignoring the fact that he hadn't answered my first two questions. 'I don't know,' he said at last.

Rich was all for going straight to the police station in town, but I wasn't sure how they'd react to the news that their brothers-in-arms were on the fiddle, so we decided to wait for someone to appear. It was another blisteringly sunny day, and the beach was too hot to sit on, so instead I sat in the cockpit of my boat. As I did so, I noticed a strong smell of petrol coming from the hold at the front. When I opened it up, I discovered that the rubber O-ring of my fuel bottle had burst, soaking everything in petrol: most of my cassettes had melted, and my fleece body warmer, my mosquito net and my cotton pillowcase were all completely saturated. All I could do was lay everything out on the deck of my boat to dry and hope that it wouldn't ignite in the heat.

In the end, we waited almost two hours for the commandant to arrive, by which time I was starting to lose patience. 'What are you going to do about our stuff?' I asked, getting straight to the point. 'There is nothing I can do,' he replied, shrugging meekly.

'What about the guards who were manning the watchtower last night?' I said, trying to contain my frustration. 'They must have seen something?' Reluctantly, he picked up the phone and tried to patch another call through to the border post. '*Alyo? Alyo?*' he squeaked into the handset. 'Is there anybody there?' Suddenly, Putin's policy of unlimited defence spending seemed to make perfect sense: if the Chinese invaded now, I realised, the border guards in Amurzet would still be saying '*Alyo? Alyo?*' into their antique phones by the time the first shipment of fake Levis rolled into Moscow.

To our considerable surprise, both the camera and the sunglasses eventually appeared, accompanied by a dishevelled-looking contingent of decidedly guilty-looking guards. Given how ineffectual the Big Cheese had been up till now, the way he dealt with the culprits was equally surprising: lining them up against the fence behind the watchtower, he admonished them one by one, raising his voice and shaking his head angrily. It might have all been for show, but he looked genuinely disappointed. He also talked to us properly for the first time, apologising for what had happened and explaining that there was good and bad in every camp. He even asked us about our journey, wondering if we were scientists studying the river, or just tourists enjoying it. I explained that we were tourists, but that I worked as a travel writer back in the UK. This prompted a wry smile. 'Make sure this isn't all you write about Amurzet,' he pleaded sheepishly.

We didn't actually get back on the water until 4 p.m., but with the help of some diligent singing, we made good time, arriving at Nagibovo (our next designated campsite) shortly after six o'clock. The village itself was set some way back from the river, so we pulled up at the first watchtower we came to and awaited further instructions.

No sooner had we dragged our boats out of the water, however, than we were greeted by a well-groomed border guard with a sharp flat-top and a big, gleaming motorbike. He spoke clearly and concisely, telling us where we could camp and how we could get hold of him if we had any problems. Then, having checked our itinerary for the next few days, he wished us luck, said goodbye, and sped off on his bike.

Only much later, when it was getting dark, did we realise that once again we'd been locked out of the village: hearing some shouting behind our campsite, we wandered along a narrow track to investigate. After a hundred yards or so we came to a barbed-wire fence, and, a little further on, a padlocked gate. Pressed up against this gate were three teenage girls, all yelling up at the guards in the watchtower to let them in. As we approached, the guard in the watchtower switched his attentions to us: 'Stop!' he shouted. 'You mustn't go any further.'

I was incredulous – there were at least twenty yards between us and the girls, plus the small matter of an impregnable barbed-wire barrier to contend with if we decided to try anything rash. 'Can't we even speak to them?' I yelled back. 'OK,' he replied, 'but only from there.' As first dates go, I thought, this was going to be tricky.

Too tricky, as it turned out: once we'd learned their names (Anna, Irina and Alena), their ages (16, 16 and 19) and their thoughts on life in Nagibovo (dull, dull and dull), the conversation soon spluttered and died, crash-landing somewhere in the wasteland between us and the barbed wire.

The guards woke us early the next morning by standing outside our tent and peering inside. By the time Tom Cruise had reappeared on his bike to see us off, we'd had enough of barbed wire and border guards, and we couldn't wait to get back on the river, which was now the only place we seemed to have any sort of freedom from overzealous officials.

The water was wrapped in a cloak of mist that took most of the morning to burn off. When it did, the river looked wider than ever, its banks barely visible. To the east, we could just make out a range of hills; according to our maps, they were over 3,000ft high, but from where we were, they hardly blotted the horizon. The only landmarks we could see were the dozens of islands which clogged up the river's main artery, and through which it was becoming increasingly difficult to navigate.

I can't have slept well, because I felt tired all day, and once or twice I even fell asleep in my boat. The next day I felt much the same, so in order to inject some much-needed excitement into proceedings, we spent the first session playing around with an inflatable rubber ring which we'd bought back in Heihe. We even filmed a short piece to camera of us both paddling the rubber ring downstream, which we affectionately referred to as our 'Rubber Ring Piece'.

Our next port of call was a small town called Leninskoye, which – coincidentally enough – boasted a small port. The latter was basically a dry dock piled high with crates and logs, and I was surprised to see that one of the barges was Chinese. We paddled downstream past the barge and pulled into a small, man-made harbour. Thankfully, the lads in the watchtower overlooking the dock knew exactly who we were, and the two customs officers who were in charge of the Chinese barge soon wandered over to say hello. When we told them we needed to buy some petrol for our stove, it was Volodya, one of the customs men, who ordered a passing dockhand to drive us to the nearest petrol station. The dockhand was built like Popeye, and had tattoos on both biceps. On the way to the petrol station, he didn't utter a single word. Once he'd filled our two tiny bottles, he tipped himself seven or eight litres before driving us sullenly back to the dock.

It was gone nine by the time we'd made camp on a narrow grass verge just below the watchtower. After we'd eaten, Rich decided to go for a quick skinny-dip, and was just tiptoeing back up to the tent in his birthday best when a gunboat roared into the cove he'd been swimming in and practically parked itself between his puckered cheeks. I'm not sure who was more surprised, Rich or the gunboat crew.

The next morning, there was a stiff breeze blowing from downstream and the water was surprisingly choppy. It looked like it was going to rain, but instead the weather just got hotter and hotter. As we paddled, I lost myself in the wind, the waves and the blissfully sunny weather, and before I knew it, I'd paddled for over six hours without having a single, memorable thought. This, I thought enviously, must be what dogs feel like every day of their carefree little lives.

We camped on an island opposite a big, industrial-looking town called Ch'in-te-li. While we were cooking supper, we were visited by some Chinese fishermen, who we'd seen pass by in a small speedboat a short while before. It was difficult to know what they wanted, but judging from the appreciative taps they were giving our boats, I guessed they'd just come over out of curiosity. In return, we showed them our letter of permission from the Chinese embassy, by way of explaining who we were and what we were doing there. At the time, we didn't think much more about it, little realising that we were in fact camped on a Chinese island, and that the words 'forbidden to land on Chinese territory' might raise a few eyebrows among our new-found friends.

The next morning, just as we were pushing off, we were approached by two more fishermen. At first, we assumed that they too had come over just to say hello, but when they got close one of the them put his hands to his eyes like binoculars, and pointed to the impressive concrete watchtower at the upstream end of Ch'in-te-li. Satisfied that we'd understood what he meant, he continued his mimed monologue by pointing repeatedly to our campsite and then his chest, as if to say 'this island belongs to us'. Finally, he pointed to his boat, indicating that we should put our canoes inside so that he could ferry us back to Russian waters. Not surprisingly, having come this far under our own steam, we were loathe to accept a lift, so we nodded our thanks, scooted off in the direction of the Russian bank, and hoped he wouldn't follow. To our immense relief, he didn't.

After five weeks on the border, this was our first run-in with the Chinese authorities, and it left us feeling liked errant schoolboys. For some reason, we'd always just assumed that the Russians were calling the shots, little realising that the Chinese had been keeping a beady eye on us all along, just waiting for us to slip up.

I had visions of getting to the end of the border and meeting our first Chinese gunship. I imagined an officer reaching inside our boats and pulling out two small tracking devices. 'Thank you, gentlemen,' he would say, 'you won't be needing these any more. Now,' he'd continue, 'as you may know, the fine for unauthorised violation of our border is $100. By my calculations, you have now committed 133 such violations. Please pay me $13,386, or I will make chop suey out of both of you. Cash will be fine. Oh, and in case you were wondering, the extra $86 is for handling, and of course bullets, should they be deemed necessary.'

At our campsite that night, however, chop suey was the least of our worries. While we were sleeping, our tent was overrun with earwigs, and our makeshift mosquito net was no match for their determined onslaught. When they weren't scuttling noisily along the groundsheet, they were scaling the sloping walls at the side of the tent. The inevitable result was that the scritchy-scratchy buggers would get about halfway up, lose their grip, and drop onto whatever happened to be directly below (i.e. chest, shoulder or face, depending on how high they'd climbed before falling).

When one eventually fell into my open mouth, I snapped (shortly after the unfortunate earwig, as it happened). Armed with a can of bear spray (this might sound excessive, but it was the first hard object that came to hand) I went on a killing spree, but, for every one of the buggers I squashed, two more seemed to appear in its place. By the time the sun had come up, I was a nervous wreck, rocking back and forth in the corner of the tent whimpering, 'I'm going to get you, little wiggie …'

As if that wasn't enough, later that morning I was scared silly by something slightly bigger than an earwig: I was just squatting down at a scenic spot to perform my daily duty, when a long, slender creature darted between my legs and made off with the toilet roll. Before I had a chance to get a good look at it, I toppled over backwards with my shorts around my ankles. By the time I'd regained my composure, the furry little felon had disappeared, leaving in its wake a long, uninterrupted trail of toilet paper.

In fact, 10 August was obviously national pest day: that afternoon, while we were paddling, we were plagued by a species of insect as voracious as anything we'd yet encountered (its scientific name, in case you're interested, was *Big Green Bastard*). I couldn't paddle more than a few strokes without having to beat my back in a frenzy, but somehow they seemed to know exactly where to bite me so that I couldn't reach them with my hand. As we neared the end of the day's paddle, we took a little side channel as a shortcut, but that just seemed to make matters worse. By the time we'd regained the main channel, I was ready to catch the next plane home.

That night, we camped at the top of a short, dirt ramp below a watchtower. We were hoping this would be our last night on the border, but after my night and day of insecticide, I was too tired to really appreciate it.

As if to mark the occasion, a big storm blew in just as it was getting dark. It was heralded by nothing more ominous than a balmy, easterly wind, but within minutes it was raining hard and fast. Nails of water slammed into the tent and bounced off the ground around us. The boys in the watchtower got quite excited, sending up flare after flare to add to the lightning that crackled across the night sky. And then, almost as quickly as it had started, it stopped, leaving behind a warm, metallic smell, and a silence that we didn't have the heart – or the energy – to break.

17 BOWLING, BABUSHKAS & BALLROOM DANCING

Our eightieth day on the river was a momentous one: after forty days and forty nights on the Russia–China border, we were finally leaving it behind. There was nothing on the river to mark the border's end – no watchtower, no flare, no brass band – but it was clear from our maps that both banks were now in Russian territory, and that we could paddle and camp wherever we liked. It's hard to explain just how much this meant to us, but after more than a month of being told what to do and where to paddle, it came as an immense relief that we were at last able to make our own decisions.

In the event, our first decision was to camp on a small, sandy island within sight of Khabarovsk, the first big town we'd seen since leaving Blagoveschensk almost three weeks before. We were still a good 25 kilometres away, but because it was perched on a hill high above the river, it looked bright and welcoming in the light of the setting sun, a promised land of ice-cold beer, clean white sheets, and flimsy summer dresses. The island we were on, meanwhile, was barely big enough for our tent, although it was divided down the middle by a neat little row of trees, which served as a convenient barrier between the main house (i.e. the tent) and the veranda (the small area of sand on the far side). There was even an outside privy, cordoned off by a well-placed twig for added privacy. Needless to say, we spent the rest of the evening availing ourselves of the pool facilities, before celebrating with a slap-up, sunset barbecue out on the deck.

The next morning, three months to the day since we'd left the UK, we began the final leg of our source-to-sea journey. We set off with great gusto, but thanks to a trick of the light, the skyline that had seemed close enough to touch the evening before now looked impossibly distant, and for the first hour it didn't appear to get any closer. To pass the time, we discussed the potential of an animated version of our video diary: we decided it would work best as a *Roger Rabbit*-style animation, complete with things like anvils, pianos and bearskin rugs that we could pull out of our boats at a moment's notice; mosquitoes the size of helicopter gunships, with loudspeakers playing Wagner slung under their bellies; and deck-mounted binoculars that were six feet long and almost as wide.

From a distance, Khabarovsk's skyline was dominated by row after row of apartment blocks, but its modern façade concealed an historic heart: the city was originally founded as a military outpost in the mid-nineteenth century by Nikolai Muraviev, who was charged with seizing the Amur back from Manchuria (it was named, you may recall, after explorer Yerofey Khabarov, the founder of the troubled little town of Albazino).

More recently, the area around Khabarovsk had been the scene of armed skirmishes between China and the Soviet Union, and in 1969 a battle over Damansky Island (a few kilometres upstream of Khabarovsk, on the Ussuri River) had propelled the two nations to the brink of war. This had set in motion a huge military build-up on both sides of the river, which had only started to ease following the collapse of communism in 1991. According to what little we'd been able to ascertain about present-day Khabarovsk, it now enjoyed substantial cross-border commerce with China, not to mention other Far Eastern countries like Japan and South Korea.

When we at last got close to the town, we noticed a marked increase in river traffic, with dozens of speedboats whizzing back and forth, and the occasional ferry nosing into the current from wooden jetties that lined the riverfront at the upstream end of the town. This current was much stronger than we realised, and because the boats and buildings now looked much closer than they really were, we almost got swept right past Khabarovsk before we could so much as order an ice cream. Understandably alarmed, we turned our boats upstream and paddled furiously against the flow.

In the event, we couldn't have planned it better. Although we missed the jetties completely, the beach downstream was heaving with bikini-clad girls sunning themselves earnestly. As we landed our canoes, for a fleeting moment I knew exactly what James Bond must feel like every day of his life. Everybody stopped and stared. Conversation stopped, jaws dropped, and worried-looking mums pulled their loved ones out of harm's way. I didn't know whether to apologise or take a bow.

It wasn't long, though, before everyone lost interest, and after recording a quick piece to camera (this was a moment to savour, after all), we hauled our boats up the beach and onto the promenade. We were just about to begin another thrilling game of hunt-the-hotel when I heard someone say, 'Where ya headed?' in a chipper Kiwi accent. It was the first Western voice we'd heard in nearly three months, and I was so surprised that at first I thought Rich was doing an impression.

It was only when I turned around that I saw a tall, tanned Adonis with curly blond hair and a grin as wide as his biceps standing right behind me. He was carrying a volleyball under one arm, and looked for all the world like he'd taken a wrong turn in Kaikowa and had somehow ended up in Siberia. Which, in a manner of speaking, he had: Dave, we soon learned, worked for a Malaysian forestry company with an office in Khabarovsk. He'd applied for the job knowing nothing about the area, and without being able to speak a single word of Russian. Now, after just two years, he was the company's operations manager for the entire region, and his Russian was good enough to cope with almost anything that cropped up (although there was no hiding his thick, Kiwi accent).

After we'd been chatting for a while, he invited us to join him for a drink. 'I'm meeting my girlfriend down here,' he drawled. 'She's local, so she might know where the nearest hotel is.' It was an offer we felt we couldn't refuse. While we watched the volleyball, we asked Dave about Khabarovsk, and whether there were other westerners living here. 'Used to be,' he nodded, 'but not any more. When the country opened up in the early 90s, foreign investment flooded in, but when the economy collapsed in 1998, it all flooded back out again. Now, there's no one here apart from us, and we're losing money hand over fist.'

Given the size of Siberia's forest reserves, I couldn't understand why it was such a curate's egg. 'Basically it's because Putin's charging us a hefty percentage for the privilege,' he explained, 'and the timber's not even that great to start with.'

The volleyball continued, and the standard was high – very high. Serious-looking lads in tight-fitting Speedos leapt around the court while cooing girlfriends looked on admiringly. There wasn't an ounce of fat on display within half a mile. 'Everyone here looks fit,' Dave mused, as if reading my mind. 'I reckon it's a combination of healthy eating, cold, harsh winters, and short, energetic summers. Also, most people don't own a car, so walking's the norm. As for the girls,' he said, nodding towards the audience, 'they're obsessed with their appearance. It's the first thing they spend their money on. No matter how little they earn, they always look like a million bucks.'

Dave's girlfriend, it seemed, was no exception. She was very slim, with short dark hair, big doe eyes, and a coy, flirtatious smile. Her name was Lida (short, I presumed, for Lydia) and her English was excellent. Dave asked her if she knew of anywhere we could stay. 'The nearest hotel is the Amur,' she said demurely, 'but I think it is too far to walk with your canoes.' I shrugged. 'How far is too far?' I asked. Dave intervened. 'It's near my office. I'll show you if you like.' That clinched it: if Dave was willing to come with us, I thought reasonably, how far could it really be?

The answer, as it turned out, was too far to walk with our canoes. The first few hundred metres were so steep it was difficult to stop our boats from rolling back down the hill. Even when the slope eased a little, Rich's canoe had a tendency to crab sideways on its trolley wheels, taking out swathes of innocent bystanders in the process.

It was only when Rich's trolley collapsed on a pedestrian crossing in the middle of a main road that we finally discovered the reason for the crabbing: one of his axle pins had popped off, and the wheel had gradually worked its way to the end of the axle. The moment Rich had bounced his boat down the precipitous kerb onto the road, the trolley wheel had flown off, sending his canoe crashing to the ground. In the event, all we needed was something to thread through the narrow hole in the axle to stop the wheel from sliding off again. After a quick scan of our belongings, we realised a keyring was the perfect solution – it was small enough to thread through the hole, but big enough to keep the wheel in place.

In all, we hauled our boats about two kilometres and run the gauntlet of a dozen different roads, and – as luck would have it – the last few hundred metres were even steeper than the first few hundred. By the time we'd got to the top, my shirt was wringing wet and my nose was dripping with sweat. We must have cut quite a dash, because initially the surly girl at the reception desk would only offer us a single night. Oddly, when she realised we were English, she extended this to three nights. Only when we'd paid for our rooms and signed the usual forms in triplicate did we produce our canoes, much to Surly Sue's dismay. After considerable persuasion, however, she finally agreed to let us store them under the stairs in the lobby before handing us the keys to our room.

The hotel itself had an air of neglected opulence, with bright, airy rooms decked out in drab colours and threadbare upholstery. The sheets on the beds, though, were as crisp and clean as they'd been in our dreams, while the fridge in the corner of the room was like a gift from the gods. Once we'd showered and shaved, we wandered back out – this time *sans canoes* – to explore the town. The city itself seemed to be built on a series of ridges running down to the riverfront, with deep troughs in between. Dipping in and out of these troughs, we made our way to Muraviev Amurskovo Street (named after the town's founder), which Dave had suggested was worth a look (having escorted us to our hotel, he'd left us to it, promising to meet us down at the beach later).

He was right: Muraviev Amurskovo was a wide, tree-lined boulevard lined with attractive, nineteenth-century buildings and fronted by dozens of modern-looking shops and cafés. Fast-food vendors vied for custom on street corners, while red-brick pediments and onion-domed cupolas jockeyed for attention overhead. The whole place was bustling with people, many of them enjoying a quick drink or a bite to eat at one of the tables scattered liberally along the pavement. And, as if by way of a finishing touch, a balmy breeze whispered through the leaves, giving the whole place an inviting, resort-like atmosphere that came as a welcome relief after the monotony of the river.

It was late afternoon by the time we got back down to the beach, by which time the promenade was overflowing with open-air bars and cafés, and fast-food stalls selling pizzas, pastries and hot dogs. Like the esplanade at Blagoveschensk, it was also teeming with girls in tight-fitting dresses, all trying desperately to look uninterested. The beach itself was still bursting at the seams with toned, bronzed bodies, while the water's edge was swimming with wiry old men made out of whipcord. Khabarovsk, I thought gleefully, was like the French Riviera without the French.

After a quick swim to cool off, we joined Dave and Lida for a drink in one of the gazebo-covered bars overlooking the river. These bars, Dave told us, were affectionately known as *greebi*, which literally translates as 'mushrooms'. Warming to the subject of slang, Dave went on to teach us a whole raft of Russian swear words, including one so obscene that it didn't even have a literal translation. Lida was not amused. 'Dave, why are you always teaching bad words or something like that?' she said, only half-joking. 'New Zealand guys, English guys – you're all the same, I think.'

A couple of beers later, Dave suggested trying out a new restaurant that was just a few streets away from our hotel. The décor was kitsch, the food expensive, and the portions pitiful. After getting by on a dollar a day for months, the thought of blowing $40 on a single (very small) meal was enough to plague me with guilt – having said that, however, I thought the unisex toilets were a nice touch.

As if that wasn't enough decadence for one night, we then paid $10 apiece to get into the best nightclub in town (as our self-appointed host, Dave was obviously keen to show us a good time), plus another $20 for two rounds of tequilas, which all told was more money than we'd spent in the last month. Still, it set in motion a memorable night of drinking and dancing that ended at four in the morning with a sad and very drunken duet of Robbie Williams' 'Angels' (by which stage, Dave had long since given up and gone home with Lida to – as he so discreetly put it – 'watch the rugby'.)

The following afternoon (we decided not to sign up for the morning) we found ourselves in a bright, soulless fast-food joint on Muraviev Amurskovo, eating limp, microwaved pizza and grainy, peanut-butter ice cream. Once the sugar had finally made it to our brains, we spent an hour at the local market picking out some new clothes. Inspired by the beachwear on display the day before, Rich went for a fetching string vest and some hot pants made out of hemp, while I opted for a tiny, navy-blue vest, and some understated tracksuit bottoms in lime green and lemon yellow.

Thus attired, we wandered over to the town's main square, which just happened to be hosting the region's annual summer festival. On one side of the impressive plaza were chessboards set up on tables, where an unkempt, middle-aged man was playing a dozen different people at the same time. Nearby was another table at chest height with sticks in opposite corners – it was only when I saw people using it that I realised it was an arm-wrestling platform, complete with handles for added leverage. Adjacent to this was a large, circus-style weight, which angry-looking musclemen pumped up and down over their heads until their faces looked like radishes.

But the highlight of the whole show was the stage in the far corner, which featured an impressive line-up of performers, from ballroom dancers in splendid, colourful costumes to a troupe of karate experts intent on kicking three shades of blue out of each other. All afternoon the crowd around the stage was dozens deep. It was all hugely enjoyable, and all the more so because it was so unexpected.

I was reluctant to leave the square, but the beach and the sunset beckoned. After a quick fashion show for the benefit of our video camera, we watched the sun set over the Amur before making our way to the Tower Café, which was on the cliff top at the far end of the promenade (according to local lore, it was here that a band of Austro-Hungarian POWs were shot dead during the First World War for refusing to play the Russian national anthem).

Would that the chef of the Tower Café had been threatened with a similar fate: for $10 a head we were served some greasy chips, half a raw cabbage, and a small chicken which had been walked quickly through a warm room.

The only reason we knew it was Monday the next day was because Dave had to go to work – it was the first time in over three months that we'd even thought about what day of the week it was. We didn't think about it for very long, mind you, because we had places to be, and people to see.

Our first stop was the laundry room in the hotel basement (we knew there was a laundry room in the hotel basement because a few minutes earlier the laundry lady had wandered into our room when we were both stark-bollock-naked). When we reconvened in the basement a short while later, she couldn't stop laughing, although I for one couldn't see what was so funny, and I said as much to Rich. 'I think you'll find that she's the one who couldn't see what was so funny, old boy,' he said, patting me sympathetically on the shoulder. Frankly, I wasn't sure I liked his tone.

Once we'd dispensed with the hilarious willy gags, I tried to explain to our still-beaming babushka that most of our clothes were made of short-string compounds like polypropylene, and that they'd melt if she so much as showed them an iron. Curiously, she must have understood exactly what I was wittering on about, because when we returned a few hours later to collect them, they smelled like a sweet summer breeze, but looked like they'd just gone five rounds with a threshing machine. When I asked how much it all was, she just shook her head and shooed us out.

The laundry fumes must have addled our brains, because the next thing we knew, we were in a chic (well, chic for this neck of the woods) hair salon on Muraviev Amurskovo. Not surprisingly, all of the stylists were female, and most of them didn't seem to be wearing much more than the girls we'd seen down on the beach the afternoon before. Come to think of it, they probably *were* the girls we'd seen down on the beach the afternoon before. The stylist assigned to me was obviously slightly nervous at the thought of cutting an Englishman's hair, because she didn't once mention the weather, or ask me where I was going on holiday this year. Rich, meanwhile, was looked after by the matriarch of the harem, a middle-aged woman with peroxide-blonde hair and beautifully manicured nails.

Halfway through my own cut, I looked across to see her snipping expertly away at an alarmingly round ball of fuzz sprouting from the top of Rich's head. It was Rich, though, who had the last laugh: in the time it took me to have my hair cut with clippers, Suzy Scissorhands gave him the same buzz-cut look using just scissors and a comb. The result was probably the best haircut I'd ever seen. In fact, it almost made Rich look quite dapper.

That evening, Dave and Lida took us ten-pin bowling at a brand new alley on the outskirts of town. In addition to being quite swanky, it was also quite empty. By which I mean we were the only people there. On arrival, we were assigned a *dyevooshka* – literally 'girl', but in this case more like a personal assistant – whose job it was to help us set up the computer scoreboard, provide assistance along the way, and generally offer encouragement and/or commiserations as the need arose. In the event, I don't think she knew quite what to make of us, because her cheers and sighs somehow lacked the conviction that was presumably called for in her job description.

Lida's short, silver dress was so tight she couldn't bend down low enough to bowl, so the boys duked it out on the boards while Lida looked diffidently on. We paid for what we thought was a single game, but after an hour and three seconds our scoreboard suddenly shut down. Now, I'd like to be able to say that I was a bit taken aback, but I wasn't; to my mind, this was typical of a country obsessed with rules and regulations. We only had a frame left, and would happily have paid for the extra minutes (or the extra hour, come to that), but rather than ask us or warn us, they just shut us down. After some carefully chosen words, we did eventually finish the game, but by that stage we'd lost interest.

We ended the night with a few games of Russian billiards at a pool bar in the centre of town. Well, I say games, but in fact we only managed one. The problem with Russian billiards, we soon discovered, was that the holes were only *fractionally* bigger than the balls, and were so precisely angled that only a direct hit would do. It also didn't help that we hadn't a clue what the rules were, and watching other people playing didn't seem to help. All of the balls were white, and as far as we could tell there was no cue ball, so we just whacked them around the table until they went in. Half an hour of whacking later, we gave up and played pool.

The next morning, we were thrown out of our hotel. Our three days were up, Surly Sue reminded us gleefully, and we had to find somewhere else to stay. Thankfully, though, not everyone at the Hotel Amur was as frosty, and one of the doormen, a young chap by the name of Alexei, agreed to watch our boats while we looked for an alternative (by remarkable coincidence, one of his friends had been in Mongolia on business a few months before, and had seen our canoes on top of Gal's jeep). We eventually ended up staying with Dave and storing our boats in his basement at work. This was more by default than by design: while Dave was driving us from hotel to hotel, he managed to U-turn his Toyota Hi-Lux right into a passing taxi, thus rendering us both homeless *and* transport-less.

The good news was, Dave had cable. We spent the night gorging ourselves on chicken chop suey and satellite TV. I'd never been a fan of satellite TV before, much less MTV, but after our weeks of isolation on the river, it was an audio-visual feast, and I vowed there and then to buy a dish in the duty-free at Heathrow the moment I got back. Disappointingly, all of the films on offer were dubbed into Russian, and we soon learned that the same actor (and I use this term very loosely) usually played every character, from sweet, innocent granny to snarling, chainsaw-wielding psychopath. More often than not, however, he'd simply stick with the voice of the latter, and hope that no one would notice.

I must have been worried about my brain turning to mush, because the next day I suggested paying a visit to the town's Museum of Local Studies. Like the museum in Albazino, it was a veritable treasure chest of ruins, relics and information: among the exhibits were a splendid stuffed bear, a relief map of the Amur, and a harrowing display about the Soviet Gulag (Gulag stands for *Glavny Upravleniye Lagerey*, or Main Administration for Camps, which was effectively a vast network of concentration camps for those swept up in Stalin's purges of the 1930s, '40s and early '50s).

Officially, twenty million Russians died in these camps or were executed under Stalin's orders, but Nobel prize-winning author Alexander Solzhenitsyn, who himself spent eight years in the Gulag for criticising Stalin in a letter, puts the number at closer to sixty million. Either way, the figures are so high as to be unimaginable. Equally disturbing is the fact that Stalin's name is still revered by many of Russia's older generation, who look back with nostalgia on a time when everything was provided by the state, and who remain resolute in their belief that only the guilty were sent to the Gulag. Perhaps it was the only way of coping with what was happening: the alternative – that everyone was innocent – was simply too horrific to contemplate.

On a less harrowing note, there was also a display of replica indigenous canoes, which were gracefully proportioned and beautifully made. But the highlight of the whole experience was undoubtedly the bristling babushkas who looked after the exhibits. Each of them ruled over their respective roosts like regimental sergeant majors. They demanded to see tickets in every room, and pounced on anyone who so much as breathed in the direction of an exhibit. But they reserved their greatest wrath for those who dared to use a video camera without forking out the required 25p supplement. Naturally I was more than happy to pay the additional fee, but every time I lifted the camera to my eye, a stuffed old bird would pounce on me and demand to see my receipt. One of them even followed me around so that she could be on hand the moment any crime was committed.

As you can imagine, this got quite wearing after a while, so I decided to have some fun: walking slowly towards an exhibit, I'd suddenly dart away in the opposite direction, just to see if she could keep up. Another trick was to raise the camera casually up to my eye as if uncertain about what to film next, and then – just as she moved in for the kill – to drop it back down again. In fact, as we played out this cat-and-mouse game, I realised that there must be an entire generation of grannies – an elite corps of museum military, if you will – dedicated to fighting an ongoing battle against good sense and reason. Still, I was glad to see it wasn't just the foreigners who were being singled out – one young lad of about seven or eight was given an earful just for thinking about standing on one of the museum's wooden display platforms.

We'd now been kicking our heels in Khabarovsk for four days and were anxious to get on with our journey, but not before Dave had cooked us a sumptuous last supper. 'There's not much to it really,' Dave enthused, doing his best bush-tucker impersonation. 'You just take a large chicken, shove a dozen bulbs of garlic up its arse, and stick it in the oven for a few hours.' That's what I love about the Kiwis – they've got such a way with words.

While we ate, we sat around the table listening to Eminem and chatting about life, love and logging. Dave even had a plan to make his fortune from a foolproof kidnapping, but we politely declined his offer to come in on it with him.

Once again, our escape from the clutches of the city was much more drawn-out than expected. We spent the day refilling out fuel bottles, restocking our larder, and replenishing our energy levels for the final push to the ocean. After lunch, we picked up our boats from Dave's office and wheeled them back down to the waterfront. Needless to say, it was much easier going downhill. We had hoped that our departure might involve some sort of groupie sendoff, with crowds of girls parting in awe as we strolled nonchalantly across the beach. Instead, it was cool, quiet and overcast, and the beach was deserted. I was willing to bet James Bond never had this sort of problem.

Dave and Lida bunked off work early to come and see us off, but they needn't have bothered. Originally, we'd planned to leave soon after they arrived, to give ourselves plenty of time to find somewhere to camp away from the city, but you know how it is: you wait for the sun to come out, you wait for the barbecue to be stoked, you wait for your *shashlick* to be cooked, and before you know it, it's eight o'clock and you're just sitting down to dinner. Dave tried to tempt us into staying another day, but the thought of wheeling our boats back up the hill was too much. Finally, after three skewers of lightly flamed cow, we said a brief and thoroughly British farewell (handshakes and backslaps all round) before pushing off at dusk into the quicksilver waters of the Amur.

It was dark by the time we got downstream of Khabarovsk proper, and all we could see were the distant lights of villages scattered along the right-hand bank. We wanted to avoid camping near an unknown village in the dark, and the left bank was over a mile away, so we had little choice but to plough on and hope for the best. Unlike our last night excursion, however, this time there was no moon to light our way, and it was quite unnerving paddling into the inky blackness ahead of us.

Just when things were starting to look a bit desperate, we noticed a vague shape looming out of the darkness. It turned out to be a small island. It looked half underwater, so before we got swept one way or the other by the swift current, we had to decide which side looked more promising. Luckily we guessed right, and it was with some relief that we pulled up a few seconds later on the island's only shingle beach. It was barely a foot higher than the river, but we decided to take our chances and – if it came to it – evacuate in the middle of the night. Not surprisingly, I spent a sleepless night peering out of the tent door every hour, on the hour. Rich, of course, slept like a baby.

The good news, though, was that we didn't have as far to go as we thought. Just after we'd left the beach, we'd passed a kilometre marker signalling the final 922km to the Pacific Ocean. At 50km a day – and with a bit of luck thrown in for good measure – that was just 18 days away, and not the 20 or 25 days we'd originally anticipated. Given that we'd already spent 86 days on the river, I thought, another 18 would be nothing, a mere bagatelle, a drop in the proverbial ocean …

How wrong I was.

18 THE WRONG SIDE OF THE RIVER

Our first full day back on the river was as tiresome as it was tiring. I spent most of it tuning into local radio, making the most of the reception while we were still close enough to Khabarovsk to pick up a signal. The only thing I listened to that made it as far as my diary, though, was an episode of *Lassie*. Naturally, it was dubbed into Russian by a chainsaw-wielding psychopath, but to my delight the English original was still faintly audible in the background (hardly ideal, you might think, but you'd be amazed at how much you can put up with when you're bored witless).

Because the river was so high, we couldn't find anywhere to camp at the end of our usual six-hour stint, so we continued for another hour and a half before pulling up on a perfect little sand island in the middle of the river. At least, it looked perfect. No sooner had we unloaded our boats and set up camp, however, than we were ambushed by a swarm of tiny black thunder-bugs. For some reason, they didn't seem all that partial to raw Boddington, but they couldn't get enough of lightly salted Grogan; they nipped, nibbled and sucked at my ankles until they'd drunk them dry, and then they went to work on the smorgasbord of capillaries between my forehead and my hair.

At dusk the local mosquitoes joined the feeding frenzy, forcing us to seek sanctuary in the tent. Usually such evasive action was enough to discourage all but the most voracious of bloodsuckers, but this time it made little difference; all night a dense cloud danced just beyond our mosquito net, accompanied throughout by an incessant, maddening drone. For every mosquito we swatted, two more made it past our defences.

By the time dawn had arrived I was hot, sweaty and itching all over, and not for the first time on our journey, I felt ready to go home. This thought had hardly even registered, however, before I realised what I was wishing for: I'd spent the last three months living my dream, and I knew that the moment it was all over, I'd wish it wasn't. Besides, I thought rationally, how could I ever expect my fungus to flourish if I wasn't prepared to get hot and sweaty from time to time?

The mosquitoes continued to plague us the following day. Up until now, we'd taken most of our food breaks on beaches, which were relatively insect-free between dawn and dusk. Now, though, most of the beaches seemed to be underwater, so instead we tried nosing our boats into the trees that lined the water's edge. We only made this mistake once: mosquitoes, like thunder-bugs, seem to operate on some sort of clever, time-delay system, whereby they only attack once you've buttered several slices of bread and laid them carefully on the deck of your boat. Now, I've no idea how much blood a forestful of mosquitoes can get through in the time it takes to inhale a round of sardine sandwiches, but if I had to guess, I'd plump for around half a pint.

I was surprised at how little traffic we'd seen since Khabarovsk. Somehow I'd expected it to be busier now that we'd left the restrictions of the border behind, but most of the time we had the river to ourselves. Perhaps it was because this section of the river was notoriously difficult to navigate in big ships, thanks to shifting sandbanks that lurked just below the water's surface, sometimes right in the middle of the river. I was also surprised at how big it all felt given that we were still hundreds of kilometres from the ocean: some of the straights we now found ourselves on were so long that we often couldn't see anything but river and sky in the direction we were paddling.

Less surprising was the fact that the sun was now setting much earlier. When we'd leaped two time zones with a single paddle-stroke back in Mangut, the sun had set well after 11 p.m. every night. Now that we were so far east, however, it was getting dark about two hours earlier, which meant we had a lot less time to sit around and loaf (this had presumably happened quite gradually, but after our week in Khabarovsk, away from our river routine, it somehow seemed quite sudden). We tried getting up two hours earlier, but this merely ate into our morning loaf instead. In the end, we continued to get up at the usual time each morning, and made up for it in the evening by staying up well past our bedtime.

Three days after leaving Khabarovsk, we decided to call in at a small town called Troitskoye, on the right bank of the river (I mention its location only because we'd spent over a month lassoed to the left bank, and it now felt quite odd to be on the 'wrong' side). Originally, we'd planned to stop short of Troitskoye, to avoid running into any holster-happy policemen, but that morning, fate intervened in the form of cheese-flavoured porridge. The reason our porridge tasted of cheese, we soon realised, was that the condensed milk we'd bought back in Khabarovsk was over a year past its sell-by date. Given that porridge *without* condensed milk tastes almost as bad as porridge with cheese, we had little choice but to resupply at the earliest available opportunity.

According to our maps, Troitskoye was just around a sweeping, right-hand bend in the river, but when we eventually rounded this bend after a solid, six-hour stint, it was nowhere to be seen. My first thought was that our maps were so out of date that it no longer existed, and that we'd have to choke back cheesy porridge for the next week. After a further half-hour of paddling, however, we discovered that it did still exist, but that somebody had moved it a few kilometres downstream.

The *dyevooshka* at Troitskoye's only hotel was already smiling when I walked up to the reception desk on the second floor; she'd obviously seen us rolling our boats up from the riverbank. 'Where are you going to put your canoes?' she asked, before I'd even had a chance to say hello. '*Nye znayoo*,' I shrugged sheepishly: I don't know. At this, she just smiled and shook her head, and without another word, she picked up the phone and began calling around for somewhere we could store our boats.

When her initial enquiries came to nothing she suggested putting them in our rooms, but I shook my head: even if the rooms were palatial (which I doubted), there was no way we could get our boats up four flights of narrow stairs. In the end, we found some space in a corridor on the ground floor. 'It belongs to a local businessman,' our smiling saviour winked meaningfully, 'but as long as you get them out before nine in the morning, he won't even know!'

Then, just when we thought the hard part was over, we had to book a room. Troitskoye was the first small town we'd stayed in since we'd left the border, so we weren't sure what to expect in the way of bureaucracy. We needn't have worried: after filling out the usual forms in triplicate, our *dyevooshka* told us we had to report to the local police station for 'registration'. When I started to ask where it was, she held up one finger to interrupt me, plucked the phone from its cradle again, and proceeded to dial the number of the nearest nick. Mercifully, the policeman who answered said he was too busy, and suggested coming in at ten the following morning. I nodded my assent, safe in the knowledge that by that time we'd be sunning ourselves a dozen kilometres downstream.

Once we'd booked into our room (too small for our canoes, as it turned out), our first priority was to find somewhere to eat. Troitskoye, like many of the towns and villages we'd visited, was a sleepy settlement boasting little more than a handful of plain-fronted shops and dozens of deserted administrative buildings. A couple of blocks back from the riverfront we found a small cafeteria that was still open. We started with a cold, stiff *cheburiki* (a kind of greasy meat pastry) and finished with a hot, floppy *cheburiki*. I'd like to be able to say that we got the same thing twice because it was so delicious, but in fact it was all they had. The only reason the second helping was hot was because the sultry Sheila behind the counter deigned to fling it in a microwave for sixty seconds. She might have even managed a smile the second time around, but I couldn't be sure.

Priority number two was finding somewhere to buy petrol, but this wasn't as easy as it sounds. Most of the people we asked didn't have the faintest idea where the nearest petrol station might be, presumably because none of them actually owned cars. Eventually, though, after exhaustive enquiries, we ended up at a one-pump forecourt a couple of kilometres out of town. We were just about to begin the long trudge back to our hotel when a policeman pulled up and offered us a lift. Fearing the worst, we clambered in, but instead of demanding to see our documents, he just chatted to us like we were old chums, asking us where we were from and where we were headed.

He dropped us down at the waterfront, which to my surprise featured a brand-new promenade complete with herringbone paving and ornate, wrought-iron streetlamps (we hadn't actually paddled this far, having landed our boats a short distance upstream). Just beyond the promenade, however, were signs that such flourishes were little more than window-dressing: a decaying dock, lined with the shells of scuttled boats and presided over by a couple of derelict cranes, was all that remained of a once prosperous port. As we took a few photographs of the cranes silhouetted against the light of the setting sun, a passing woman asked me if I thought they looked beautiful. 'Yes and no,' I said, smiling, partly because I didn't want to offend her, and partly because I didn't know. 'That's Siberia,' she laughed in acknowledgement, before continuing on her way.

We finished the night with a cold beer on the promenade, but by the time my bottle was half empty, I was ready for bed. What I wasn't ready for was a pair of pissed-up lads asking us to take photos of them and inviting us into the 'woods' for some vodka. Call me Old Mr Unadventurous if you will, but the thought of wondering into the darkening forest with a couple of half-cut cowboys was enough to send me scuttling back to my hotel room. Wandering home along the water's edge, we passed a cloud of papery white moths that flickered and danced in the dying embers of the sun.

The next morning, after stocking up on bread, sardines and condensed milk, we repacked our boats on the pavement outside our hotel, much to the delight of some local schoolchildren who were gathered nearby. Before any of them had plucked up the courage to speak to us, however, they were hurried along by an anxious-looking teacher who eyed us suspiciously. If only she'd made the effort to return my greeting, I thought disappointedly, she might have been able to give her class an impromptu geography lesson, complete with a couple of real, live Englishmen.

There was a stiff breeze blowing upstream when we got on the river, and the water was decidedly choppy, but the clear blue sky meant it was still shorts and T-shirt weather, and for once it felt good to be battling the wind and the waves. What didn't feel so good was my stomach: I don't know if I'd eaten one too many *cheburiki* for breakfast, or if my twice-daily dose of iodine was finally starting to take its toll, but that afternoon I had to forego my share of sardines in tomato sauce. Thankfully, though, my ailing appetite seemed to recover the moment the chocolate appeared, which was obviously a great relief to all concerned (and by all, of course, I mean me).

The highlight of the day, however, was yet to come. That afternoon, we spotted what looked like a small yacht tacking into the wind behind us. When it got closer we realised it wasn't a yacht at all, but a makeshift catamaran made out of oil drums, planks of wood and other odds and ends lashed loosely together with bits of rope; the only thing that looked even vaguely serviceable was the sail, which bowed reassuringly in the breeze.

When it got closer still, we hollered hello to its two crew members. One of them had thick curly hair, while the other had a shaved head and wore beady, John Lennon-style glasses – together, they looked like a couple of students on their way to Glastonbury. In fact, they were on their way to Komsomolsk, a big, industrial city about 100km downstream. They'd left Khabarovsk two days before us, they said, but they hadn't had much luck with the wind. At some point we'd obviously passed them, so I was surprised we hadn't seen them before now. I was just about to ask them about this when they waved farewell, gybed their mainsail (well, their only sail), and tacked ponderously back across the river. For my part, I'd have liked to know more about where they were from (I was fairly sure they were Russian, but I had no idea if they were local or not) and why they were sailing to Komsomolsk on a home-made raft. For some reason, though, they decided to keep their distance, and although we continued to catch occasional glimpses of their sail, we never got the chance to speak to them again.

The day after we ran into our fellow adventurers, we almost ran into a passing hydrofoil. Or rather, it almost ran into us. We knew from our research that hydrofoils plied the 300-odd kilometres between Khabarovsk and Komsomolsk every few days, but we had no idea how fast they travelled. We later learned that the journey took just seven hours, which translated to an average of nearly 50km an hour. On a still day the skipper wouldn't have had any problem spotting our brightly coloured canoes from miles away. Today, however, was the windiest day we'd experienced on the entire trip, which meant there was every chance he'd lose us in the chop (so to speak). Needless to say, when I suddenly saw a great, white canoe-slicer heading straight for me I was a little anxious. I had no idea whether the pilot could see me or not, but after a few agonising seconds, he changed course and thundered past, trailing a giant plume of white water behind him.

Our campsite that night felt like a desert island, thanks to the stiff breeze, darkening skies and waves that thumped onto the beach. After six hours of being buffeted by the elements, I was cold, wet and exhausted, but I was also strangely exhilarated, and I got a real buzz from wandering in amongst the sand dunes in search of somewhere to pitch our tent. For the first time in weeks, I felt like I was in my element again, and I didn't want it to end. As I sat in my camp chair that evening, my body wrapped up against the wind and my toes curled up in the warm sand beneath my feet, I made a point of taking it all in; this, I thought contentedly, was what it was all about.

Despite the warmth of the sun on our tent the following morning, there was no let-up in the wind or the swell. On the water, our boats pitched and rolled in the waves, some of which broke alarmingly over our bows. I have to admit, getting wet came as something of a shock, particularly as we'd spent the last three months trying to avoid it, and for a fleeting moment we considered calling the whole thing off. Once we were as wet as we were ever going to get, however, we stopped mincing and started paddling, ploughing through every wave with unabashed enthusiasm.

Despite – or perhaps because of – this enthusiasm, the day was dominated by a piercing pain at the base of my neck. It wasn't the first time I'd felt it on the trip, but it was certainly the first time it had made me swear out loud in frustration. It felt as if an endlessly long pin was being pushed slowly but continuously into the neck muscles just to the left of my spine. It came on early in the day and throbbed for every second of every minute of every hour that we paddled. Still, I knew we'd both been quite lucky in terms of our physical health thus far, so to be stricken with such a minor complaint at this late stage was something of a blessing. I also knew that as soon as I stopped paddling the worst of it would wear off within minutes, leaving behind little more than a numb, aching sensation in my vertebrae. In the meantime, all I could do was grin and swear at it.

Because of the wind, we didn't chat that much, but even if it had been still, I'm not sure we'd have chatted any more. The fact was, we'd now spent every day of the last three months together (four if you counted the weeks leading up to the source) and although we were still like a pair of old women at every campsite – and indeed at every food break – on the water we both tended to switch off and let our minds wander. Increasingly, I found myself thinking about friends and family back home. At one point, I saw the vapour trail of a jet passing high overhead, and imagined myself sitting on a plane home, watching an in-flight movie and sipping a glass of wine. As I continued to gaze at it, I realised it was the first plane we'd seen since leaving Ulaan Baatar.

The only landmark of the day was the sprawling, industrial town of Amursk. We'd been able to see it from our campsite that morning, and four hours later we still hadn't reached it. Its skyline was dominated by the smokestacks of a huge power station, and dozens of high-rise apartment blocks that were well past their prime (assuming that they'd ever had a prime). One, though, was unfinished, and looked much more pristine, with rows of perfect, dark squares punched into its plain white façade. It had an almost neoclassical feel to it – or at least, it would have until the verandas and washing lines were added.

The town planners had obviously made more of an effort on the promenade, which featured a grand staircase leading down to an inviting beach, but the beach, like the promenade, was completely empty. From the river, the whole place looked oddly lifeless, as if it had been abandoned a decade earlier and had never been resettled. In the event, we decided not to stop at Amursk – it just didn't look that inviting. Instead, we made straight for Komsomolsk, now just a day's paddle away. What we didn't realise (until it was too late) was that it was billed in our guidebook as one of the most depressing places in all of Siberia.

Komsomolsk, we knew, was a more modern city than either Blagoveschensk or Khabarovsk, having been founded by an enthusiastic band of young communists who first arrived here by boat in 1932, intent on creating a utopian paradise on the banks of the Amur. In reality, it became little more than a massive manufacturing plant, churning out planes, ships and submarines for the Soviet military. It was also supposed to be the last stop on the Baikal Amur Mainline, a secondary branch of the Trans-Siberian railway (which was barely ten years old at this point), but the line wasn't completed until the 1970s, at the height of the city's productive powers. The collapse of communism spelt the beginning of the end for Komsomolsk: factories were closed and thousands were laid off. Those who could find work often didn't receive any wages for months on end. Almost overnight, it became a city without a purpose, manufacturing products without demand.

As we approached the city the following afternoon, our view downstream was dominated by a massive railway bridge at the upstream end of town, and beyond it the ubiquitous jumble of apartment blocks littering the bank. We also saw – and heard – a few speedboats buzzing back and forth, despite the choppy conditions and the dark, brooding clouds that covered Komsomolsk like a shroud.

Once again we found ourselves paddling past kilometre after kilometre of built-up waterfront without having a clue where to stop. Eventually, though, we pinpointed the hydrofoil terminal, and landed our boats on the quiet beach just downstream. We asked a ruddy-faced, beefy-looking lad for directions to the nearest hotel. He was surrounded by a gaggle of giggling girls, and seemed only too glad to help, pointing us in the direction of the aptly named 'Amur', which he assured us was just a few hundred yards away. It turned out to be almost a kilometre away but it was easy enough to find, and was certainly much easier to get to than its namesake in Khabarovsk.

The neat-looking *directora* at reception thought it was just wonderful that we'd paddled all the way from Khabarovsk (I'd long ago given up telling people where we'd really come from). 'Oy yoy yoy,' she exclaimed kindly, '*kak maladyetz!*' (as you may recall, this literally means 'what fine fellows', although a more modern translation might be something like 'good lads' perhaps, or – I don't know – 'would you like my eldest daughter's hand in marriage?'). As she spoke, I noticed an old man in a straw panama tinkering away with an electric heater in the far corner of the room. He seemed to have more bare wires than he had holes to put them in, and every time he tried to plug one in, the *directora* would grab my hand and wince in anticipation.

Form-filling took the usual half-hour, as did squeezing our boats and other belongings into a storeroom on the ground floor. Only then, when we were free from the twin burdens of bureaucracy and baggage, could we at last step forth into the thriving resort town of Komsomolsk.

To our surprise, it was considerably more open and attractive than we'd been led to expect by the brief and somewhat flippant entry in our guidebook. The streets and squares were wide and spacious, and even in the grey light of an equally grey day, the whole place had a feeling of hustle and bustle that was reminiscent of Khabarovsk. Admittedly there were fewer girls wearing next to nothing, but it was cooler now than it had been a few weeks ago; instead, a more modest, autumn collection was on show, complete with faded jeans, faux-fur coats and long, soft-looking scarves.

There was also an inescapable atmosphere of enterprise about the place: while we wandered, we stopped for some barbecued *shashlick* at a makeshift café, complete with a bar area and a broad canopy. The *shashlick* was delicious, the chef was as enthusiastic as he was efficient, and the tables were filled to capacity with carefree young students sharing a joke over a cup of coffee. In the event, we were too tired to do much more than walk down the city's main street and back, but this turned out to be about four kilometres long, so we had our work cut out. By the time we'd got back to our hotel, the best we could manage by way of a night on the town was to mooch down the two flights of stairs to the hotel restaurant. 'Restaurant' is perhaps overstating things a little: it was more of a backroom with a few tables and a food counter, but it did the job.

We were served meat stew and potato parcels by a slender-looking blonde who seemed to have about 63 children, although at least two of them belonged to the Gwyneth Paltrow lookalike who worked in a little shop down the hall. In due course the chef appeared, to ask us how our food was and to get us to sign her visitors' book (curiously, ours was the very first entry). Her daughter, she told us proudly, taught English at the local technical institute. They'd often had Chinese and Japanese guests staying at the hotel, she said, but never Englishmen. Disappointingly, neither of the two blondes seemed to share her enthusiasm for Englishmen, but that might have been because they were both too busy running around after kids with enormous fluffy pompoms in their ponytails.

The very next day, the police paid us a little visit.

19 CAUGHT IN A CLOSED TOWN

It all happened quite quickly. One minute I was sitting on the edge of my bed, scratching my scrotum and rubbing the sleep from my eyes, the next I was being interrogated by a couple of plain-clothes policemen wearing holsters. They may have knocked, but if they had done they certainly hadn't waited for an answer. One of them had a soft-edged, oriental-looking face, while the other had narrow, furtive features and dark, darting eyes. Rich, oddly, was nowhere to be seen.

'Yes,' I began, as indignantly as I could manage in my boxer shorts, 'what do you want?' Jackie Chan showed me his police card and asked to see my *dokumenti*. 'Of course,' I nodded, knowing better than to make a fuss. There was an expectant pause as he flicked through our papers. 'There is a problem here,' he announced at last, handing them back to me. 'What problem?' I demanded, starting to get a little anxious. 'You do not have permits to visit Komsomolsk,' he said simply.

'But we have permission to travel all the way along the Amur,' I insisted, thrusting the relevant letters back into his hands.

'These are not official documents,' Jackie shrugged. 'Foreigners are not allowed in Komsomolsk.' I asked why not. 'Komsomolsk is a closed town,' Shifty chipped in, helpfully. A moment later, Rich wandered in, but if he was surprised to find two policeman sitting on his bed, he didn't show it. I explained what was going on and asked him how he thought we should play it.

'Lie,' he said. 'Tell them it's taken us three months to get here, and that in all that time we've not had a single problem.' I said exactly that, but they obviously didn't buy it, because the next thing we knew we were both being marched down the corridor to the hotel reception. Jackie put through a call to the police station, and after a quick rush of syllables, he handed me the receiver. To my surprise, the man at the other end spoke excellent English: 'You can only stay in Komsomolsk for three days, but you need permits to stay. If you haven't got these permits, then you must pay a fine.'

Here we go, I thought wearily. 'How much?' There was a pause at the other end, as if he was trying to decide what he could get away with. '170 roubles,' he said finally. That was about $6. 'And if we pay the fine we can stay for three days?' I said, just to be sure I'd understood. 'Yes, no problem,' the voice said, reassuringly. I thanked him and handed the receiver back to Jackie, who spoke briefly into the handset before hanging up. It turned out to be $6 each. Cash was splashed, hands were shaken, and Shifty suddenly became less shifty. 'It's just the way of things in Siberia,' he shrugged chummily. 'There are many military factories here, building ships and planes. Komsomolsk has always been closed to foreigners for this reason.'

That afternoon, we continued our *cheburiki* tour of the Russian Far East, devoured two giant skewers of barbecued beef, and ate an ashtray full of peaches and ice cream at a dingy café near the riverfront. We did a few things in between – buying petrol, posting letters, that sort of thing – but basically we just ate for England. We also found a shop that sold books in English:

not surprisingly, Sherlock Holmes was well represented, but in amongst the study guides and dictionaries, I was delighted to find a copy of my favourite book, Raymond Chandler's *Farewell My Lovely*. As if that wasn't coincidence enough, Rich also found his favourite, Jerome K Jerome's *Three Men in a Boat*. Even more bizarrely, they were literally the only novels in English in the shop not written by Sir Arthur Conan Doyle – it was almost as if they had been stocked in our honour.

We also spent some time down at the waterfront, which was dominated by a garish, Soviet-era mural and a collection of conspicuous sculptures. Of these, the biggest was a memorial to the founders of Komsomolsk, mounted on top of a huge marble plinth. In the scene that was played out in brass high above our craning necks, an athletic young man carrying picks and shovels over his shoulder was beckoning with his free arm for the masses to follow; gathered in front of him were the youth of the old Russia, eagerly rushing forth to found a new world order. The youth of the new Russia, meanwhile, were skidding their bikes in the shallow puddles around the statue's base.

Those who were too old to be messing around on push-bikes were gathered in the appropriately named Harley Blues Café, a dark but cosy bar a few blocks back from the river. We sat in a booth drinking an ice-cold American beer and watching Ali G and Madonna carousing on French MTV. It was now early evening, and the place soon began to fill up. When there were no spare tables left, two girls asked if they could perch on the end of ours. I waved my hand in agreement and carried on talking to Rich.

They must have assumed that neither of us spoke any Russian, because a couple of beers later, I heard one of them say to the other, 'So, which one do you like best?' When the second girl shot us a furtive glance, it was all I could do not to laugh. 'Do you speak Russian?' asked the first girl, trying not to look flustered. 'Of course!' I said, as nonchalantly as I could. In the stunned silence that followed, her face seemed to fill with crimson from the bottom up.

The blonde who'd spoken to us had pale skin (when she wasn't blushing), bright red lips and heavily made-up eyes; her friend, meanwhile, had olive skin, lips that didn't need any lipstick, and the sort of dark brown eyes that could make you forget your name. It was the blonde who did most of the talking. She told us that her name was Victoria, and that she was a teacher in a local school. Her friend, she said, was called Nastia, and was training to be a paralegal.

For our part, we tried to explain what we were doing in Komsomolsk and how we'd got there, but either they didn't understand, or they didn't care, because the next thing I knew, Victoria was asking us if we liked dancing. 'What, here?' I said anxiously. 'No, of course not,' she said with a smile. 'There's a club down on the promenade. Perhaps you'd like to come with us?' Needless to say, we didn't need much persuasion.

What followed was much like our nights out with Julia back in Blagoveschensk, except for one crucial detail: the girl who had been carted off in the back of a police van for simulating sex with a bar stool at a busy, open-air bar was now doing much the same thing to Rich in the middle of a heaving club. Obviously I'm not trying to suggest that Nastia was the same girl, merely that she subscribed to the same school of dancing. When she wasn't clamping her legs around Rich's unsuspecting waist, she was hitching her already illegal dress up around her hips, caressing her breasts, and stroking her groin in a most unladylike manner. Frankly, he was lucky to get out alive.

Victoria was older and wiser, and while Nastia was busy blowing Rich out in bubbles, she chatted to me about her family, her job, and her life in Komsomolsk. Although she enjoyed her work, she said, it was badly paid – she wanted to move to Khabarovsk, where the pay and prospects were better. As for Komsomolsk, she said, she was lucky to have a job at all. 'There are many people without work here,' she admitted, as if it was her fault, 'and the men do nothing but drink.' I knew from experience that she wasn't just talking about the occasional nightcap at closing time.

At 3 a.m., Nastia announced she was leaving, and grabbed Rich by the hand. 'I think we're going to dance some more,' I said quickly, anxious to offer Rich a way out. He nodded gratefully in agreement. Nastia clearly wasn't impressed and gave Rich her best, doe-eyed pout, but she knew as well as we did that she'd lose face if she changed her mind. Victoria could see what was going on, and offered to walk her home. In reply, Nastia gave Rich a last, longing look, kissed him lightly on the cheek and left without another word, closely followed by an apologetic Victoria.

We left a short while later, when the coast was clear, but instead of doing the sensible thing and heading straight back to our hotel, we went for a quick dip down at the beach; in the dark shadows cast by the promenade, the water was black and still, and refreshingly cool after the stifling heat of the club. At the time, we actually had no idea just how hot things were about to get.

A few hours later, I was lying in my bed hoping fervently that the day would go away and leave me alone. This was our third day in Komsomolsk, and I knew we risked another fine (or worse) if we stayed any longer, but just thinking about packing our boats and stumbling down to the beach brought me out in a cold sweat. Fortunately, the booths of the Harley Blues Café were as dark during the day as they were at night, and a few stiff, black coffees later, I no longer wanted to die.

By the time we emerged from our burrow in the small hours of the afternoon, the sun was blinking through the clouds and the town was starting to warm up. The orange and white façades of *Ulitsa Lenina*, and the trams that screeched and trundled back and forth, gave the place a distinctly European feel. Once my head had stopped screeching in time with the trams, I went in search of some new tapes to replace the ones that had melted when my fuel bottle had burst, and was surprised to find the latest Moby album in a kiosk just off the main street; for some reason, I'd just assumed that Siberian music shops would still be wallowing in the swinging sixties, but MTV, it seems, waits for no man.

All of that walking left me feeling a bit peaky, so while Rich went in search of a bank, I retired for a quick kip. An hour or so later, I was rudely awakened by a knock at the door. I was just about to curse Rich for not taking his key with him when I noticed that he was asleep on his bed. There was another knock, this time more insistent. I assumed it was Jackie and Shifty, and decided to ignore it, earnestly hoping that Rich had remembered to lock the door when he'd come back.

Presently, though, the knocking became a hammering, and I couldn't ignore it any longer. When I finally threw open the door, however, there was no sign of Jackie and Shifty. In fact, there was no sign of anyone, not because there was no one there, but because the corridor was filled with thick, acrid smoke: our hotel was on fire. Peering into the gloom, I could just make out a hazy lady in a pinafore. She wailed something incomprehensible in Russian and disappeared into the darkness.

Unsure if we'd ever see our room again, we decided to throw everything that was irreplaceable – passports, diaries, exposed camera film – into a couple of dry bags, before legging it after the hazy lady. We had no idea if we'd even be able to get down the corridor, let alone the stairs, and the smoke was so thick that we couldn't see more than a few feet in front of us. Staying as low as we could, we crabbed our way down the corridor towards a dancing orange light. It turned out to be a fireman's torch, beckoning us urgently down the stairs. Outside on the pavement, we found a handful of hotel guests milling around and looking remarkably unconcerned, and it soon became apparent that the fire was already under control. Just twenty minutes later, we were allowed back in.

Our friend the *directora* was clearly shaken by the whole experience, but she wasted no time in showing us the damage. Luckily, no one had been hurt and only one room had been completely gutted, although the adjoining corridor was black with soot. From what remained of the charred room, it looked like the blaze had been started by an ancient dial-a-channel TV set in the far corner. I couldn't help noticing that it was – or at least had been – identical to the one in our room.

Not surprisingly, we both felt too on edge to go back to bed, so we decided to make the most of the sunny weather by heading back down to the waterfront. To our surprise, it was packed: there were kids swarming all over the plinth of the city memorial, ice-cream vendors and beer bars every couple of dozen yards and, at the far end, an open-air stage surrounded by a sizeable crowd. Not for Komsomolsk the ballet and ballroom dancing of Khabarovsk, though – this was, after all, the city of youth: here, thrash metal was the music of the masses, and anarchy was the order of the day. Well, just so long as no one tried to clamber up onto the stage.

Although this was supposed to be our last day in Komsomolsk, we didn't actually make it to the river until ten o'clock the following morning (not that we were trying to put it off, you understand). Part of the problem was that we had trouble finding the sort of food that we were used to: the first few shops we tried seemed to specialise in items like sunflower oil and Brillo pads. Only by combining goods from a number of different establishments were we able to find everything that we needed but, by then, it was too dark to set off, so we had little choice but to stay an extra night and hope that Jackie and Shifty didn't come knocking.

When we did eventually wheel our boats back down to the river, the sky was cloudless for the first time in days, and the water was reassuringly still. Even then, we managed to delay our departure by another half-hour, with a quick drink at an open-air café overlooking the beach. Well, it was a nice day, after all. When at last we ran out of excuses, we carried our canoes down to the water's edge, clambered in, and pushed off into the waiting water.

As the Komsomolsk skyline receded imperceptibly behind us, I took a good look at our new surroundings. The river, I noticed, was gradually narrowing, forced between the foothills of the Sikhote Alin Mountains, which rose up to over 4,000ft on either side of us. It seemed odd to think that they were almost as high as the source of the river, some 4,000km upstream. I also realised we were now just 500km from our goal, which to all intents and purposes meant we were practically on the home straight. The problem was, it didn't feel like that at all. Maybe, I mused, it was because until recently the end had seemed so distant that it wasn't worth thinking about; now that it was so close, it was difficult to think about anything else. It might also have had something to do with the fact that 500km was still a bloody long way.

The weather remained clear and calm the following day, although it was now noticeably cooler. The change was even more marked at night: for the first time since we'd left Mongolia, we were compelled to zip up our sleeping bags, and to twist them around our legs to eliminate unwanted air pockets. Getting up in the morning was getting more and more difficult, as the warmth of our dry sleeping bags was invariably more inviting than the chill of our damp paddling clothes. Still, it certainly beat putting on a jacket and tie and battling for a seat on the Northern Line.

The next day was the same, and the day after that, as the seconds, minutes and hours blended into one another. Often, the only thing that distinguished one session from the next was the sort of mood I was in: one minute, I'd feel upbeat and positive, sculling across the water like a water boatman across a millpond; the next I'd feel down and dejected, cursing the river and all who paddled on her. One of the things that really got to me was the fact that Rich was always so far ahead, no matter how hard I paddled. There was nothing rational about it – that's just the way it was. It never occurred to me to ask him if he cursed me for being so far behind.

Apart from food breaks, one of the few things that provided us with any distraction was stopping for a wee, not because it was interesting in its own right, but because it often presented something of a challenge. Usually if we were caught short we'd just pull over at a suitable beach and jump out, but now that beaches were so scarce, we had to come up with a workable alternative. The solution we eventually hit upon involved paddling alongside a mud-bank or overhanging branch that was low enough to stand on. Then, easing ourselves gently upright in our boats, we'd put one foot on the bank or branch while the other foot remained in the canoe. Once we were stable, it was simply a matter of fertilising the foliage and then sitting carefully back down again. The only things we had to be wary of were strong currents and a facing wind, for obvious reasons. Because this technique usually involved one foot being higher than the other, it became known as 'the explorer's stance', after all the admirable men and women who have ever gazed out over land or sea with one foot boldly going further – and slightly higher – than the other.

Surprisingly, this technique worked quite well, even if we did occasionally get the wind direction wrong. The only time I *did* almost come a cropper was when I stopped at what looked like a solid mud-bank: as I stepped onto it, my foot began to sink, slowly at first, and then more quickly. I assumed that after an inch or two it would hit something solid, but it just kept on sinking. Because I had nothing to hold on to, my body keeled over alarmingly, until I looked like ... well, someone with one leg shorter than the other.

I thought about asking Rich to get out our EPIRB, just in case, but the ignominy of being airlifted from a muddy puddle five days short of the finish would have been too much to bear

(EPIRB, you'll remember, stands for Emergency Position Indicating Radio Beacon). Eventually, when the mud was just below my knee I stopped sinking, much to my relief and much to Rich's all-too-obvious disappointment. The bastard even had his camera out.

Every evening we'd make a point of poring over our maps, willing the Pacific closer. It was only when we unfolded them and spread them out that we realised how close it really was. Although the kilometre markers were still promising another 400-odd kilometres of tedium, the ocean was now tantalisingly close, just 150km to the east.

Every morning, meanwhile, we'd wake to heavy dew and thick fog, which would gradually evaporate to leave tendrils of mist draped over the dark, forested hillsides on either side of us. This other-worldly landscape provided a welcome change from the monotony of the swamps and flatlands further upstream. In fact, this was exactly how I'd pictured the Amur back in the UK all those months before: downriver, the vast bluffs formed by the gentle bends in the river overlapped like the wings of a theatre set, getting fainter and bluer until they eased off to the right and disappeared into the haze.

We celebrated our hundredth day on the river by laying out all of our equipment in front of our tent and taking a picture of it. It was one helluva party. We also started a new bottle of insect repellent, which was rather enigmatically called 'Ben's 100'. The number apparently indicated that it contained 100% DEET (the active ingredient in many mosquito repellents). The name Ben, meanwhile, seemed to refer to the burly, bearded character in a lumberjack shirt on the front of the bottle. Given the pinprick velocity with which the DEET sprayed from the nozzle, I can only assume that Ben must have been a fireman before he turned to chopping down trees for a living.

The following day was 1 September, and the continued drop in temperature made us realise that the summer was definitely coming to an end. Barring a major disaster, we now knew that we'd reach the Pacific before it froze over, but judging by how quickly the weather was changing, we guessed that it wasn't as far away as we might have expected just a few weeks before.

The day after that we crossed over to our final map, which was something of a momentous occasion. We'd now been through nine maps, some of which were well over a metre across (to give you a sense of scale, 2cm represented 10km, so a single sheet covered 500km, or roughly the distance between London and Glasgow). But what struck me most was the fact that our surroundings were every bit as mountainous at the end of the river as they had been at the source. Not only that, but the swift current which had swept us downstream since day one was still showing no signs of letting up. Before we'd left the UK, and indeed when we'd set off from the source, we'd assumed the current would dwindle to nothing in the first few days, when the river lost most of its height. And yet here we were, just inches above sea level, and we were still being swept along like logs in a flash flood – all *we* had to do was dip our paddles in the water every so often for appearances' sake.

With a little over 100km to go, we started the day with a following wind, and managed a brisk 43km before lunch. I don't know why we were paddling so fast – perhaps it had something to do with the fact that we could practically smell the sea, or maybe it was because we were chatting to each other on the river for the first time in days. The subject under discussion was teenage fashion disasters: Rich confessed to wearing winkle-pickers, studded armbands and death metal T-shirts in his youth, despite the fact that his musical tastes veered more towards Simon & Garfunkel and The King Singers, infamously known for the immortal line, 'I just want somebody to be gay with …'

The best (or worst) I could come up with was a pair of silver, aviator-style glasses, a tweed flat cap (worn forwards, not backwards) and a collection of matching tartan scarves. In fact, thinking about it now, it's probably little wonder that I ended up in the depths of Siberia fifteen years later.

After our daily six-hour quota, we couldn't find anywhere to camp, so we didn't have much choice but to push on. And on. And on. For miles and miles we could see nothing but dense, impenetrable reed beds on both sides of the river. By the middle of hour eight, the wind was really starting to gust, dousing me in water with every stroke of my paddle (and you already know how much I hate to get wet). When we finally found ourselves somewhere level and dry to pitch our tent, we'd been paddling for over nine hours, and had covered the best part of 75 kilometres.

The campsite that eventually presented itself was a beach just upstream of a small village called Takhta. The beach itself was strewn with massive, rusting chunks of metal and machinery. It seemed like a fittingly dark and depressing place to end the interminable slog of the last few hours. It wasn't that nine hours was too long to be on the water – after all, we'd managed it for weeks on end back in Mongolia – but that we'd only been expecting six. When we at last dragged our boats out of the water, we were tired, wet and very fed up. And, as if that wasn't bad enough, later that night a freak storm almost threw our tent into the river. While we were inside it.

20 PUSHING THE BOAT OUT

It looked like rain when we set up camp, so we put the outer on, just in case. It was just as well we did. In the middle of the night, a gust of wind blasted through the open door of the tent, eliciting an ear-splitting slap from the flapping fabric. It was so loud it even woke Rich up. 'Hmmm,' he mumbled uncertainly, 'that sounds interesting.'

Rich often used the word 'interesting' when he meant 'worrying' or 'dangerous'. There was another gust, followed by another loud slap. 'Oh well,' he decided, 'if the pegs don't hold the tent down, our bodies will.' And with that, he rolled over, sighed contentedly, and went back to sleep. Twenty seconds later, a third gust blew through the doorway so ferociously that it plucked all of the pegs out at the front of the tent, lifted the groundsheet from the sand, and deposited us both in a heap at the back. I didn't realise all this at the time – I just knew that Rich was on top of me, and that I had no idea why. The problem, we soon realised, was that the tent was facing straight into the wind, which meant that it was behaving like a miniature balloon, with us as its unsuspecting passengers.

Once we'd worked out which way was up, I held the front of the groundsheet down while Rich frantically zipped up the porch, before throwing his bodyweight onto the fabric to stop it from being wrenched from his hands. This seemed to help, and for a moment the slapping stopped. 'Maybe if I just stay here for a minute...' He hardly had time to finish his sentence before another blast hit, followed by the first heavy smacks of rain on the outer. After the fourth smack, the heavens opened, and the wind began to buffet the tent relentlessly, bending the poles almost to breaking point; in the darkness, it sounded like we were being stampeded by a herd of wild horses.

Clearly, something had to be done. Our waterproofs were in our boats, so I slid into the fleece that I'd been using as a pillow before taking over in the porch so that Rich could do the same. Yelling over the din of the wind and the rain, we quickly decided on a plan of action, leaped from the tent, and got soaked to our short and curlies in a matter of seconds. Our plan involved lashing the two main guys at the front of the tent to hooks in the cockpits of our upturned boats, as the sand was obviously much too soft to hold any pegs. We then had to roll both boats on top of the outstretched porch – making a V shape at the front of the tent – to stop it from catching in the wind.

Once the boats were in place and the porch was tamed, Rich scampered to the back of the tent to peg out the remaining guys as best he could. The only way to stop the pegs from pinging straight back out again was to put heavy stones on top of them, but this was easier said than done on an empty beach in the middle of the night. While Rich went off in search of rocks, I lashed our boats together with a sling, hoping vaguely that two together would be harder to blow into the river than one on its own.

As I worked, naked from the waist down and legs akimbo to steady myself, I was acutely aware of the water pouring off my testicles, which were dangling somewhat unhappily in the breeze. Needless to say, for a fleeting moment I felt rather exposed, and I was quite glad when the last knot had been tied and I could at last return to the relative comfort of the tent.

By the time our fortifications were finished, the wind seemed to have relented a little, but I was still concerned that my canoe would be rolled over and pitched into the river by a sudden gust, so I lay awake for almost an hour, trying to think warm, dry thoughts in my warm, dry sleeping bag.

But the night was yet young: at five in the morning I was woken by a sound that I felt sure was born of neither man nor beast. It sounded like a cross between a galloping horse and a cat having a fight, and it was loud, close and very unnerving. This was closely followed by some scuffling at the foot of the tent, some tramping up and down in the sand, and then nothing more. When I finally fell into an anxious sleep, I'd decided that a mad old crone on horseback had galloped down to the beach, sacrificed a cat to the river, howled at the moon a few times, and then disappeared into the forest. Rich, meanwhile, had a dream that the cause of the cacophony was an emu chick fighting with a little ginger tomcat. Still, he must have thought more of it at the time: the next morning I woke to find the can of bear spray nestling conspicuously between our pillows.

Later that morning we stopped at Takhta, to stock up for the final push to the ocean. For the first time on the entire journey, the shop was right on the riverfront, which we couldn't help but interpret as a good omen. The simple wooden sign above the door read ВСЁ ДЛЯ ВАС, or 'Everything for You', and it was true to its word: the bread was still warm, the condensed milk was still in date, and the chocolate was still tasteless. In the time it took us to shop and pack the extra food in our boats, we'd managed to attract the usual crowd of well-wishers: there was the clucking babushka, who couldn't believe we were still wearing shorts at this time of year, and who wanted to know where we'd sheltered during the storm; there was the earnest young lad on a motorbike, who wanted to hear all about our journey; and there was the obligatory village drunk, who couldn't understand why we'd want to go to Nikolayevsk when there was already plenty of vodka in Takhta.

Soon after we left, we passed a speedboat sprawled with the limbs of half a dozen fishermen who looked like they were sleeping. A few minutes later, though, we heard the ominous buzz of an outboard motor approaching from behind (I say ominous because we were never quite sure what was going to come of being pursued). When they got closer, it became apparent that they hadn't been asleep, so much as semi-comatose: two of them could hardly stand, and a third was slurring so much I wasn't even sure if he was speaking Russian. Another looked like he'd recently been whacked in the face with a spade, and had blood caked on his upper lip and all down his chin. The first two were less out of it, but even they boasted big grins and glazed eyes. One of them, who introduced himself as Pavel, was clearly delighted to meet us: he said he loved England, gave a big thumbs-up to London, and tried to convince us that Russia was … well, 'Whoooaaaaah!'

On Pavel's insistence, Rich took a photo of them all, and in return they produced a generous handful of marijuana from the glove compartment of their boat. Pavel gave a knowing grin as he held it out for me to take. 'Shhhhh,' he slurred, missing his lips with his finger. I tried to explain that we didn't smoke, but he wasn't listening. Not wanting to appear ungrateful, I took it from him and placed it carefully in the bottom of my boat, between my legs, so that I could toss it overboard later. And with that, he wished us luck, waved goodbye and – by way of a parting gesture – stood up and pissed over the side of the speedboat.

Although the rain never came, it was a grey and dreary paddle, and we made slow progress, partly because of the interruptions early in the day. Thankfully, though, we found somewhere suitable to camp after just five and a half hours – it was a flat area of sand and gravel hemmed in by forest and tucked away at the end of a long reed bed. Reeds had been the dominant feature at the water's edge for a few days now, but something I hadn't noticed was how colourful the forest had become – when the sun set that evening, the bank of trees behind our tent wouldn't have looked out of place in the height of a New England fall. The other thing that was starting to look quite colourful was my fungus, but Rich managed to hide the EPIRB before I did anything rash.

That night, I woke in the small hours to hear the familiar patter of rain on the tent. And by 'tent', I mean 'inner'. You'd have thought that by now we'd have learned our lesson, but because the sky had been clear when we'd gone to bed, we'd decided not to bother with the outer. Even when it started raining we didn't move until the patter became a downpour. For the second night in a row we found ourselves flapping around in the dark getting soaked to the skin.

Thankfully, it wasn't as windy this time around, but it was noticeably colder; by the time I'd scrambled back into my sleeping bag, my hair was dripping and my teeth were chattering. Which, by happy coincidence, was more or less when the rain stopped. Once I'd dried off and warmed up, I peered outside to see if there was any more rain on the way. To my surprise, stars blinked back at me from every direction, save for a tiny cloud just to one side of our tent, and seemingly just a few feet above it. It was like one of those rain clouds you get hovering over umbrellas in cartoon strips. It was also, I felt sure, the smallest cloud to produce rain in the history of weather.

We woke the following morning to blue skies and glassy waters. Nikolayevsk was now only 30km – yes, 30km! – away, and from our campsite we could just make out the smokestacks of the town's power station (it's a curious characteristic of Siberian power stations that they're invariably built right in the middle of towns, and that their smokestacks are always bright orange, presumably to make them even more of an eyesore than they already are). Soon after we set off, the river braided into numerous channels, which snaked their way through dozens of reed-choked islands. We followed what looked to be the widest of these channels, but were soon slowed to an energy-sapping crawl by acres and acres of hull-sucking weeds that grew just below the water's surface.

Halfway along this channel Rich stopped to relieve himself at one of the few solid sections of bank we'd seen all day, and almost came a cropper: because the bank was too high for him to beach his bow, he positioned his boat parallel to the bank, stood up slowly, and carefully adopted the 'explorer's stance'. When he tried to sit back down, however, he lost his balance and fell back into his cockpit. The boat tipped alarmingly, and as it stood balanced on its edge, I willed it to capsize, not because I had it in for Rich, but because I would have been highly amused if he'd taken his first swim on the very last day of our journey. Except he didn't capsize, and it wasn't our last day.

At least, not quite. You see, we'd decided that the real end of the Amur was a small and probably very muddy island about 30km out into the estuary. This, we reasoned, would be far enough out to quell any lingering doubts we might have had about where the river ended and the sea began (naturally I apologise if you were hoping to get this over with, but if you've come this far, you may as well see it through, if only to find out what happens with the local prostitutes in Nikolayevsk).

Emerging from the braids, we became increasingly bogged down in the vast expanses of bright-green lily pads that covered the water's surface. We'd seen isolated patches of these lilies for a few days now, but here they overwhelmed the shoreline, reaching hundreds of yards out into the river. They were so thickly clustered that we often couldn't find a way through, and had to follow wide, sweeping curves to avoid them. As we neared Nikolayevsk, however, we had little choice but to paddle straight into them; with their heavy pads dragging on the hulls of our boats and their densely packed roots clutching at our paddle blades, it felt like trying to toboggan through treacle.

Like Khabarovsk, Nikolayevsk was founded by Nikolai Muraviev in the middle of the nineteenth century, as part of his campaign to wrest control of the Amur back from Manchuria. As a staging post for convicts being sent to the penal colony on nearby Sakhalin Island, it became a thriving port town, and by the beginning of the twentieth century it boasted British and Japanese Consulates, an American club (established by traders from California), and even a French brothel. All of this came to a sudden and bloody end, however, when the Bolsheviks rode into town in 1920 and killed every Japanese they could find, in retaliation for the humiliating defeats suffered by the Russian navy in the war against Japan fifteen years earlier. Since then, its importance as a seaport has been eclipsed by the city of Vladivostok, which for seventy years was home to the Soviet Pacific Fleet.

Somewhere we'd heard Nikolayevsk described as a charming old fortress town of tsarist style, but from where we were sitting it looked more 'industrial style': the skyline ahead of us was dominated by the orange-and-white smokestacks of the power station, while the water's edge was interrupted by two harbours, one of which was home to a large barge and a corral of derelict cranes. There were also a few smaller boats moored up at intervals around the harbour walls, while far out in the estuary we could just make out the distinctive shapes of a couple of tankers.

This apparent incongruity, however, was neither here nor there, because for us Nikolayevsk was something of a holy grail, a place of myth and legend. We'd been counting down to it for the final thousand kilometres, and indirectly we'd been counting down to it for the last hundred days. Now, all we really needed was to get some rest in preparation for our moment of triumph the following day.

Once again, we had to guess where to pull in, but it was a relief to realise that this would be the last time we'd have to go in search of a hotel dragging our boats behind us. As we neared the second of the two harbours, I was surprised to see a fish leaping out of the water just in front of our boats. It was closely followed by another, and then another. They were quite big – maybe a foot or so long – and looked a bit like rainbow trout. Admittedly they didn't leap very high – it was more a sort of rolling breach really – but they were still impressive, if a little startling.

Even more startling was hearing someone shouting my name when we eventually pulled up at one end of a long wooden jetty, particularly given that I was nine time zones from the nearest person I knew. When I looked around to see where the voice was coming from, I saw someone gesticulating urgently at us from the deck of a fishing boat at the far end of the jetty. We were too far away to make out what he was trying to say, but acting on the assumption that it might contain the words 'stop', 'I'll', 'or', and 'shoot', we paddled obediently over.

Only when we got closer did I realise that we'd actually met our heckler the day before, when he'd come over in a small speedboat to say hello. Based on that single meeting, it seemed we were now best comrades: 'Would you like some fish soup?' he called out cheerfully as we pulled up alongside his boat. I glanced at Rich, who shrugged his consent. 'Sure,' I replied, 'why not?'

After securing our canoes to the boat's railings, we clambered onto the deck. Our host, a big, ruddy-faced man called Yevgeni, invited us to sit at a table laden with food. In the middle was an enormous bowl of what looked like strips of raw chicken dipped in egg yolk. 'Eat, eat!' Yevgeni insisted, pouring us each a bowl of soup and sliding the bowl of meat towards us. 'What is it?' I asked uncertainly. 'It's called *Tala*,' he replied, making a point of stressing the second syllable. 'It's a Siberian speciality.'

I must have still looked doubtful, because he speared a few pieces on a fork and handed them to me. 'Try it,' he nodded reassuringly, 'it's delicious.' He was right: it tasted a bit like smoked salmon in a delicate cheese marinade. The soup, by comparison, was decidedly less appetising: there were all sorts of once-aquatic innards floating around at the bottom of my bowl, most of which looked disturbingly like inch-wide sections of surgical tubing. In reality they were nothing more sinister than the intact spinal tissue of a giant sturgeon.

While we ate, we were joined by half a dozen of Yevgeni's colleagues: two of them wore smart-looking uniforms with NYPD-style badges on their sleeves, while the rest sported the traditional tracksuit and T-shirt combo so beloved of the Russian military. 'We're all fish inspectors,' Yevgeni told us, pointing proudly to the badge on his own sleeve. 'We've been patrolling the river between here and Khabarovsk for the last two weeks.'

Assuming they were interested in more than just the quality and sheen of individual scales, I asked him what they'd been looking for. 'Red caviar,' he said sternly, tightening his face into a frown. 'It's a big problem here.' Although I didn't catch every word, he went on to explain that the mouth of the Amur was swimming with sturgeon, and as such was something of a hotspot for poachers looking to make a quick buck from the fish's salty, blood-red eggs (unlike black caviar, which traditionally comes from the overexploited waters of the Black and Caspian Seas, and is – pound for pound – more expensive than gold, red caviar is relatively cheap: when we'd been in Khabarovsk, for example, £1 would have bought us about a hundred grams of red, compared to just one or two grams of black).

While I had Yevgeni's attention, I decided to ask him about the tidal currents out in the estuary, and immediately wished I hadn't. They were very strong, he said, and big waves were common, particularly when the wind was blowing against the tide. 'Even in this big boat,' he said sagely, 'we don't risk it.' The problem, it seemed, wasn't so much what the weather was like when you set off, but what it might be like when you got out there. He advised us to stick as close as we could to the left bank, and to avoid the island completely. It didn't help that no one seemed to know when high tide was, or even what the weather was supposed to be like the following day. By way of an on-the-spot forecast, Yevgeni sniffed the air a few times, gazed out to sea, and eventually pointed to the moon, which was low on the horizon and almost hidden by haze. 'When the moon is like that,' he said, as if the evidence was irrefutable, 'bad weather is on its way.'

Thus reassured, we went in search of somewhere to stay, promising Yevgeni and his henchmen that we'd join them later for a drink. Two young lads showed us the way to the nearest hotel, which was only a few hundred yards from the harbour. It was without doubt the least prepossessing hotel we'd seen in Siberia, which – given the competition – was quite something. There was no obvious reception, and no sign or plaque outside: in fact, the only indication that it was anything other than a disused office building or a block of run-down apartments was a tatty, red-leather door which looked almost as heavy as the cow it had been crafted from.

As if determined to make up for the hotel's unwelcoming exterior, the middle-aged woman at the front desk was as sweet as honeyed pancakes. She wore enormous glasses with an elaborate silver frame, and was shy and effusive by turns, as she wasn't sure what to make of us. Still, she seemed quite happy for us to store our boats under the stairs in the lobby, and when I mentioned we were thinking of going for a wander into town, she promised to keep an eye on them while we were gone.

Considering how unimpressive Nikolayevsk had looked from the river, we were quite surprised to discover that it did indeed retain a great deal of its original tsarist charm, thanks to its narrow, leafy boulevards, its beautifully preserved wooden houses and its lush green park, which overlooked the river. In the warm glow of the setting sun, even the waterfront looked inviting.

All too inviting, as it turned out. No sooner had we wandered down there than we were called over by Yevgeni. As we clambered aboard his boat, Rich presented him with his fishing rod to thank him for his hospitality earlier in the day (given that Rich had now been carrying it on the deck of his boat for three and a half months without catching so much as a minnow, it seemed unlikely that we'd need it for our last day on the river). Not surprisingly, Yevgeni was delighted, and wasted no time in presenting us with a long, red-and-white pennant in return: it was about four feet long, with a red border around the outside, and the silhouettes of two stylised red fish forming a circular motif in the centre. 'It's the official flag of the Fish Inspectors' Federation,' Yevgeni explained, waving it towards the boat's stern. 'We fly it when we're patrolling the river.'

With the goodwill and camaraderie flowing unchecked, it was only a matter of time before the vodka followed suit, and we were soon bolting our first shot of the evening. This was closely followed by a second and then a third, each slightly bigger than the last. 'Russian tradition,' Yevgeni assured us with a wink. It was enough to send even the most rosy-cheeked of sea dogs over the rails. For two baby-faced young cherubs from England, it was the beginning of the end.

Long after I'd lost count of what round we were on, Yevgeni gave me his watch, which in my vodka-stewed stupor looked like a Rolex. Closer inspection, however, revealed the word 'Capitan' on its bezel. Yevgeni's wrist wasn't much bigger than a beer barrel, and of the six 'diamonds' set into the face, two were missing, but I couldn't have cared less: for now, at least, I was the 'Capitan', and I promptly ordered the crew to weigh anchor and hoist three sheets to the wind.

I hardly even noticed when the two girls arrived, much less when one of them slipped below deck with a member of the crew. Frankly, I was too busy telling the time. The girl who was left behind grew increasingly bored with the constant drinking, and it was only when I proposed a toast to England that she suddenly perked up. As she grabbed my hand and led me into the shadows down the side of the boat, I had just enough time to flash Rich a nervous grin.

All too aware that now was the time to turn on the charm, I slurred my way through a few evening-class staples ('What a beautiful night …') before she came to my rescue by asking about life back in England. We'd hardly got much further than *Beeg Byen* when we were joined by the second girl, who led us both up to the empty bridge with a mischievous giggle, before passing around a No. 9 beer (on the sliding scale of Siberian beer strengths, No. 9 is what they typically use to power space rockets). Not long after this – ten, maybe fifteen seconds – the entire crew appeared on the bridge to announce that it was time for us to leave. I didn't know if this was because we'd moved in on their girls or if they were just ready for bed, but either way, we'd clearly outstayed our welcome. Rich, though, wasn't having any of it: 'No, no, no, *Vodka Nada!*' he pleaded, in a confused cocktail of English and Russian. 'Let's drink some more and talk to the lovely girls; go on, Paul, ask how much they are!'

I hadn't noticed quite when Rich had gone and gotten himself smashed – only later did I realise that his limited Russian meant that while I'd been talking he'd been drinking – but he was clearly in all sorts of trouble. Thankful only that he couldn't remember the Russian for 'How much?' I persuaded him to say '*Dasveedanya,*' before dragging him reluctantly back to our hotel. Passing the lovely lady at the front desk, I tried to maintain some semblance of sobriety myself, only to discover that someone had rudely put a step in front of my feet while I was looking the other way. The last thing I remember was the yellow linoleum rushing up to meet my grinning chops. I didn't feel a thing.

We had hoped to make it to our little island in time for lunch, but it was gone eleven before either of us could manage much more than a wincing, bleary-eyed blink. When we did eventually wheel our boats down to the river, Rich soon found himself doubled up by the side of the road, noisily parting company with the light lunch he'd eaten just a few minutes before. Still, he felt much better when he finally got back on the water and his boat started lurching and heaving in the choppy waves; all in all, it wasn't quite the auspicious finale we'd been hoping for.

The weather wasn't as bad as Yevgeni had predicted, but it was bad enough: the first stretch involved battling into the wind across a wide bay, while our boats thumped and splashed through the frustratingly irregular waves. For the first few hours Rich's face looked as green as the water we were paddling through, and I was quite relieved when the colour returned to his face at our first food stop. After that, the estuary opened out, although the mountains that rose up from the south bank, three or four miles distant, were still impressive, rearing a thousand feet or more above the river. We had no way of telling if the tide was coming in or going out, but we made steady progress, and we could soon make out the island we were heading for, far in the distance.

Because the weather was showing no sign of worsening, we took the decision to abandon the bank and make a beeline for the island; it took us another hour to work out that the horizon was playing tricks with us, and that we were in fact heading towards the wrong island. The right island, we realised with a growing sense of gloom, was still another two hours' paddle away, which meant we couldn't even see it yet. Adjusting our course slightly, we pointed our boats towards the open sea and hoped for the best. Soon after this, a huge tanker crept past us: it was probably more than a kilometre away, but it looked incredibly close compared to the mountains on either side, and it made us realise just how far we were from dry land.

As it turned out, the island we were hoping to reach was so small and so low that we didn't see it until it was just a few kilometres away. As we got closer, we had to contend with the same, paddle-grappling weeds that had ensnared us just upstream of Nikolayevsk, but at least this time they had the effect of calming the swell a little. We saw dozens of fish darting in and out of the greenery, and at one point a seal popped his head above the surface as if to show us the way.

The final twenty minutes felt like an hour, but eventually we pulled up alongside a low mud-bank on the north shore of the island and threw our paddles wearily into the undergrowth. After 107 days, 4,400km, and over four million paddle strokes, we'd finally arrived at journey's end. I'd like to be able to say that I felt a due sense of joy and elation, but instead I just felt hung over and slightly sick.

EPILOGUE

As I lifted myself gingerly out of the cockpit of my boat, I realised that my arms felt more tired now than they had at any other time on our journey – it was almost as if they'd only been putting in the effort over the last four months on the understanding that they'd be allowed to turn to jelly the moment they were no longer required.

As we'd expected, the island we were on was little more than a muddy mound strewn with shrubs and bushes. The one thing we hadn't expected, however, was to find a small, home-made picnic table within yards of our chosen campsite. At the time, I couldn't help but feel slightly aggrieved at this discovery: there just seemed to be something quintessentially civilised about a picnic table that didn't fit in with our pre-conceived notions of how our journey would end. After all the hours, days and weeks we'd spent in anticipation of this moment, it hardly seemed fitting that (a) someone had been here before (b) that they'd found time to build a picnic table and (c) that they'd almost certainly used it to dine on red caviar and Russian champagne in the meantime. It was only later, when I wasn't feeling so tired and emotional, that I realised how apt the picnic table really was: it provided a timely reminder of every little town and village we'd visited along the Amur, and every experience we'd shared with the river's inhabitants along the way, and in so doing it gave the lie to the idea that we were on some godforsaken river in the middle of nowhere.

Once we'd got over our initial disappointment we shook hands, as much to formally mark the end of our journey as to congratulate each other. It was, I realised, the first time we'd ever shaken hands, and – in a way that only we Brits can manage at such an emotional moment – it was perfunctory and to the point. Besides, we were both too drained to be more effusive, and it was still too soon to reflect on what, if anything, we'd actually achieved. I'm not sure what emotions I'd expected to experience at that end, but in the event it just felt like the end of another day on the river. I wasn't even overwhelmed with relief that it was all over – all I really wanted to do was slide into my sleeping bag and sleep for twelve days. My one concession to celebration was to leave my diary in my dry bag – for once I didn't want to have to think about anything.

Once I was all bundled up in my sleeping bag I could hardly move, not because I was particularly stiff (this would come later), but because I was completely spent. Outside it was already getting cold and dark, but inside it was warm and dry, and for the first time since we'd tossed our paddles onto the island, I felt very contented indeed.

Thus cocooned, I snoozed for over an hour, but it was only a matter of time before hunger became more pressing than sleep. We cooked from the comfort of our sleeping bags, positioning the stove beneath a small opening in the outstretched porch of our tent. We had planned to bring a beer to share, but somehow it had been forgotten in our rush to get on the river before midday. Actually I didn't mind in the least: all I really craved was what we'd eaten more or less every day for the last 100 days: soup with bread left over from lunchtime, pasta with garlic and tinned fish, and hot chocolate with lashings of sugar. Unfortunately, we were out of instant soup, so we had to make do with boiling up a handful of Oxo cubes instead. Still, it wasn't all bad news: in lieu of drinking half a bottle of warm beer each, we decided to prise open our final mystery tin, which contained what looked like flattened silly putty. It turned out to be some kind of chicken paste and, to our surprise, it was actually quite edible, if a little waxy.

Once we'd had our fill, we slid the few inches required to reach our respective sleeping positions, and it was only then that I realised just how uneven the ground was beneath our tent. Even with a camping mat it felt like I was lying on top of a herd of camels huddled tightly together. Mercifully, however, the bumps seemed to fit the contours of my body precisely, and within minutes I was sleeping like a puppy after playtime.

Because my new watch didn't actually work, when I awoke the following morning I had no idea what time it was, but there was just enough light inside the tent to tell me that dawn was on its way. Rich stirred at around the same time and, despite the cold, we decided to watch the sun rise over the Pacific (I suppose that, strictly speaking, it was actually the Sea of Okhotsk, but somehow this doesn't have the same ring to it). We stuck our feet out at the bottom of our sleeping bags, and waddled over to the water's edge looking like penguins wrapped in Pertex. We didn't have long to wait, although we couldn't tell exactly when the sun first peeped over the horizon because it was obscured by a low, distant bank of cloud.

Gradually, though, the world around us brightened, and with it our mood. A deep, dreamless sleep was obviously all that I'd needed to bring me back to life, and when the sun finally appeared, I experienced the surge of elation that I'd been hoping for 12 hours before. Suddenly, and quite unexpectedly, I felt as energetic as I'd been on the morning that we'd set off from the source. This, I thought, was it: we'd done what we'd set out to do, and in doing so we'd achieved all of our goals: we'd paddled one of the world's great rivers from source to sea, we'd met some extraordinary people along the way, and – perhaps most importantly – we'd both been able to grow beards that David Bellamy would have been proud of.

And yet, despite this belated sense of satisfaction at a job well done, any feeling of completion continued to elude me. Contemplating this for a moment, I began to realise what the problem was: we hadn't actually finished paddling. At some point, we still had to cross the estuary to reach Arameef, a small village on the north bank almost directly opposite the island we were on. We had no idea whether the tide would be going in or out, or even whether we'd be able to cross it without getting swept further out into the estuary. We weren't unduly concerned about this, as we were quite confident that we could look after ourselves in open water, but my mind had now shut down the paddling part of my brain, and I didn't want to exert myself for any longer than was absolutely necessary.

For once, there was no sense of urgency as we struck camp and packed up our boats. Up until now, we'd always stuck rigidly to our routine of setting off at 9 a.m. every day, even when we hadn't had any deadlines to meet. It was, I suppose, our way of coping with the distance we'd had to cover, of motivating ourselves to get on the water each morning. Now that we'd reached our goal, that motivation was gone, and with it the schedule that had provided some much-needed structure to our days on the river.

Although it was only 3km to the mainland, the current was quite strong, and we had to point our boats more or less straight back up-river to make any headway. As a result, a journey that should have only taken half an hour took well over an hour, which gave me plenty of time to think back over the events of the last four months.

Needless to say, many of our expectations had been completely overturned. From the information that we'd been able to gather before we'd set off, we'd assumed the weather would be cold and wet at the start, warm and wet in the middle, and cold and wet again at the end. In actual fact, it had rained no more than half a dozen times since we'd set off from Mongolia. Apart from that, it had been hot enough for us to wear nothing but our river shorts from dawn to dusk. More often than not the beaches we'd stopped at for lunch had been too hot to walk on in bare feet, and even at night we'd only really needed our sleeping bags at the very beginning and the very end of our journey.

The variety and quality of the food and provisions we'd been able to buy along the way was also something of a revelation. Far from having to make do with 'bits of sheep', we'd been able to buy everything we needed, not to mention a few things (rose-petal jam and cocoa-flavoured butter spring to mind) that we could definitely have managed without. Occasionally we'd had to buy enough food to last us for two or three weeks, because we'd never been sure if the villages marked on our maps would stretch to a shop, but in retrospect we needn't have worried: even the very smallest settlements had boasted a bakery, invariably stocked with an incongruous selection of other tasty treats, from sun-dried fruit to tins of salty seaweed.

And then there was the river itself, which, despite our concerns to the contrary, quite literally carried us to the ocean. We'd expected there to be little or no discernable current after the first few weeks, but if anything the river had actually picked up speed with every passing kilometre. This slow but merciful increase in pace had been caused by seasonal flooding, which at times had turned the river into an unrelenting freeway of fast-moving water. In fact, it's probably fair to say that if we'd forgotten our paddles altogether, we could still have reached the river mouth – albeit a little later than was actually the case – merely by steering our boats with our rudders.

But the biggest surprise of all was how sociable our journey had turned out to be. We'd expected – and indeed hoped for – a wilderness experience, an escape from the rigours and responsibility of day-to-day working life, but in the villages, towns and cities of the Amur River, we'd found something far more memorable, and infinitely more rewarding.

What struck me most was the generosity of the people we'd met along the way, and the kindness they'd showed us: in fact, this book could equally well have been called *The Kindness of*

Strangers if Kate Adie hadn't got there first. There was Andrei the poacher, who'd offered us his first catch of the day back in Mongolia, and Maria in Olovannaya, who'd thought nothing of inviting two hairy foreigners to join her for a champagne picnic on the beach; there was the stranger in Shilka who'd given us money to pay for a phone call to Moscow, and Victor in Sretensk, who for all his bluff and bluster had shared his only loaf of bread with us; then there was Igor and Alexander, who'd delivered bread and milk to us on the river, and the nameless beauty of Chernayevo, who'd brought us freshly-made pancakes; and let's not forget the equally anonymous man from Kasatkino, who'd passed a jar of milk to us through a barbed wire fence, and Yevgeni the war veteran, who'd wanted to give us his bearskin rug, if not his daughter's hand in marriage.

Of course, much of the attention we'd received came from military – and occasionally militant – personnel, but for all the excitement this had afforded, I wasn't really sure what to make of it. Over the last few months we'd been pulled over, guided, guarded and arrested, but we'd also been welcomed, wined, dined and entertained. We'd witnessed a lot of different styles of leadership, and enjoyed the company of a whole host of memorable characters: 'Top Secret' Dennis, who'd tried to convince us that a charging bear could be stopped with a forked stick and small penknife; Valera and Robbie Williams, who'd shown us the time of our lives in Novovaskresenovka; Viktor, who'd given us a guided tour of his border post, dried our clothes and showed us how to use a flare gun; and of course Alexei - a.k.a. the Fonz - who couldn't have been more officious, but who had inadvertently been responsible for the most memorable night of the entire trip.

On the one hand I felt grateful that we'd been allowed near the border at all, given the sensitive nature of the region we'd been travelling through, but on the other hand, I felt disappointed that we'd seen so little of China. Our occasional encounters with Chinese fishermen (not to mention the odd barrage of fruit and veg) had offered us only a fleeting glimpse into the Chinese way of life. It was ironic, and not a little frustrating, to think that if we'd been travelling in the region by bus or train, we'd probably have been free to go anywhere we pleased. In some ways the Chinese authorities took the sensible path: by forbidding us access to their side of the river, they eliminated the red-tape nightmare that might otherwise have ensued. The problem with this is that the bureaucratic nightmare exists at all, a situation which is understandably shaped by a great deal of history, not to mention bad blood, between two vast and highly competitive nations.

The biggest discrepancy between the regions to the north and south of the Amur, it seemed, lay not in the cultural differences, but in the economic differences: the exploitation of natural and human resources on the Chinese side of the river had resulted in a burgeoning local economy, while the lack of investment and infrastructure on the Siberian side had resulted in widespread unemployment and rampant alcoholism. The distance between Moscow and Siberia was as much political as it is geographical, and as a consequence Siberia had become marginalised, a distant and almost forgotten backwater that just happened to be the size of mainland America. The resentment felt by many Siberians towards both the authorities in Moscow and their neighbours across the river was symptomatic of a malaise for which there was no quick fix.

History was also doing its best to conspire against progress in the region. While the emerging middle-classes of Moscow and St Petersburg were enjoying the perceived benefits of capitalism, many people in Siberia seemed unable to shake off the fear of poverty and authority that had been a part of everyday life in the region for decades. As we'd discovered to our cost, there were still 'closed towns' in Siberia which foreigners weren't even allowed to visit. It was almost as if, in

Siberia at least, Russia was suffering a Cold War hangover that it couldn't shake off.

Not surprisingly, it was the older generation who seemed least able to let go of the past: although they were all convinced that Mother Russia would one day rise to be a great nation again, they seemed resigned to the fact that it wasn't going to happen in their lifetime. The younger generation, meanwhile, were intent on finding their fortunes – or at least improving their prospects – elsewhere. When Helena, the precocious ten-year-old we'd met in Olovannaya, had said that she wanted to travel for ten years before she got married, she'd expressed the sorts of hopes and dreams that would have earned her grandparents a spell in the Gulag. The hope for Siberia was that once she'd seen the world, Helena and others of her generation would return home to share their knowledge and experiences, and to contribute to the region's economy and culture. Whether there would be any incentive to return was another question, and one which only the policy-makers in Moscow could answer.

But what Siberia lacked in terms of investment and infrastructure, it more than made up for in terms of its community spirit, and it was this spirit that provided the key to its future. A common history, a shared sense of struggle against the odds, and the fact that most of the region's towns and villages were so small that everyone knew everyone else, all contributed to a stoicism that was born of generations spent living in a harsh climate, both literally and metaphorically. But it was more than just stoicism; it was also a feeling of optimism, a sense that things would get better with time, and it was perhaps this more than anything else that defined the lives of the people we'd met along the river.

As for us, we'd realised our dream, and we'd even managed to do it somewhere warm and sunny to boot. For a few glorious months, we'd slipped the surly bonds of our day-to-day lives and enjoyed the unmitigated simplicity of life on the river. There's something distinctly liberating about travelling under your own steam and - quite literally – just going with the flow. There's also something satisfying about living for months on end out of two small hatches with neoprene covers, carrying with you only what you need to eat, sleep and travel in comfort. Throughout our journey our only parameters had been the rising and setting of the sun, and the right and left banks of the river. Apart from when we'd had to re-supply, the only decision we'd had to face each day was whether to have porridge or semolina for breakfast. The rest of our diet, and indeed the rest of our journey, had followed a routine that was as regimented as it was comforting, and it was this routine that had defined our own lives for the last four months.

In fact, we'd sometimes been so wrapped up in our hour-to-hour, day-to-day existence that it had been easy to forget that it wouldn't go on for ever, and occasionally we'd had to remind ourselves to breath deeply and suck it all in. Throughout it all, though, there was nowhere else on earth I'd rather have been than Siberia, and no-one I'd rather have been there with than Rich. I have, in the past, tackled a number of long and occasionally tedious journeys on my own, and there are those who would argue that this is the only way to travel, but I would suggest that there's nothing better than sharing such experiences with friends. In fact, I'd go one better, and venture that there's nothing more important than friendship: if it should then take you to the ends of the earth with someone you like and admire, so much the better.

The question is, would I do it again? Absolutely. Even back then, if someone had told me that I had to do the whole thing again, I honestly don't think I'd have batted an eyelid. Today, looking back at everything with 20/20 hindsight, my answer would still be the same, although the next time around I think I'd prefer slightly fewer armed guards and rather more Swedish dancing girls.

As our boats crunched up Arameef's long shingle beach, it finally felt like we'd reached the end of our journey. Now all we had to do was get our enormous red and yellow boats back to Mongolia ...

INDEX